I want to go to Heaven the moment I die

By Thaddeus Doyle (Rev)

For a full list of all Fr. Thady's books, booklets and CDs, and how to order these by post including current pricelist, or to see the list of Fr. Thady's coming missions and talks, see website

www.jesuspowerministries.org

(This website can also be called up by asking Google for any of the following, "Fr Thady Doyle", or "Fr Thaddeus Doyle", or "The Curate's Diary".)

(Or send a stamped self-addressed envelope to Fr. T. Doyle, Shillelagh, Arklow, Co Wicklow, Ireland asking for the pricelist.)

Cover

The faces on the cover are in the shape of a heart, inspired by the remrakable dream of four year old Hannah Curtis of her brother entering Heaven through the Sacred Heart of Jesus. See P. 160. Jesus, the one and only Saviour is at the top left; Mary, Queen of Heaven, at the top right.
For the photos of ordinary and extraordinary people, I felt 'led' to just go to my own photo albums, and select a range of photos of deceased of different ages who in their own way had sought to live the dedicated Christian life. They are, in clockwise order, Fr. Kevin Lanigan, (former classmate), Little Nellie of Holy God, taken from her picture when I visited her room; Matty O Neill, Tinahely, Co Wicklow; Sr. Lucia of Fatima, Kathleen Canavan, Enniscorthy, David Curtis, London, (see P. 160), Mary Doyle (my mother), Tommy King, Tinahely, Bl. Mother Theresa, Barry Monaghan, Murrintown, Co Wexford, Harry Goldsmith, Killinick, Co. Wexford, Canon Matty Doyle, Camolin, Minnie Madden, Murrintown, and Deborah Palmer nee Jordan, Tinahely, at whose wedding I officiated when she was already terminally ill.

Cover consultant, Martina Davis.

"My sheep hear my voice, and I know them, and they follow me; and I give them eternal life, and they shall never perish, and no one shall snatch them out of my hand. " John 10:27-28 RSV

1

Acknowledgements

All Scripture quotations denoted RSV are from the Catholic Edition of the Revised Standard Version of the Bible, copyright 1965, 1966 by the Division of Christian Education of the National Council of the Churches of Christ in the United States of America. Used by permission. All rights reserved.

(Scripture verses not denoted RSV, I have used my own words to shorten or simplify.)

All quotations from St. Faustina's Diary, Divine Mercy in My Soul, © 1987 Congregation of Marians of the Immaculate Conception, Stockbridge, MA 01263. Used with permission.

Quotations from St. Elizabeth of the Trinity From the Complete Works of Elizabeth of the Trinity Volume One translated by Sr. Aletheia Kane, O.C.D. Copyright © 1984 by Washington Province of Discalced Carmelites ICS Publications 2131 Lincoln Road, N.E. Washington, DC 20002-1199 U.S.A. www.icspublications.org Volume Two translated by Anne Englund Nash Copyright © 1995 by Washington Province of Discalced Carmelites ICS Publications 2131 Lincoln Road, N.E. Washington, DC 20002-1199 U.S.A. www.icspublications.org Used with permission.

Quotations from the visionary 'Anne' taken from her book "The Mist of Mercy". Published by Direction For Our Times. © 2006, Used by permission. See www.directionforourtimes.com re Anne's ministry.

Quotations from Marino Restrepo's book "From Darkness into the Light", © Pilgrims of Love. See www. marinorestrepo.com.. Used by permission.

Quotations from Dr. Howard Storm are from 'The God of Miracles' by Michael Brown, Queenship Publishing Company, ©. Used by permission. See also "Spirit Daily" website.

Quotations from Barbara 'X' are from 'The God of Miracles' by Michael Brown, Queenship Publishing Company, ©. Used by permission. See also "Spirit Daily" website.

Quotations from Linnie Smith are taken from the "Spirit Daily" website ©.

Quotations from Don Piper are from his book "90 Minutes in Heaven" co-written by Cecil Murphy is published by Revell, a division of Baker Publishing Group, ©, 2004, Used by permission.

Quotations from Fr. Steven Scheier, from his interview on EWTN. Used by permission.

All quotations from Gloria Polo are taken from gloriapolo.neuevangelisierung.org/indexeng.htmls ©. See also www.apostolat.org/gloriapoloCOM/contactoeng.html. Used by permission.

Quotations re Don Bosco are from "Stories of Don Bosco" by Peter Lappin, © 1979, Don Bosco Publications.

Quotations from Denise Curtis' book, "A Song For David", © 2008, published by Lulu.com. used by permission

Quotations from Stanley Villavicencio, are taken his talks at Divine Mercy Conference, Dublin.

Quotations from Barbara Harris Whitfield, www.cbwhit.com/barbarahome.htm, ©, Used by permission.

Quotations from 'Beyond the Darkness' by Angie Fenimore, copyrighted © 1995 by Angie Fenimore. Foreward copyrighted © by Betty J Eadie 1995. Used by permission of Bantam Books, a division of Random House, Inc.

Quotations from George Rodonaia taken from extracts of his testimony on www.near-death.com which are taken mostly from Phillip Berman's book 'The Journey Home', © copyrighted by Phillip Berman, 1996.

All quotations from Lee Ezell are from her book "The Missing Piece". © copyrighted 1987 by Lee Ezell. Published by Servant Publications. Used by permission. See her website

Quotations from David Oakford and from Dr. Richard Eby are taken from www.near-death.com, ©.

Quotations from Fr. Tomislav Ivancic from his talks at the Priests' Retreat, Medjugorje '07.

Quotations from Fr. Joe Bill taken from his healing retreat talks.

— —

"And I heard a voice from heaven saying, "Write this: Blessed are the dead who die in the Lord henceforth." "Blessed indeed," says the Spirit, "that they may rest from their labours, for their deeds follow them."
Rev 14:13 RSV

2

Contents

Before you even read the table of contents, stop and pray: "Lord, I invite you to speak to me through this book."

————————————————————————————

"Our true home is in Heaven and from Heaven will come the Saviour, the Lord Jesus Christ, who will transform our lowly bodies into copies of His own glorious body." Phil 3:20-21a

3

You Are An Eternal Spirit

We have an eternal spirit that lives on when our mortal bodies die. **In fact it is far more true to say that we are eternal spirits now conjoined to mortal bodies.** We take it that the mortal body is the more essential part of who we are, and that the eternal spirit is some sort of vague shadowy reflection inside, but in fact the opposite is the case:- our eternal spirit is the more essential element of who we are. As you will see in the next few chapters, from people's near-death experiences, and even, in the cases of Don Piper and George Rodonaia, from what were clearly after-death experiences, not merely does one's eternal spirit live on when one's mortal body dies, but it is able to see, hear, smell, touch, feel, think and to come to understand new truths.

People who were blind all their lives, are able to see and to describe in vivid detail what they saw. People who had good sight all their lives, discover that this is nothing compared to how they see things on the other side. People who were deaf all their lives are able to hear perfectly. People with good hearing all their lives, experience hearing with a new sensitivity. From studying genuine near-death experiences, one discovers that the real capacity to see is in our eternal spirit. One's physical eyes merely enable one's spirit to see while one's spirit is conjoined to its mortal body. One's real capacity to hear is in one's eternal spirit; one's physical ears merely enable one's spirit to hear while conjoined to one's mortal body. Likewise each of one's senses are antennae of one's eternal spirit.

People who did not believe that life continues after death, discover that it most certainly does. People who did not believe that God exists, encounter Him. People who have committed their lives to Jesus have a tremendous experience of His love and of being loved. People who had little capacity to recognise the truth about their lives, including the truth about their own selfishness and the truth about how they have brought hurt into the lives of others, are enabled to see the full truth about their lives, the good and the bad, and after their near-death experience, there is often a major conversion.

In dealing with near death experiences, we do, however, need to be cautious. All near-death experiences are partial. Some mistake their partial near-death experience for the full thing. Worse still, those who through their own fault, rejected God and lived selfishly in this life, may come under the influence of satan masquerading as an angel of light. But even where this happens, the person has a real out-of-body experience. That person too experiences an afterlife.

"We know that while we are at home in the body we are away from the Lord, for we walk by faith, not by sight. ... We would rather be away from the body and at home with the Lord." 2 Cor 5:6b, 8 RSV

If one approaches near-death experiences with an open mind, and examines all the evidence, one has to accept that at the centre of one's being is an eternal spirit. One's eternal spirit is the most essential element of who one is. **Indeed one is not truly alive until one's eternal spirit is enabled to come alive within.** One's intellect, one's conscience, one's will, one's spiritual heart, one's inner personhood are all components which enable one's eternal spirit to operate through one's mortal body.

We also discover that during near-death experiences, while one's spirit is away from one's body, one can have one's life transformed. Sometimes people who have been victims all their lives, have their lives transformed as a result of their eternal spirits being embraced by God's unconditional love. Barbara Harris Whitfield suffered all her life, but after her spirit was embraced by God's love during her NDE, she was a new woman. Often being permeated by God's unconditional love is accompanied by being challenged about one's life. Angie Fenimore, another victim of much abuse, attempted suicide after a life of despair, then after she was embraced by God's love and challenged about her actions, she was able to come back into her mortal body and live as a new woman. Marino Restrepo abused drugs, drink and sex for thirty three years, but after first finding himself at the gates of hell, then being embraced by God's love, he was able to come back into his body and to dedicate his life totally to God.

The bottom line is:- heal one's spirit and one's life will be transformed. Even where people have had a lifetime of suffering or even of being addicted to drugs, drink and sex, once their eternal spirits have been forced to face the truth about their lives and then embraced by God's love, they can come back into their mortal bodies and live the new life, leaving their addictions behind. In the first half of this book there are stories of where people had this happen for them during near-death experiences. There are three chief elements to these life transforming near-death experiences:- being embraced by God's love; being shown the full truth about one's life; and, if one through one's own fault has made wrong choices, being faced with the eternal consequences.

In the second half of the book I will look at how to become open to God's love and to have one's life transformed while still in one's mortal body. God desires to help each of us to experience His love and to have our lives transformed here on earth. Become open to this, and we can look forward with joy and anticipation to the next life.

— —

"God himself will be with them; he will wipe away every tear from their eyes, and death shall be no more, neither shall there be mourning nor crying nor pain any more, for the former things have passed away."
Revelation 21:3-4

5

He Was Dead For 90 Minutes

In January 1989, Don Piper attended a Baptist Conference at Lake Livingston in Houston. On his way home, as he was crossing the bridge over Trinity River, an oncoming juggernaut, an eighteen wheeler, crossed to his side of the road, hit his car head on, and went right over his car crushing both the car and Don inside it.

Don was badly broken up. Sections of bone from one of his arms and from one of his legs were never found. He clearly had massive injuries. There was blood coming from his eyes, nose, ears and mouth. When the medics arrived, they examined him and declared him dead. That was at 11.45 am. Before his body could be removed to the mortuary, he had to be certified dead by a more senior doctor. So at 1.15 pm, his body was again examined. **He was still dead.** A cover was draped over the car until his body could be removed.

Meanwhile traffic had backed up for miles. Dick and Anita Onerecker were also on their way home from the Baptist conference. They were now stuck in the tailback of traffic, and eventually decided to walk up to the scene. They saw the red car that was covered over, and were told that the man in it was dead. They didn't know that it was their friend Don. **Baptists do not believe in praying for the dead, but suddenly Dick heard an inner voice speaking to him, "You need to pray for the man in the red car."** His first instinct was to dismiss the idea as ridiculous, given that the man was dead. Yet he became convinced that God had spoken; that God was asking him to pray for the dead man.

This was Baptist country. Everyone on the scene was a Baptist. When he said that he would like to pray with the man in the covered-over car, he was emphatically reminded that the man was dead. When he said that he would still like to pray with him, he was told in no uncertain manner that not merely was the man dead, but that the scene was so horrific it would be best for him not to see it. Dick explained that he had been a medic in Vietnam and so would be well able to cope with the sight of the man's injuries. "You haven't seen anybody this bad" was the reply he got. However he was given permission to pray with the dead man, if that was what he really wanted.

Don's car was crushed, but the hatchback part had been torn off, so Dick was able to crawl in that way. Getting far enough in to be able to reach Don's body, he checked for a pulse. There wasn't one. **Don was still dead!** Dick still didn't know who the man was. All he knew was that even though the man was dead, God was asking him to pray with him. So he started to pray. When he ran out of

---

"The righteous will shine like the sun in the kingdom of their Father"
Mt 13:42 RSV.

6

words, he sang a hymn, then continued to pray and to sing as he felt led. As he prayed, he felt an inspiration to pray that the man be healed of unseen injuries - meaning brain and internal injuries. It was a rather strange prayer to make for a man who was clearly dead - and whose obvious external injuries were massive. Dick found himself praying with a passion and an intensity he had never before experienced. Then he began to sing again. This time he started to sing, "What a friend we have in Jesus." **Guess the shock he got, when suddenly, the 'dead' man started singing it with him.**

Dick got out of the car as fast as he could, and running over to the doctor, started to shout, **"The man's alive! He's not dead! He's alive!"** The doctor thought Dick was nuts. Don had been checked and pronounced dead not once but twice. The doctor had seen for himself that Don was not just dead, but utterly crushed. Now here was a preacher claiming that he was not merely alive but singing. **"He's alive! The dead man started singing with me."** Claiming that the 'dead' man was alive was bad enough. Claiming that he was singing certainly was pushing out the boat. The doctor was convinced he was dealing with an utter nutcase. Nor was the situation helped when Dick continued to shout, **"He's singing! He's alive!"**

Nobody would listen to Dick. After all Don wasn't just dead, he was crushed and mangled. Finally Dick threatened to lie down across the road if they wouldn't check Don again. Eventually the ambulance driver agreed that if it would make Dick happy, he would check that the dead man was still dead. He walked brusquely over to the car, pulled back the cover, reached inside to prove that Don was still dead - and then let out an almighty shriek! Suddenly everyone rushed into action - or at least they attempted to rush into action! But the car was completely crushed down on Don's mangled body, so he could not be stirred without heavy cutting equipment. That had to be ordered in from over thirty miles away.

During the wait, Dick got back in and continued to pray with Don. Don's injuries were massive. The wheels of the lorry had gone right over him. The dashboard had come down across his legs crushing his right leg and breaking his left in two places. His left arm was dislocated and had swung backwards over the seat. It was barely still attached, with a section of bone missing. The lower left arm was just a piece of flesh that held the hand to the rest of the arm. The same was true of his left leg. Four and a half inches of the femur were missing and never found. His calf and foot were just attached by skin and flesh. Why he didn't lose all the blood from his body defies medical explanation.

Blood seeped from his eyes, ears and nose. It was clear that he had originally sustained massive head injuries and internal injuries. When Dick prayed that

— —

Jesus said, "Young man I say to you, arise." And the dead man sat up and began to speak. Luke 7:14-15

he be healed of hidden injuries something must have happened. But his injuries were still massive. His journey to hospital was to prove utterly horrific, and then he was transferred from one hospital to another by ambulance as the weather was too bad for a helicopter. Worse still, they had to keep him awake, so there was a limit to the medication that he could be given. It was an utter nightmare. He thought that the journey would never end. Eventually it did. But terrible pain was to be his constant companion for many months. There were times when he just wanted to die; "God, is this what I came back for?" he cried out many times. "You brought me back to earth for this?"

Of the accident itself, all Don remembered is seeing the bridge, and then suddenly being enveloped in a light with a brilliance that could not be described in words. He says "In my next moment of awareness, I was standing in heaven. Joy pulsated through me as I looked around, and at that moment I became aware of a large crowd of people. ... As the crowd rushed toward me, I didn't see Jesus, but I did see people I had known. Their presence seemed absolutely natural. They rushed toward me, and every person was smiling, shouting, and praising God. .. Although no one said so, intuitively I knew they were my celestial welcoming committee. It was as if they had all gathered just outside heaven's gate, waiting for me."

First to greet him was his grandfather, Joe Kulbeth. Next was his childhood friend, Mike Wood, who had himself been killed in a tragic car accident, and whose death, Don had never got over, but now as they met, all the grief was swept away.
Then he was met by a great throng of people that he had known on earth, all radiating immense happiness and joy. Earthly words, he says, are inadequate to describe the "unimaginable joy, excitement, warmth, and total happiness" as "everyone continually embraced me, touched me, spoke to me, laughed, and praised God".

Interestingly Don speaks of seeing people of different ages, "old and young and every age in-between"; all of them people who had influenced his life in some way. Don's family was big into reunions, but this reunion surpassed them all. He say, "Heaven was many things, but without a doubt, it was the greatest family reunion of all." And the ambiance was terrific:- "Warm, radiant light engulfed me. As I looked around, I could hardly grasp the vivid, dazzling colours."

Don says, "Never, even in my happiest moments, had I ever felt so fully alive. I stood speechless in front of the crowd of loved ones, still trying to take in everything. Over and over I heard how overjoyed they were to see me and how excited they were to have me among them. I'm not sure if they actually said the words or not, but I knew they had been waiting and expecting me."

Every creature in heaven and on earth was singing: "To him who sits on the throne and to the Lamb, be praise and honour, glory and might, for ever and ever!" Rev 5:13

"I wasn't conscious of anything I'd left behind and felt no regrets about leaving family or possessions. It was as if God had removed anything negative from my consciousness, and I could only rejoice at being together with these wonderful people. They looked exactly as I once knew them - although they were more radiant and joyful than they'd ever been on earth."

His great-grandmother, Hattie Mann was Native American. She was an old woman when Don knew her, her head and shoulders bent forward, an extremely wrinkled up face, and usually not a tooth in her head, as she seldom wore her dentures. Now she was here to greet him, standing totally upright, her face radiant, and with sparking white teeth that were clearly her own. As she smiled her entire face lit up and radiated, nor did she any longer look old in the sense of being worn out. All the ravages of living on earth were gone from everybody, and even those who hadn't looked beautiful in earthly terms, now looked just perfect.

Don says, "They embraced me, and no matter which direction I looked, I saw someone I had loved and who had loved me. .. I felt loved - more loved than ever before in my life. .. When they gazed at me, I knew what the Bible means by perfect love. It emanated from every person who surrounded me, and I felt as if I absorbed their love for me."

Up ahead was what Don describes as the entrance to Heaven. Coming out from it was, he says, "a brilliance that was brighter than the light that surrounded us, utterly luminous." Earthly words, he says, cannot describe what he was now seeing, nor the feelings of wonder and awe he experienced.

"There was absolutely nothing but intense, radiant light. ... The powerful light I had encountered when I met my loved ones paled into darkness as the radiance and iridescence in front of me increased. It was as if each step I took intensified the glowing luminosity. I didn't know how it could get more dazzling, but it did.

"I wasn't blinded, but I was amazed that the lustre and intensity continually increased. Strange as it seems, as brilliant as everything was, each time I stepped forward, the splendour increased. The farther I walked, the brighter the light. The light engulfed me, and I had the sense that I was being ushered into the presence of God."

On earth when we step into a bright light, our eyes take time to adjust, but now his eternal spirit had no such difficulties. He could see with ease. He says, "In heaven, each of our senses is immeasurable heightened to take it all in. And what a sensory celebration! ... A holy awe came over me as I stepped forward. I had no idea what lay ahead, but I sensed that with each step I took, it would grow more wondrous. Then I heard the music. ... It was like a song that goes

— —

"The city has no need of sun or moon to shine upon it, for the glory of God is its light, and its lamp is the Lamb. By its light shall the nations walk; ..... and there shall be no night there." Rev 21:23 -24 RSV

on forever. I felt awestruck, wanting only to listen. It seemed as if I were part of the music - and it played in and through my body. I stood still, and yet I felt embraced by the sounds."

It wasn't just the humans who were singing and making music. The angels were using their wings to create a tremendous ongoing holy melody. He didn't see the angels, yet he is totally convinced that this is what he was hearing. Nor was that the only thing he heard. There was music, but it was totally unlike anything that he had ever heard on earth. He says, "The melodies of praise filled the atmosphere. The nonstop intensity and endless variety overwhelmed me. The praise was unending, but the most remarkable thing to me was that hundreds of songs were being sung at the same time - all of them worshipping God."

The whole atmosphere was one of praise, with the praise totally centred on God. He says, "Praise was everywhere and all of it was musical, yet comprised of melodies and tones I'd never experienced before. 'Hallelujah!' 'Praise!' 'Glory to God!' 'Praise to the King!' Such words rang out in the midst of all the music. I don't know if angels were singing them or if they came from humans. I felt so awestruck and caught up in the heavenly mood that I didn't look around. My heart filled with the deepest joy I've ever experienced. I wasn't a participant in the worship, yet I felt as if my heart rang out with the same kind of joy and exuberance."

Despite the fact that thousands of hymns were being sung at the same time, it was all in total harmony. Every sound blended with and complemented the rest, yet despite this great multitude of hymns being sung in harmony, Don could distinguish each song. They included many of the hymns and choruses that Don himself had sung over the years, but also there were hundreds of hymns that he had never heard before. He says, "Hymns of praise, modern sounding choruses, and ancient chants filled my ears and brought not only a deep peace but the greatest feeling of joy I've ever experienced."

No wonder when Don came back to earth, he came alive joining Dick in singing, "What a friend we have in Jesus"!

Evaluation of Don's Testimony

Don was dead. His experience is an after-death experience rather than a near-death experience. He is a committed Christian from the Baptist community. Committed Baptist's tend to have a truly living relationship with Jesus. Not merely did Don know and love Jesus, but he was living the love-filled transformed life. He was

— —

"After this I looked, and there was an enormous crowd, far too many to possibly count! They were from every race, tribe, nation, and language, and they stood in front of the throne and of the lamb, dressed in white robes and holding palm branches in their hands" Rev 7:9

actually coming from a Christian convention when the accident happened. He was ready to go to Heaven the moment he died. That, I would suggest, is why he had no experience of undergoing a life review during his near death experience unlike most people who have near-death experiences. He didn't need a life-review. That had all been taken care of while he was here on earth. He was ready to go straight to the gates of Heaven the very moment he died. He had this experience while outside the gates. Just think what it must be like inside!!

Don was ready to go straight to the gates of Heaven. This should be our aim also - to so live that we will be able to go to Heaven the very moment we die. When we walk with Jesus, Heaven becomes something to look forward to, while the Bible tells us that God desires to deliver us of all fear of Him and all fear of death and judgement. Perfect love, and God is love, casts out all fear. If you are walking with God, He wants you to know that He loves you. If you are truly walking with Him, then He wants you to look forward with joy and anticipation to the next life.

The visionary Anne, (see page 22), was once praying beside a dying priest who had lived the dedicated priestly life. As she prayed, she had a vision of the preparations that were already underway to welcome the priest to Heaven. The Heavenly equivalent of the red carpet will be rolled out for us too if we walk with Jesus in this life, and like happened in the case of Don Piper, we too will be met by a welcoming committee comprised primarily of people who have assisted us in our faith journey, or whom we have assisted.

Meanwhile we Catholics would do well to read again what Don has written about singing in Heaven. We Catholics have not taken to congregational singing. Sometimes there is a stubborn resistance to it. But our eternal spirit was made with both a love for singing and a need for singing, especially in our relationship with God. Spiritual singing nourishes our eternal spirit. Where there is vibrant singing that comes from the heart, in Church or in Prayer Groups, it often leads to real spiritual growth - and indeed to miracles. What is more, one cannot enter Heaven until one has been delivered from all resistance to spiritual singing.

Footnote

Don Piper's Book, **"90 Minutes in Heaven"** co-written by Cecil Murphy is published by Revell, Grand Rapids, Michigan. While it comes from the Baptist community, it is a book that I would recommend all Christian bookshops to stock. It is a book that truly has the power to touch lives. I have no hesitation in rating it amongst the ten best books I have ever read.

— —

They fell on their faces before the throne and worshipped God, saying, "Amen! Blessing and glory and wisdom and thanksgiving and honour and power and might be to our God for ever and ever! Amen!" Rev 7:12 RSV

Purgatory And The Bible

Don Piper was fully ready to go to Heaven the moment he 'died'. He arrived straight at the entrance to Heaven without any life-review or having to deal with any unpleasant experiences. He had truly loved God and lived for Him and for his family. Jesus was His best Friend. But what of those whose love for God is at best lukewarm, or who are in rebellion against God, or who have caused real moral and spiritual hurt to many people?

What some claim to have experienced while 'dead' can best be understood in the light of the Catholic understanding of Purgatory. Christians of other denominations have a problem with Purgatory on the basis that they hold it isn't Biblical, so I invite you to briefly bear with me as I show that Purgatory is a Biblical doctrine. (Or you can feel free to jump to the next chapter.)

Rev 21:27 tells us that "nothing unclean shall enter Heaven". Yet it is very clear that many who call themselves 'saved' are also deeply attached to a sin or sins. Often much transformation, even very difficult transformation, is required. If it doesn't take place in this life, it still has to take place before they enter heaven.

The only question is:- how does this transformation take place? Some believe that we are simply 'covered over with the robe of righteousness'. But Jesus said, "There is nothing now hidden that shall not be brought to light, nor anything secret that shall not be brought out into the open." Luke 8:17

St. Paul warned, "When the Lord comes, He will bring to light the things now done under the cover of darkness, and He will reveal what was really in people's hearts. Then each person will be rewarded accordingly." 1 Corinthians 4:5

Again he said, "Each man's work will become manifest; for the Day will disclose it, because it will be revealed with fire, and the fire will test what sort of work each one has done. If the work which any man has built on the foundation survives, he will receive a reward. If any man's work is burned up, he will suffer loss, though he himself will be saved, but only as through fire." 1 Cor 3:13-15

The word purgatory comes from the Latin for fire, but there are two different types of fire mentioned in the New Testament, and it is very important that we distinguish between them. There is the fire of the rubbish dump which goes on and on, and which is used as an image of hell. But there is also another fire. Jesus says, "Everyone will be salted with fire" Mk 9:49. This is the fire which will test each man's work; the "refiner's fire" mentioned in Malachy 3:2. This

---

" I died and behold I am alive for evermore, and I have the keys of death and Hades" Rev 1:18 RSV

fire does not destroy. Instead it purifies. One fire represents the destruction that is Hell, the other fire is an image of the cleansing that is Purgatory. Fire is used as an image of what happens in Purgatory, but remember it is an image. It doesn't mean that there is an actual fire there. The phrase used by St. Paul in 1 Cor 3:15 is "as through fire".

In **2 Maccabees 12:40–45**, when Judas discovered that his fallen soldiers had sinned grievously by wearing pagan symbols, he took up a collection to send to Jerusalem to have prayers offered for them. "Thus he made atonement for the dead, that they might be delivered from their sin."

While 2 Maccabees is not in the Protestant Bible, a very strong case can be made that it should be. Furthermore 2 Maccabees very definitely represents what was then commonly believed, and what was still commonly believed in the time of Jesus. Had Jesus rejected this belief, surely He would have said something. Instead He refers to a sin that will not be forgiven either "in this age on in the age to come". "Whoever sins against the Holy Spirit will not be forgiven, either in this age or in the age to come" Matthew 12:32.

At the very least, this implies that Jesus knew that people believed that some sins could be forgiven in "the age to come". Once again He did not reject such belief, but instead spoke in a way that could be interpreted as supporting such a belief. On top of that, we discover a teaching that is at least partially similar to Maccabees in **1 Peter 3:19–20**. "Being put to death in the flesh, but made alive in the spirit, Jesus went and preached to the spirits in prison."

Who were these souls in prison? They were those "who formerly did not obey" 1 Peter 3:20. Peter explicitly mentions those who tried God's patience in the time of Noah, but clearly they represent all who "did not obey" in past times.

Why did Jesus preach to these souls in prison? Peter gives the answer:- "This is why the gospel was preached even to the dead, that though judged in the flesh like men, they might live in the spirit like God" 1 Peter 4:6. In other words, even though they had disobeyed God while here on earth, they were being given a second chance to respond to Jesus on the other side so that they might enter Heaven.

As you will see from the following chapters, this is exactly what Dr. Howard Storm, Angie Fenimore, Gloria Polo, George Rodonaia, and several others claim to have happened to them during their near-death experiences. Dr. Storm had rejected the gospel when growing up. George Rodonaia had never been introduced to it. Angie Fenimore had committed suicide. Gloria Polo had sponsored abortions. Each of them claim to have encountered Jesus when outside their bodies. Each of them had a very definite Purgatory experience as they faced the truth about

— —

"The Father disciplines us for our good, that we may share his holiness."
Hebrews 12:10

13

their lives. Dr. Storm and Gloria Polo could be said to have escaped hell by the skin of their teeth. Angie Fenimore visited the very depths of Purgatory.

But each of their experiences, while they occurred in recent times, correspond to what the Bible says happened when Jesus, on His death, went to minister to the souls in prison.

It should also be noted that while Jesus said to **the good thief**, "This day you will be with me in Paradise," Jesus did not enter Heaven until the Ascension. It is possible that Paradise here corresponds not to Heaven but to the upper realms of Purgatory. Remember that following His death, Jesus went to preach "to the souls in prison". So Jesus visited Purgatory, not Heaven, on the day He died.

Dr. Richard Eby had a genuine near-death experience which changed his life, and led to his retiring from his prominent and successful medical practice to become a minister. He claimed that Jesus told him during his near-death experience that "Paradise is a holding place for the souls who have accepted me as their Saviour ..... Paradise is also my heavenly school for perfecting the saints. You must be taught how to become priests and kings in my kingdom so as to teach others to worship My Father in spirit and in truth."

This sounds very much like the upper 'realms' of Purgatory. It would make sense of how Jesus promised the good thief that he would join Him in Paradise that very day, even though Jesus did not ascend to His Father until the Ascension. However one needs to be cautious concerning the teaching people claim to have received during near-death experiences - including Dr. Eby's claims. See pages 94 - 95

Then there is the story of **Lazarus and the rich man.** We normally take it that the rich man went to Hell, but he calls Abraham, "Father Abraham", which is totally consistent with the reverence of a soul in Purgatory. Souls in Hell would only call Abraham, "Father Abraham" when trying to be cunning. Even more clear-cut is the fact that the rich man wanted his brothers to be warned about their lifestyle. This corresponds with our belief that the souls in Purgatory intercede for us here on earth. The souls in Hell most certainly do not intercede for us or want us to be warned about our lifestyle. However the story of Lazarus and the rich man is merely a story told to make a point, so it is important not to read too much into the minor details.

There are also some contradictions in Bible passages about salvation that can best be explained by there being the possibility of Purgatory as well as Heaven and Hell. One the one hand, there are passages in the Bible that make it all appear so easy:- "Everyone who calls on the name of the Lord will be saved" Romans 10:13. "If you are faithful to His covenant, his salvation will reach to your children and children's children" Ps 103:18

Sirs, what must I do to be saved? And they said, "Believe in the Lord Jesus and you and your household will be saved" Acts 16:30-31.

"Whoever gives to one of these little ones even a cup of cold water because he is a disciple, truly I say to you, he shall not lose his reward." Matthew 10:42 RSV

On the other hand, there are the passages that make it appear very challenging. "Enter by the narrow gate, for the gate is wide and the way is easy, that leads to destruction, and those who enter by it are many. For the gate is narrow and the way is hard, that leads to life, and those who find it are few." Mt. 7:13-14 RSV

The tension between these different passages could be explained if some passages refer to going straight to Heaven, whereas other passages are speaking in terms of 'being saved' - that is avoiding Hell.

Jesus also spoke in terms of there being stages of salvation. "He who believes has eternal life and I will raise him up on the last day." He did not say "he who believes will go straight to Heaven, yet it is clear that we do not just stay 'sleeping' until the Last Day - as some believe. Moses and Elijah came to be with Jesus during that special event we call the transfiguration, so clearly they were not 'sleeping'. Jesus promised the good thief, "This day you will be with me in Paradise", so clearly he wasn't going to be 'sleeping'. So then it appears that there will be stages to salvation:- what happens when we die and what happens on the Last Day.

Some explain this in terms of "the resurrection of the body". But what is the resurrection of the body? In Heaven we will have a body but it will not be a material body. Jesus rose body and soul, yet this did not prevent Him from entering locked rooms. Our Lady's 'body' in her apparitions clearly is a spiritual body even though we Catholic's affirm that she is now enjoying the fullness of Heaven - including whatever "the resurrection of the body" consists of.

The more logical explanation of all this is that there are stages to salvation:- that the fact that one "has eternal life" does not guarantee that one will go straight to Heaven the moment one's dies. It merely means that one will escape eternal damnation. It is possible that some people will remain in Purgatory until the Last Day.

Footnote

In the messages of Fatima, which are accepted as genuine by the Catholic Church, one area of controversy concerns what Our Lady said when Lucia asked concerning two young ladies who had died. Our Lady apparently said that one of them would remain in Purgatory until the Last Day. This is not inconsistent with Angie Fenimore's testimony - see P. 34.

— —

"Then the eyes of the blind shall be opened, and the ears of the deaf unstopped; then shall the lame man leap like a hart, and the tongue of the dumb sing for joy, for waters shall break forth in the wilderness, and streams in the desert." Isaiah 35:5-6 RSV

They Were Organising His Funeral

Stanley Villavicencio was raised with a great devotion to the Divine Love (Sacred Heart) of Jesus Christ, even from his school years. He married a nurse, Melissa, in Cebu in the Philippines. They deliberately bought a house close to a little chapel dedicated to the Sacred Heart. But when the house was bought, they discovered that the chapel was only a temporary structure. Stanley then led the efforts to have a permanent chapel built. He also became a member of the Perpetual Dawn Rosary Association in Cebu. So Stanley was a dedicated Christian. But he also had his faults. He loved God, but he was also sinning in different ways. His life had yet to be truly transformed.

There is a beautiful local tradition in Cebu that when a special family occasion occurs, the head of the family receives into the home a large pilgrim statue of the Virgin Mary. March 2, 1993 was the birthday of one of Stanley's children. The statue duly arrived that morning. Stanley, as head of the household, was to receive it. But they couldn't wake him, so his mother-in-law did the honours. Then they heard him moaning. Entering his room, they found him lying in bed, convulsing, with blood coming out of his mouth, forcefully. He was rushed to Chong Hua Hospital. Here he was put on a life-support machine, but the doctors said that his chance of survival was one in a million.

The following day, the doctors declared him brain dead. They called his wife and asked permission to take him off the life-support apparatus. Preparations were then put in place for his funeral.

Meanwhile Stanley was having a near-death experience. Stanley already had a living relationship with Jesus. Because of this, on leaving his body, he quickly saw the light, and then Jesus was standing before him.

He says, "At first I saw a light, a very big bright light, but not glaring. You can stare at it. It is like a fountain. It is like a fog as it slowly evaporates. Then I notice someone standing in front of me. Looking at His face, I recognized Jesus. As we are looking at each other, He raised His left hand and as he did, the clouds above were sucked downwards and when they reached just above us, the clouds keep on turning and changing in colour and when they stopped, they became like a video screen. Then Jesus showed me the film of my life, from my childhood up to my present. As I watched the times I did good, the video flowed normally, but every time I committed a sin, it was shown in slow motion, highlighting the sin

---

"They will see the Son of Man coming on the clouds of Heaven" Mt 24:30.

and its effects. I had also committed some bigger sins, what we call the mortal sins. When it came to them, the video would stop, zoom in and enlarge. I said to myself, 'This is too painful to look at.' I tried to shut my eyes, but shutting one's eyes only works when still in our mortal bodies. Even when I closed my eyes I could still see it.

"During this life-review, I also saw that every time I committed a sin, deep within I could feel the heaviness. I could feel the weight. I was not conscious of this weight when committing the sin, but deep in my spirit, it was there. The more I committed a sin, the more the heaviness, the more the weight. And I had a deep sense that before I enter Heaven all these must be completely cleansed away.

"On the other hand, every time I did good, like for example giving to the poor, there was joy in my spirit. During the life-review, this came across as if my spirit was floating, and I had a deep sense that in helping the poor or whoever, it was really Jesus I was helping. 'Whatsoever you do to the least of My brethren, that you do unto Me.'

"I also noticed that the sins I did not confess to a Priest, I still feel a great heaviness when viewing them, but that with the sins which I did confess to a Priest, it is lighter. We cannot deny anything because the screen is so big and very clear and also the pictures are also big and below the pictures are written the day, the month, the date and the year. And below that it is also written the hour, the minutes and the seconds. So, we cannot deny anything, even the seconds are recorded.

Stanley's life was reviewed not once but three time, going back over the more significant events, especially the more serious sins. Then Jesus told him that he was to go back, that Jesus had much work for him to do on earth. Jesus promised that He would direct him by means of dreams, saying, "When I have a message for you, I will appear to you in your dreams."

When Stanley came back into his body, he caused chaos in the hospital by suddenly disconnecting himself from all the tubes and getting up. The nurse in charge of the ICU ran from the unit so fast that she broke the heel off her shoe. But that was nothing to the shock that his family got when he walked in home while they were in the middle of setting up the house for his wake.

Word soon reached the media. In the Philippines it made the news on TV, the radio and the newspapers. Following this, Cardinal Vidal of Cebu set up a commission to investigate what had really happened. It was set up immediately, that very March, while everyone had a clear remembrance of the events. Cardinal Vidal himself led the investigation.

— —

"When the Lord comes, He will bring to light the things now done under the cover of darkness, and He will reveal what was really in people's hearts. Then each person will be rewarded accordingly." 1 Corinthians 4:5

After the investigation, Cardinal Vidal released a letter confirming what happened to Stanley. He gave Stanley an endorsement letter, so that he could give his testimony around the world. He also appointed for him his own spiritual director, Msgr Chris Garcia, an expert in these things. This is because Stanley has continued to receive messages from Jesus by means of the dreams.

All who witnessed what happened were profoundly effected. The head specialist in Chong Hua Hospital, who had been in charge of Stanley when he was in the ICU, was so impressed by the miracle he had witnessed, that he left the hospital, entered seminary and is now a priest.

Stanley himself now devotes his entire life to witnessing to Jesus, travelling around the world in so far as his family commitments allow. Jesus has led him to become a promoter of the Divine Mercy. He knows all about the Divine Mercy, having experienced Jesus and how the divine mercy works, first hand!!

He is a strong believer in the power of the special prayer that Jesus gave St. Faustina called the Chaplet of Mercy, and tells many beautiful stories of prayers answered. One involves a poor man in the Philippines, whose wife needed special medicine, and having no money, he bartered his pig for the medicine. He got the medicine, started administering it to his wife, but that evening, the pig took sick and appeared to be dying. What would he do when the chemist came to collect the pig the next morning? So he got his young children together and asked them to say the Chaplet of Mercy around the pig!! Guess the giggles from the children!! He had to restart the chaplet several times!. But as they finished it, the pig got back on its feet.

In the case of Stanley's near-death experience, we see how people who love Jesus move almost immediately into the light and into the presence of Jesus. However, if there is sin in their lives, that has still to be dealt with. A key element of the purgatory phase is seeing the full truth about one's life. In Stanley's case, this was shown to him in the form of a film - it is usually shown in the form that best suits the person. Stanley, a dedicated Christian, found his life-review tough going. He wanted to shut his eyes to what he was seeing. Think of how utterly painful it must be for the person who, through his or her own fault, has rejected God and caused serious moral and spiritual hurt to others.

In Stanley's case also we see the importance of making good Confessions:- this in one of the ways given to us by God for facing the truth about our lives while here on earth.

Stephen's Near Death Experience

"But he, full of the Holy Spirit, gazed into heaven and saw the glory of God, and Jesus standing at the right hand of God; and he said, 'Behold I see the heavens opened, and the Son of Man standing at the right hand of God'." Acts 7:55-56 RSV.

Barbara's Visit To Purgatory

Don Piper was a totally dedicated Christian living the transformed life. Stanley Villavicencio was a dedicated Christian who still had certain sins to deal with. Barbara 'X' was an ordinary person, living an ordinary life, but didn't have a real relationship with Jesus. She had a near-death experience during what should have been a routine operation. The doctors thought they had lost her. Eventually they got her back.

She says, "The first thing that happened was that I realized I was in a void. It was a total black place in space, and for a fraction of a second, I was very scared. But as quickly as that came, I was directed to the left side of me, and as soon as I turned, there appeared a Light in the distance to the left side which immediately comforted me.

"At that point I just started heading toward that Light with my being (I don't know how) and I was surrounded by what I would describe as a tunnel. .. Besides the Light, which was very bright, there was a prism and music unlike any there is on earth. I don't know how to explain it. The music was so welcoming, so comforting, and so angelic that it became a part of you."

"I was moving up this tunnel and getting closer to the light and there was some kind of companion with me, because every time that I thought to ask a question, everything was immediately answered. I remember briefly stopping because within the walls of this tunnel were beings. I didn't have a great religious upbringing and never thought of Purgatory, but when I came back it seemed like part of that, probably the last level of Purgatory. The souls existed on the outside of the tunnel and were resting, as if they were sitting or standing or lying down.

"The light was brilliant. You can't describe its brilliance. It was filled with love, peace, and the knowledge. As you move through that tunnel, you are more and more consumed by it. And then I was in the presence of the Lord. I was prostrate. I was not able to withstand the majesty and the awesomeness of what was before me! I was nothingness compared to that. And then there was a period of being embraced by this love and peace and serenity and knowing I had reached my final destination, that this was truly a home."

Barbara's description of the light is very similar to that of Don Piper's. He wrote,

---

The souls in Purgatory died "in God's grace and friendship" and are "assured of their eternal salvation; but after death they undergo purification. ... The Church gives the name Purgatory to this final purification of the elect, which is entirely different from the punishment of the damned."
New Catechism 1030 - 1032

"There was absolutely nothing but intense, radiant light. ... The powerful light I had encountered when I met my loved ones paled into darkness as the radiance and iridescence in front of me increased. .... The light engulfed me, and I had the sense that I was being ushered into the presence of God."

Her description of the music is also similar to that of Don Piper's. He said, "It seemed as if I were part of the music - and it played in and through my body. I stood still, and yet I felt embraced by the sounds."

One of the major element in Don's testimony is meeting with loved ones. This is not in Barbara's testimony. I would suggest that while she met Jesus, unlike Don, she did not reach Heaven's entrance. As she said herself, hers was more an experience of Purgatory.

As part of her 'Purgatory experience' Barbara underwent a review of her life. Because her near-death experience was brief, this should not be seen as the complete review, but rather an inkling of how such a review works.

Her story is carried in Michael Brown's book, "The God of Miracles". Michael interviewed her himself. He says, "What Barbara thought as small achievements in her life - barely remembered - were magnificent to God. ... She was shown the day she had spent time listening to an acquaintance who had lost her fiance in a car accident. This was crucial to Christ; it was one of the highlights of Barbara's life, and she didn't even know it."

She was also shown the time she had placed her hand on the shoulder of a woman grieving at church. Michael Brown says, "Christ considered this one of her great achievements in life - just that little gesture, just that moment, and when we see life from that perspective, we realize that every person we encounter is meant to be encountered and is often set there as an opportunity for us to become a little miracle. It is not great feats the Lord is looking for - not feats as men describe great feats; it is how much we help others. It is how we make each other feel. It is kindness. It is the personal touch."

Here we are getting Michael Brown's 'editorial'. Yet concerning the importance of our every contact with people, he is spot on. **Each day we receive many opportunities to be the hands and voice of Jesus. What may appear small to us, has a real eternal significance.**

Michael quotes Barbara as saying, "When you see it through the eyes of the Lord, you see your life as a whole. You see how in the course of all creation your life makes a difference and you see how it affected the Creator - and how it stops at the Creator when you offend one of His own.

— —

"Whoever gives to one of these little ones even a cup of cold water because he is a disciple, truly I say to you, he shall not lose his reward."
Matthew 10:42 RSV

"We don't see things the way the Lord does, and for me it was a tremendous eye-opener. At this point, the way I was offending the Lord the most in my life was my attitude and in the way I spoke to my husband and children - my nearly verbal abuse. It was the tone and the things that I said that were very offending to another's soul and heart. You can be firm with your kids, but the Lord doesn't want you to use an insulting tone. I was shown my vocabulary and the tone with which I said things, because it was a condescending one."

Michael Brown says, "In this trip to the other side, Barbara was shown how particular events bore tremendous repercussions. When she rose grumpily from sleep and was negative to her family, she saw how this spread to others throughout the day at school, at the workplace, at stores and then through the families of those who were touched by the negativity. She was shown a drop of light that started in one spot and went around the globe in a band of light. That was the way it was supposed to be. But she was also shown that when she awoke and was negative, a circle of darkness went over the circle of light, erasing it."

Barbara told him, "When I got up in the morning, smiled, and presented breakfast hugging the children, it went from my house everywhere. I was shown a drop of light that falls on the ocean and has a rippling effect."

This is another theme that comes up again and again. Gloria Polo was shown how she had brought hurt into the lives of millions. If we cause severe spiritual, moral or emotional hurt to someone, they in turn will end up hurting others, including their children. This starts a cycle of hurting that can be passed down through the generations. Thus it is possible for us today to hurt people who will not even be conceived for another 200 years or even 500 years. I have seen some situations of hurt within families, where I would consider it an absolute miracle if in 200 years time, the descendants of those families were not still caught in an ongoing cycle of being hurt and hurting.

Likewise, if we learn to walk with God, we will bring blessing into the world, and this blessing keeps spreading outwards in the present era and also downwards through the coming generations.

Footnote

All quotations from Michael Brown's beautiful book, "The God of Miracles", Queenship Publishing Company. A very uplifting book.

———————————————————————————

"Sharp words can wound as deeply as any sword, but wisely chosen words can heal" Proverbs 12:18

Anne's Visions Of Purgatory

There is a visionary, who to protect the privacy of her family, uses the name Anne. She now lives in Ireland. Nothing is published without first being submitted to her bishop. This means that her messages and visions can be considered 'safe'. It is not for me to discern whether the messages received through Anne are supernatural, but I have found them very uplifting and inspiring.

In April, 2007, she had a series of visions concerning Purgatory. Again it is not for me to discern whether these visions are supernatural, but, for the first time ever, I feel that I have come to understand the nature of Purgatory in a way that is consistent with God who is love. There is also a great consistency between Anne's visions of Purgatory and some near-death experiences.

We have traditionally looked upon Purgatory as a place of punishment. This is a mistake. In Anne's visions, Purgatory is above all a 'place' or process of God's mercy, not of punishment. It is a place or process provided by God for sinners who are not eternally lost, but who yet are not ready for Heaven. Those with unrepented sin are not ready for Heaven. Those who have caused serious spiritual or moral hurt to others, and who have not repented and sought to make reparation, are not ready for Heaven.

In Purgatory, God allows one to see the full truth about one's life. The full truth about one's life includes all the hurt and damage one caused through one's past sins. Purgatory is a place where one takes responsibility for the damage that one has done, and intercedes for those that one has hurt. During her visions, Anne witnessed several people in various stages of the purgative process.

On her first mystical experience of Purgatory, Anne says, "Jesus stopped me at one soul and I listened. This man sat up against a tree. He was completely isolated by the mist. He sat with his back to this tree praying. I could hear him. He pleaded with God, saying, "I'm sorry. I'm sorry." Grief for his sins poured out of him. He felt so much regret. Jesus said that this was a place where souls came to be purified. I understood that there were souls all around us. I also understood that as the mist thickened, so did the isolation and remorse.
I said, "Jesus, his prayers are so beautiful, so pure." Jesus told me that all

"Each soul will have to come to terms with their response to the grace that was given to them on earth. This is what purgatory does for us. It aligns our life on earth, our service and non-service, to the reality that is Heaven. We see Heaven before us. Behind us is our response to the truth given to us on earth, otherwise known as the truth of our life. We must make the journey from one to the other." 'Anne' in "The Mist of Mercy"

prayers in this place were beautiful and pure. The man was praying passionately that souls on earth, some of them his loved ones, would be spared such dreadful remorse. Jesus explained to me that this soul had worshipped a false god. He said that **this man worshipped the god of materialism** and had rejected Him, Jesus. This man was being purified. This was Purgatory."

Concerning this encounter Anne writes, "I have to say that I would be quite content to sit in the mist at that tree and tell God how much I loved Him and how sorry I was for my sins. You could pray for everyone on earth, you could praise God, you could do plenty of good there. If Jesus wants me there, I'll be happy to go. I would hate to feel that sad about not serving Jesus, though. I assure any reader that this remorse is dreadful. Also, these souls did not see Jesus or experience Him as He went through there, so they must be denied any awareness of God's presence, much as we are here on earth."

The woman who ridiculed her husband's faith

Many people not merely refuse to respond to God themselves, but they block others who wish to respond. Anne describes another encounter she had, "Jesus brought me to a woman praying in the mists. She prayed heartbreakingly for her husband. I understood that she had blocked God's grace in their family. Her husband, destined for a high level of holiness, had not been allowed to bring his faith into their home and family. This woman had ridiculed him and mocked him until he remained silent about his feelings for God.

"Her remorse was painful. She begged God selflessly not to allow her husband to be held accountable. She was asking that she be allowed to take responsibility for his not achieving the level of holiness he should have achieved. Jesus answered her prayer and told me that in the last days of his life, her husband would advance in holiness at a miraculous pace, allowing him to be as holy as he would have become given a sympathetic and accepting atmosphere in the home.

"I gather he did not fight for his faith with his wife and it is for this she fears he will be held accountable. But I see that this man chose to keep the peace in his family with good motives of family unity. God is rewarding this and granting exceptionally gracious graces in response to the prayers of this wife and mother because their children will be affected profoundly by their father's holiness in this, his last agony on earth."

The priest who lacked reverence for the Host

Anne says, "I saw a man praying. He was a priest. This man was filled with remorse because when he served on earth, he did not pay the proper respect to Jesus in the Eucharist. He believed in the true presence, but did not pay homage

_ _

"There is nothing now hidden that shall not be brought to light, nor anything secret that shall not be brought out into the open." Luke 8:17

to this presence. He set an example of casual indifference and even disrespect to God this way. I understood that this poor man ridiculed others who did respect God's presence in the Eucharist. This was causing him the greatest pain now and He prayed passionately. He was not exactly praying for forgiveness. .....

"This priest was begging Jesus to allow him to take responsibility for the sins of others who were led astray by his mistreatment of the Eucharist. He felt responsible. I asked Jesus if this were accurate, that he was responsible. Jesus said it was not entirely accurate because many of the souls affected should have known better. For those who did not know better, the sin is less. This man wants to accept some responsibility. He does not wish to leave Purgatory until all those he negatively impacted have moved through. Jesus will decide if this is just but I got the feeling that God is about to put this lovely man into heaven. Jesus has mitigated the damage to others, partially through this man's prayers. Some of the responsibility comes from the omission of graces that could and should have been obtained by this priest had he kept his eyes on Christ in loving obedience."

She had had an abortion

One of Anne's encounters in Purgatory was with a woman who had an abortion when she was young, and was praying that others might be spared from making this mistake. Anne saw this woman move to the higher levels of Purgatory where one is no longer in isolation, but is able to interact with the other souls. A great welcome awaited her. It was revealed to Anne that because she (Anne) had offered up a difficult day yesterday, this soul had been greatly helped.

Jesus told her, "You, Anne, will be credited for the merciful speed with which she progressed. Do you see My generosity? Proclaim that generosity so that souls will live their lives in union with Me. ..... This woman would never have chosen to reject her child in another time. You saw her goodness. You saw her love for Me. She, like many others, suffered from the grave deception of the enemy. I protected her in the end, of course, and she will give glory and joy to others for all eternity. There will be a joyous reunion for her and her child."

The Fortune Teller

Anne says, "I stopped at a woman praying. She was nearly curled up in a ball and rocking, so great was her distress at the damage she had done through her disobedience to Jesus on earth. Jesus revealed that she was a fortune teller and that she led many people astray. This woman was repeating over and over again, 'I'm sorry. I'm sorry. I'm sorry.' She was in terrific remorse, deservedly so, of course. That is a given. Everything here is just and fair. Jesus drew me away. .... I could not leave her in this condition and said, 'Jesus please. What can I do?' He was so kind and gentle. He said, 'She will benefit from your intercession.' At that very moment she stopped saying, 'I'm sorry' and began saying, 'Praise you, Jesus. Thank you, Jesus. Thank you for your goodness, Lord Jesus Christ'."

The Mist of God's mercy

To give souls privacy they are surrounded by mist. Anne calls this **the mist of God's mercy.** It enables them to come to terms with themselves and with their past in privacy. "The mist is not punishment, but rather a mercy, because the mist in Purgatory ensures privacy. Souls would not like their sins to be exposed for others to see, and the work that needs to be done in the misty part of Purgatory is a private thing. For Jesus to allow souls to complete this work in the mist is another act of mercy for souls . God allows us the grace of examining our soul in privacy so that our grief and remorse will be visible only to Him and to the saints who wish to help us. The work done in our souls is very deeply personal. As I understand it, purgatory is a process of forgiving ourselves and coming to terms with our decisions against our good God. Depending on the sins and the level of malice, it takes more or less time."

The Depths of Purgatory

There are different levels to Purgatory. Some souls are on the point of entering heaven. It is beautiful where they are. But others barely escaped hell, and are still only in the very early stages of a very difficult process. For those, Purgatory isn't a pleasant place. Anne says, "Souls in this cheerless, dark place are wrapped into themselves. They are studying each of their actions and the impact their actions had on everyone affected. It's not a pretty thing to have to do if you have spent your life rejecting Christ and indeed working against Him."

Anne's description of the depths of Purgatory is remarkably similar to that of Angie Fenimore following her near-death experience. Yet even though the depths are a cheerless dark place, souls are safe here.

Anne says, "Souls are safe here. They are protected. Nobody can hurt anyone else. This area, after all, is God's area and God has custody of each soul. God has all the power. This is His jurisdiction and all is orderly. God would never allow a soul to be injured in His care and these souls, while they are in their own private 'hell' if you will, with remorse, are safe and protected. What a contrast to the real hell, where souls constantly prey upon each other."

On another occasion Anne had a further glimpse of these, the darkest parts of Purgatory. Here one is being challenged to see oneself exactly as one is, but coming to terms with this truth is not easy. Anne says, "This is the Land of Perfect Truth and any nonsense will dissipate immediately upon entry. Falseness is not

---

"Jesus spoke to them, saying, 'I am the light of the world; he who follows me will not walk in darkness, but will have the light of life'."
John 8:12 RSV

even an option or a possibility here. It cannot be. All is Truth." In this Anne's teaching does not quite do justice to the struggle some souls will have in admitting the truth about their lives. For the person who has a degree of openness to Jesus, the admission comes quickly, but for those who have just been rescued from hell by the skin of their teeth, it may take ages.

In Purgatory one sees how one's sins brought hurt into the lives of others, not just the people one directly hurt, but also the knock-on consequences, that is all the other people who were hurt by the people that one hurt. For those who through their own fault caused great hurt, it isn't easy to come to terms with that. In the depths of Purgatory this can be a real struggle. It explains why some people may be in Purgatory for a very long time - perhaps even to the end of time.

Those Approaching Heaven

As souls draw closer to heaven, they enter into communication with one another. The image Anne uses to describe it, is that of people in AA or other twelve step programmes, helping one another to understand and come to terms with their past mistakes.

Anne writes, "Souls were voluntarily examining where they had rejected God in their lives, thereby rejecting His grace so that they would not have to change. Souls were helping each other to understand where and how they had taken turns against Christ. These souls had long since been confronted with their sins and made reparation for them. In this, the end of the purification process, there was a more gentle, higher level of self-acceptance and awareness. A big part of the healing came from the acceptance and understanding of their brothers and sisters around them, who were involved in the same part of the process."

"What struck me most in this area was the love that these souls had for each other. There was such camaraderie and understanding and acceptance. I noted different races, by the way, as well as different periods, which told me that souls take different amounts of time to get through Purgatory because some souls were from a more modern era than others. All were at peace and all were content and contemplative in their self-examination.

"Another feature that jumped out at me was the total absence of falseness. There is no phoniness, no fake humility or pretending to care about someone.. It's all perfectly honest and perfectly safe, emotionally speaking, as well as every other way of speaking. .... In this area, the last area before Heaven, souls are coming to a final acceptance of their mistakes. This acceptance will last them for eternity. There is no judging of each other in this land of God, which includes Purgatory

— —

"Continue to strive to complete your salvation with reverential fear, cooperating with God who is continuously at work within you to guide you and enable you to carry our his plan" Philippians 2:12b-13

and Heaven. Souls are far too busy coming to terms with their own mistakes to point fingers at anyone else. I love it here. I love the honesty, directness, calmness, beauty, and certainty of God and his goodness. There is complete safety from ridicule or attack."

The Woman Who Loved Her Fags

Anne saw a woman who had lived a deeply religious life, but who had had a nicotine addiction. She was now praying with total trust in God, thinking not of herself at all, but praying for all the people she knew on earth. Jesus revealed that she was merely in Purgatory while separating from her addiction.

This is a challenging vision - a reminder to us that, before entry to Heaven, we need to experience total transformation. The challenge facing us is to ensure that this transformation takes place here on earth or at least that we have a firm desire for this transformation. I tend to the view that the woman in Anne's vision had no desire while on earth to be delivered from her nicotine addiction. To enter Heaven the moment we die, we need to at least desire total transformation. If you have a compulsive tendency or an addiction, bring it to Jesus. Ask for it to be broken, and start taking reasonable steps for that to happen.

But the woman who 'loved her fags' only visited the uppermost regions of Purgatory. This is a wonderful place, a place of joy, love and happiness.

The graces we missed

It isn't just the bad things we do, but also the graces that we weren't open to, that we will have to face. If I fail to take the steps to grow in my relationship with God, then countless other people will miss out. In Purgatory I will see all that.

Anne says, "Each soul will have to come to terms with their response to the grace that was given to them on earth. This is what Purgatory does for us. It aligns our life on earth, our service and non-service, to the reality that is Heaven. We see Heaven before us. Behind us is our response to the grace given to us on earth, otherwise known as the truth of our life. We must make the journey from one to the other. The two have to be merged in order for us to be ready for eternity. ... This process is a good thing. It is another aspect of God's great and perfect mercy."

'Ghosts' and souls that are not at rest

Anne does **NOT** mention ghosts in her book, yet some of what she says has a **POSSIBLE** relevance. She says that some souls may visit the scene of their past sins while still in the deeper levels of purgatory. She says, "It is possible that God will decide that a soul revisit the scene of his sin so that he can rest in it in order to absorb it fully because the soul must take responsibility for his sin. This may

"Bring these and all the departed into the LIGHT of your presence."
Eucharistic Prayer 2, which dates back to around 150 AD

be the only way the soul can heal and come to full unity with God. In a situation where a soul struggles with this, God will place him there for a period."

"The priest I saw could have spent time in the churches where he so badly offended God. While he is there, you can bet that if there is another priest struggling with a similar temptation, this priest would have beseeched Heaven to help the struggling one to avoid the same sins. This is how they love in Purgatory and Heaven. Everyone is pulling for everyone else. God allows this. It is all part of the family model that is the Communion of Saints."

Clearly the souls in Purgatory would not knowingly cause hurt to people here on earth. God's souls do not seek to cause hurt. On the contrary, their desire is to help. In Anne's visions, they are continuously interceding for those on earth. The claim that if souls are not at rest, that they will seek to draw attention to their plight by hurting the living, is **not** consistent with Anne's visions. It is true that the souls in the depths of Purgatory will beg for help, just like the rich man in the story of Lazarus and the rich man, but they will not deliberately cause hurt. If damage or hurt is being caused, it is far more likely that the evil one is in some way involved. It is possible that the person or persons responsible for the 'evil' entering the place or the family tree are still in Purgatory, coming to terms with how their sins allowed evil to enter the world. They may be begging for help, but it is not they who are causing the hurt. Instead of causing hurt on earth, the souls in Purgatory are interceding that the cycle of hurting be broken.

It is possible however that Mass being offered may at once deliver the area or family tree from whatever evil is affecting it, and at the same time bring blessing to the soul in Purgatory. Indeed, if they sense that the cycle of hurting that they started, has been broken, it will certainly bring them relief and joy.

Anne also mentioned the possibility of the souls of the damned returning to the place of their sins, but she didn't elaborate. If they return to the place of the sins, then they will certainly seek to cause hurt. It is also possible for an evil spirit to take the form of a person from the past, and to cause hurt.

Sometimes too, when bad things happen in a place, it is as if a power of evil in some way attaches to that place, and then more bad things happen. Sometimes a person may incorrectly think that the problem is a holy soul, and have Mass offered for this soul. The power of the Mass is such that it will likely bring deliverance from the evil. We do however need to regularly pray against the power of evil and how it may manifest itself.

Anne was also shown how the time of a person's death, wake and funeral is a special time when the deceased can be helped by prayer. What a shame today that there is a drop-off in the recitation of prayer during wakes. Anne saw that

"Father Abraham have mercy on me, and send Lazarus to dip the tip of his finger in water and cool my tongue with it." Luke 16:24

some people may have the process of purgation complete by the time that the funeral Mass is over.

Dealing With Our Past

God's most perfect plan for us is that we go to heaven the moment we die. Going to Purgatory is like having to do 'repeats' after an exam. One only has to do the 'repeats' when one has failed. Jesus wants us to be able to go straight to heaven. But, for this to happen, if we have either sinned seriously or even blocked God's grace, then it is important that we get very honest with ourselves about the hurt we have caused.

Anne says, "**We will have to do the work before or after death.** Nobody will enter heaven without a good long think on their behaviours and actions. This deepens my understanding of the Lord's constant urging that souls spend time in silence. If we are always distracted by noise and entertainment we will not be inclined or able to scrutinize ourselves. This self-scrutiny must be done."

Better to grieve over our past sins now and to intercede for anyone we have hurt or let down, than to end up doing so in Purgatory. Anne says, "I asked Jesus about all of our past sins. I know many souls who grieve deeply about the sins in their past. Jesus said that these souls will not suffer from their past sins if they confess them and are sorry for them.

"Grief over sins is an indication that a soul is doing the work here on earth, which will free the soul from doing the work after death. Penance, in the spirit of holding oneself accountable, is not a bad thing. By this I refer to little sacrifices in the day, small fasts, completing an action for another, and generally offering extra service or love in the spirit of reparation. Holy souls (on earth) often offer sacrifices and penances in reparation for the sins of others, which is good also."

Not merely will a holy soul do this for their sins, they will also seek to do so for the sins of others. This is entering into the spirit of reparation.

Anne's Vision of Hell

Anne says, "Our Lord showed me a glimpse of one small area of hell at this time. I saw a soul with the ugliest red eyes. They are vacant, devoid of all humanity. They are evil. This demon's eyes locked onto something and for a moment I thought it was me but he went right past me and began to assault another one such as himself. They are fighting constantly here. They are assaulting each other. They are molesting each other. They are shaming and humiliating each other. They are in the right place. I felt no fear as they cannot hurt us and I know

---

"Do not be afraid of those who kill the body but cannot kill the soul; the one to fear is the one who can destroy both body and soul in hell"
Matthew 10:28

it. I shifted my gaze and saw the most ominously evil being. It sat in a place by itself, immersed in darkness of thought. I said, 'Jesus, what is he doing?' Jesus explained that he was plotting against the Church. I felt a momentary fear for Pope Benedict. Jesus said that he could not hurt Pope Benedict because of the Holy Father's obedience. He explained and I 'saw' clearly that if a soul is obedient to the Church, that soul seals off gaps where the enemy can enter and work. This wretch could plot against the Pope until the cows come home but our beloved leader will always be safe through his obedience.

"Other poor souls will allow this demon influence through their pride and subsequent disobedience, but those who stand firm under the protection of Church authority will be safe. **I was amazed at how impenetrable a soul can become this way, through obedience.**

"Suddenly, like a snake striking, this demon lashed out and grabbed another soul, pulling him into his dungeon-like area to torture him. This victim, far from being a sympathetic figure, would be tortured for a while and then move off to plot against and victimize another.

"Again, I did not feel sympathy for any of these. I felt that Christ was smart to contain these ones where they could make war on each other and leave God's children alone. God's children are vulnerable through sin and persistence in sin, but where there is any remorse or humility or even a little bit of love, God protects. I must say, I was repelled, disgusted, even a little upset, but not afraid and not startled. I have seen souls behaving in similar manners in life."

Anne's description of hell is very similar to the experience of Dr. Howard Storm who found himself at the mercy of evil spirits that were seeking to drag him to hell. See page 43.

Anne's visions also help us to understand Hell in the light of God who is love. Hell is indeed a place of great suffering, but, contrary to popular belief and to the less than perfect understanding of hell in some sentences in the Bible, it is not God who is doing the punishing. The spirits there are well able to punish one another. Hell is the provision of a merciful God who desires to protect us from these vindictive bullies. Outside hell, we can see their power at work in people who become evil and vindictive, yet their power is to a degree limited.

Footnote

All quotations are taken from 'The Mist of Mercy' by Anne. Published by Direction For Our Times. A beautiful book. It would make a lovely present also. See www.directionforourtimes.com for full details about Anne's ministry.

— —

"You shall know that I am the Lord, when I open your graves, and raise you from your graves, O my people." Ezekiel 37:13 RSV

The Lukewarm Priest

Over the years, Mother Angelica interviewed many people on EWTN, but when asked later which testimony most impressed her, she immediately replied that of Fr. Steven and his account of his near death experience.

Fr. Steven said, "I was ordained in 1973. My life as a priest was a day to day existence. I didn't handle my life very well. I was more concerned about what my peers thought. My priesthood was not in service to God's people, but in how people thought of Fr. Steven Scheier - especially my brother priests. That's what I was like for eleven years after my ordination. Deep down I knew that I was not doing what I should be doing - I was not the priest that I should be. I hid this to the point that people thought that I was a good priest, and so this was a sugar coating for everything that I was doing which was wrong."

On 18 October, 1985, he was involved in a head-on collision with a truck while travelling back to his parish in Kansas after visiting another priest. He was thrown from his car by the impact and suffered major head injuries. In fact the entire right side of his scalp was torn off, and even part of his brain. He describes himself as having been "pretty much unconscious" after the accident.

By God's grace, there was an experienced nurse in the car behind. She was a lapsed Catholic, and tried to pray the 'Hail Mary' into his ear, but didn't know all the words. Prompted by her, Fr. Steven found himself saying the Hail Mary over and over again within himself even though unconscious. The nurse knew immediately that he had suffered a broken neck; that the second vertebrae in his neck was broken. This is sometimes called 'the Hangman's Break', because it is what happens to those who are hanged. They then asphyxiate. Had Fr. Steven's head been turned or moved, he too would have died. Thankfully the nurse recognised this, and he was moved with great care, being taken first to a small local hospital. From there he was taken by helicopter to a huge hospital in another part of Kansas. He was unconscious during this.

His friends were told that there was only a 15% chance of his survival. That night, all the Christian Churches in his parish held vigils for his recovery. Thankfully he recovered in record time and was released from hospital on 2 December 1985. He says, "I still had the halo on my head - that is a metal circle around my head screwed into the skull to prevent my head from moving." The halo was eventually removed the following April.

— —

"I know your works; you have the name of being alive, and you are dead. .... If you will not awake, I will come like a thief, and you will not know at what hour I will come upon you." Rev 3:1b, 3b RSV

When he regained consciousness, he didn't remember what he had experienced while unconscious. It was only when a Gospel passage came 'alive' for him, that the memories came back. (So it is possible that some people may have near-death experiences but don't remember them.)

The memory of what he had experienced while unconscious, suddenly started to come back on day while he was celebrating Mass in his parish. He was reading the Gospel of the parable of the farmer who went out to inspect his vineyard. One tree had been there for three years, but still hadn't borne fruit. The farmer asked the vinedresser, "Why don't you cut it down and throw it into the fire? Why should it clutter up the ground?" The vinedresser replied, "Sir, give it one more chance. I will manure it and hoe around it, and then see if it bears fruit. If not then I will cut it down." Luke 13:7-10

Fr. Steven says, "When I was reading this Gospel in church, the page became illumined, enlarged, and came off the lectionary towards me. I'm a German! Things like this don't happen to me! But it did happen. I finished Mass as best as I could, went back into my rectory and had a number of cups of coffee."

Then he began to remember what he had experienced while he was unconscious. He says "I was before the Judgment Seat of Jesus Christ. I have no way of telling how long it lasted. God went through my entire life accusing me of various things, to all of which I said 'Yes'."

Fr. Steven had always believed that there was an excuse for his failures; that given the circumstances of his life and his needs, that he wasn't really at fault for his sins. But now he found that those excuses just didn't stand up. He says, "I had always been able to find excuses for my actions. But now I was talking to the Truth, and when you're talking to the Truth you can't give excuses. All you can say is 'yes' - 'that's the truth'. And that's all I said: 'Yes, Lord, I know'.

"At the end, He said to me that my sentence is Hell. Again, I said: 'Yes, Lord, I know.' I knew this is what I deserved. I didn't see Him, I just heard Him. Then I heard a female voice. She said, 'Son, will you please spare his life and his eternal soul.'

"He said, 'Mother, he's been a priest for twelve years for himself and not for Me. Let him reap the punishment he deserves.'

She continued by saying, 'But Son, if we give him special graces and strengths, and then see if he bears fruit. If he does not, then your will be done.'

"There was a very short pause. Then He said, 'Mother, he's yours!' Ever since then I have been hers."

—— ——

"This is the Land of Perfect Truth and any nonsense will dissipate immediately upon entry. Falseness is not even an option or a possibility here. It cannot be. All is Truth."
The visionary 'Anne' describing Purgatory in 'The Mist of Mercy'

Before the accident, Fr. Steven says that his faith did not come from his heart. He says, "One believes in Our Lord, Jesus Christ, our Blessed Mother, the angels and the saints, in one of two ways: with the head - intellectual assent - and with the heart. It is the heart that is important. I believed up here, in my head. I didn't know anything about this in my heart. So the angels, the saints etc., I believed in them but they were make-believe friends. They were not real.

"When I regained consciousness and the ability to think again, that's one of the things I was very, very aware of; that they are the only real things that exist, that we are the ones in the 'shadow world'. We have only one home and it's not here! A lot of my priorities were mixed up. My priorities should have been to save my soul and to help save others - which is what a priest should do anyway. Had I died, if you asked my parishioners would they have thought that I went to Hell, they would have said no."

People see the surface. God sees exactly what is in our hearts and minds. When we go before God, it will not matter what other people think of us. People may think that we are great, but God sees the actual truth.

Naturally, following his NDE, Fr. Steven has a great love for Our Lady. He says, "We have a Mother. I didn't have any special devotion to her. But since then she has become everything to me. At the foot of the Cross, Jesus looked down upon her and on the apostle He loved, and said, 'Woman, behold your Son' - meaning 'Mother, I give you the whole Church now as your sons and daughters; they're yours.' She takes this very literally and very seriously."

Following his NDE also, Fr. Steven's priesthood has been transformed. He says, "Before the accident I had no problem in saying Mass, but I had no problem in missing Mass either. None. I was not a priest for Him, I wasn't prepared to suffer for Him. I was a priest for myself, and I always ran from the cross - always. I've found out since then that if we run from the cross there's always a bigger one awaiting us. Crosses are not long-lasting, they are not eternal, and He's always there to make them as sweet as He possibly can. But I was a coward those twelve years. There was no spirituality in those twelve years. I had little training in the spiritual life when I was in seminary. A priest once said, "This life is a life of sacrifice. Love it, or don't be a priest!"

Nor was it just the way he was living the priesthood that had brought him under judgement. He says, "I had broken commandments, too. How I lived the priesthood was but the icing on top of the cake. The cake was rotten, and the icing was bad; it was bitter. During those twelve years, I pantomimed being a priest. I'm sorry to say I was not a priest! I always needed assurance: about my homilies, about how well I was doing. All these served to uplift me. I sought ways

— —

"What will it profit a man, if he gains the whole world and forfeits his life." Mt 16:26 RSV

to comfort myself when I suffered. Priests are also liable to the commandments. My mission is to let you know, to let priests know, that you are liable to Hell, and that Hell exists. But also, His Divine Mercy exists; His love outweighs justice.

"To priests, I say be a priest in the service of Our Lord, Jesus Christ. Be a priest of prayer. Once prayer goes, your priesthood goes. And do not be afraid of telling things as they are, as we see them, as God sees them; to say what should be said. This won't make you popular, but that's part of what being His follower is. He never promised that we would be popular by being His follower. He only promised crosses. But the crosses are bearable because He's there, and because His Blessed Mother is there to lighten them.

"Let me say that a priest without prayer - is dead. A priest without the Blessed Sacrament - is dead. A priest without the Blessed Mother - is dead. I learned my lesson, but it took Him to break my neck and the threat of eternal damnation just to get my attention. But I would go through the same thing in order to arrive at where I'm now at! I would never want to go back to the way I was before - never!

"Before the time of the accident I knew I was in mortal sin. At that time it didn't make any difference to me. I used Confession regularly, but not appropriately."

There are stages to repentance. There is the person who confesses his sins but has no intention of changing. That he confesses his sin is good. It is accepting that he is a sinner. It shows an openness to God. But normally a real desire to break the habit of sin is also required. Fr. Steven says, "But I wasn't about to change my life. I was using the sacrament as a sort of Fire Insurance! I wondered how many of my Confessions were valid because I had no firm purpose of amendment. I felt sorry for my sins, but the kind of sorrow I had was not religious sorrow.

"At the time of my accident I was not caring about all this. I took for granted certain things, and assumed things I shouldn't have. For example, that there's time - time later on to convert. What God pointed out to me was, **"Steven, there is no time."**

Evaluation of Fr. Steven's NDE

It is clear from Fr. Steven's testimony that it is possible to be a popular priest and yet have much to face on the other side. Believing in God's existence isn't enough. Saying prayers and receiving the sacraments isn't enough. If you desire to go to Heaven the moment you die, or even to the upper realms of Purgatory, then come to a living relationship with Jesus, and allow Him to transform you from within.

Jesus said that the first and greatest commandment is "You shall love the Lord

Jesus answered him, "Truly, truly, I say to you, unless one is born anew, he cannot see the kingdom of God" John 3:4 RSV

your God with all your heart, with all your soul, and with all your mind" Mt 22:37 RSV. This is the most important COMMANDMENT, not some optional extra. Loving the Lord with all our heart and all our soul, involves a very definite relationship with Him, one that is deeply experienced by us. Loving the Lord with all our mind involves embracing His teaching, and seeking to be guided by Him in all things.

If you truly love the Lord your God with all your heart, soul and mind, He will become the most important reality in your life. The temptation which Fr. Steven faced as a young priest, and which I think we all face, is to put people's opinions of us before God's opinion. There is a basic human need to be well thought of, but it is a need that can give rise to the temptation to seek to impress. The need will be all the more powerful if we do not admit to it and do not open it up in Confession. Then it can have a major subconscious influence over us, and lead us to seeking to make a name for ourselves rather than witnessing to God. An important step in the spiritual journey is identifying the temptation that arises from this inner need to be well thought of, and then to take the practical steps to overcome it and to be delivered of it.

Footnote re the role of Our Lady

The one difficulty in Fr. Steven's testimony is that in it, it sounds as if Our Lady is more merciful than Jesus. But Our Lady's mercy is totally derived from the mercy of Jesus. He and He alone is Saviour.

After people's life-review comes judgement. This often comes in the form of an interchange between two voices. "Your life deserves this" one voice says, "Have mercy on him" (or words to that effect) a second voice says. Fr. Steven says that it was Jesus who delivered the judgement. This is unusual. Usually people, after their NDE's, believe that it was the Father who delivered the judgement. But even in this one needs to be careful. One's intellect plays a major role in 'hearing' these voices, and before actual entry to Heaven, one's intellect, as we shall see from other people's near-death experiences, is quite capable of getting it wrong. It could be the case that the judgement is 'automatic', but that one's intellect 'hears' it as if it comes from the Father. Or it could be that Fr. Steven presumed that it was Jesus who pronounced the judgement when in fact it was the Father. He says that he heard the voice but didn't see the person.

After the accident, a nurse tried to say the Hail Mary in his ear, and he found himself asking her intercession while unconscious. In these circumstances, it is totally natural that Our Lady would play a role in asking for mercy for him. But in this, she is merely expressing the merciful plea of Jesus, (see Angie Fenimore's testimony).

— —

"The Son of Man is to come with his angels in the glory of the Father, and then he will repay every man for what he has done." Mt 16:27 RSV

His body was in the morgue for three days

What about atheists? Where do they go after their death?

George (Yuri) Rodonaia's mother was born in London, his father lived in Georgia, then part of the Soviet Union. They believed in personal freedom and used every opportunity to campaign for it. Very quickly they came to the attention of the KGB. George said, "They were courageous people, perhaps too courageous, because the KGB banished them to the gulag in the late 1940s for openly expressing their opposition to totalitarian government. So they spent many years in that horrid detention system made so famous by Alexander Solzhenitsyn."

Around 1948 they were forced to work on the Tran-Siberian Railroad. Many other dissidents were also forced to assist in this massive construction project. They worked on the railroad for about six years before George (Yuri) was born, in 1956. Then Khrushchev came to power in Russia. George's parents were first charged with spying and then murdered by the KGB. George was only seven months old. He was lucky in that a childless couple adopted him and gave him a truly loving home. They loved him as their own, and gave him every help they could, including with his early education. While excellent people, they were not however religious. Sadly his adoptive father died of lung cancer when George was only nine. Just three years later, his adoptive mother died, also of cancer, when he was only twelve. George, while only twelve, was now living in the house on his own, but the neighbours looked after him.

He was a brilliant student, and realised that the future lay in getting top marks. He was invited to attend the University of Moscow when only fourteen. Here he developed a great love for the physical sciences and medicine, but had no interest in religion. He said, "I was very much a typical young research scientist and a pretty sceptical one, too. I was not religious at all. I was an atheist. I had basically accepted the materialistic perspective of the hard sciences that everything can and should be reduced to a material cause. There was no room for spirituality for me at all; out of the question, totally out of the question."

Yet George had a vision of a 'free' Russia, free that is from its totalitarian Communist government. This led to his involvement in the publication of 'Iberia', an underground freedom newspaper. This in turn brought him to the attention of the KGB. Then in 1974, when he was 18, he was invited to study at Yale University

----

"The Godward journey is a journey on which every individual is launched, unknowingly, at birth." Christopher Bryant

in the United States. But the KGB knew that if he once got to the United States, he would seek asylum, so he was refused permission to go.

Meanwhile he married and in quick succession had two sons. Now he had a definite tie with Russia, and was no longer considered such a high risk in terms of defection. He also had friends campaigning for him in the United States. Even Henry Kissinger became involved. The stage came where it was embarrassing for the Soviet government to continue to refuse permission for him to travel, so permission was granted.

But some KGB agents had no intention of letting him go. The day before he was due to leave, he was standing on the footpath in Tbilisi waiting for a taxi. Suddenly a car swerved, and drove at speed up on to the footpath. It was not out of control, as it was driven between and around the trees. George was hit head on, then part dragged, part driven for about ten meters. Then the car reversed and drove over him a second time. It then sped off, leaving him for dead. Being declared dead, his body was taken to the mortuary.

George had been what might be called a good atheist. He didn't believe in God, but he loved his wife and child. He believed in freedom and was working for it, and he had sought to develop his natural gifts. But he didn't know Jesus who is the light of the world. This may explain why he now found himself in "a realm of total darkness". He said, "The first thing I remember about my NDE is that I discovered myself in a realm of total darkness. I had no physical pain, I was still somehow aware of my existence as George, and all about me there was darkness, utter and complete darkness - the greatest darkness ever, darker than any dark, blacker than any black. This was what surrounded me and pressed upon me. I was horrified. I wasn't prepared for this at all."

As an atheist, George had been 'living in the dark', and now had to find his way to the Light. However, he had done no one real harm. Indeed he himself had been a victim of very serious wrongs from the moment he was conceived. Based on the knowledge available to him, he had sought to live a life of love and to work for liberty. So his intellect was open to the truth even if he had yet to come to know the Truth. This may help explain the process that happened next.

He said, "I was shocked to find that I still existed, but I didn't know where I was. The one thought that kept rolling through my mind was, 'How can I be when I'm not?' That really troubled me. I was trying to analyse what was going on, but it didn't make sense. Then I remembered **Descartes'** famous line: **'I think, therefore I am.'** That took a huge burden off me, for it was then I knew for certain I was still alive, although obviously in a very different dimension. Then I

———————————————————————————————

"He will transform our weak mortal bodies into copies of his own glorious body, using the same power by which He is able to bring all things under his rule" Philippians 3:20-21.

37

thought, if I am, why shouldn't I be positive? I am George and I'm in darkness, but I know I am. I must not be negative. Then I thought, how can one be positive in darkness, positive is light? Then, suddenly, I was in light; bright white, shiny and strong; a very bright light. It was like the flash of a camera, but not flickering – that bright. Constant brightness."

Not having known the Light, coming into the light involved a painful adjustment. He said, "At first I found the brilliance of the light painful. I couldn't look directly at it. But little by little I began to relax. I began to feel warm, comforted, and everything suddenly seemed fine.

While George hadn't known the Light, he had been a scientist, and was enthralled by the composition of reality. When we die, we will still have the same intellect when we go to the other side, and we will at first see the eternal realities through the way our intellect has been developed in this life. On death, if one has not known Jesus, the Light, but has loved God, regardless of whether one called Him Allah or Buddha, it is likely that one will first either see or experience God just as one has understood Him. This does not mean that this limited vision of God will be one's permanent experience, but rather that it will be one's starting point.

If one has not known God, but has appreciated beauty, then that may well be one's starting point when one's eternal spirit leaves one's mortal bodies. George hadn't known God, but he had appreciated the beauty of creation through a scientist's eyes. He said, "The next thing that happened was that I saw all these molecules flying around, atoms, protons, neutrons, just flying everywhere. On the one hand, it was totally chaotic, yet what brought me such great joy was that this chaos also had its own symmetry. This symmetry was beautiful and unified and whole, and it flooded me with tremendous joy. I saw the universal form of life and nature laid out before my eyes."

As he experienced this, he relaxed and let go. He no longer needed his body; he could leave it behind, and with it all concept of time as we understand it here on earth. Somewhere along the line he had his life-review, seeing his life right from its beginning. For him, it was as if he saw his entire life all at once. He says, "I participated in the real life dramas of my life, almost like a holographic image of my life going on before me - no sense of past, present, or future, just now and the reality of my life. ... There I was. This was my life. I didn't experience any sense of guilt or remorse for things I'd done. I didn't feel one way or another about my failures, faults, or achievements. All I felt was my life for what it is. And I was content with that. I accepted my life for what it is."

Concerning his experience of his life review, and his not experiencing any guilt, it should be stressed that in life, he had been a victim rather than a victimiser:- his

"Truly, truly, I say to you, the hour is coming, and now is, when the dead will hear the voice of the Son of God, and those who hear will live."
John 5:25 RSV

parents murdered when he was a baby; his adopted parents dying when he was still a child. Then there was his work for liberation within Russia which resulted in him being persecuted. He was also a loving husband and father. His being an atheist was through little fault of his own.

Secondly, it is extremely common for people to have an experience of being embraced in God's unconditional love during their life-review, but sometimes there is judgement to face later. Read Angie Fenimore's testimony. Read Gloria Polo's testimony. Being embraced in God's unconditional love is not a guarantee of immediate entry to Heaven or that one will not have to go through a purgative phase in which one grieves for the hurt that one has caused to others and for the opportunities that one has missed in this life.

George didn't experience judgement, but he describes the experience of being enveloped in God's unconditional love as follows. "During this time the light just radiated a sense of peace and joy to me. It was very positive. I was so happy to be in the light. ... I learned that all the physical rules for human life were nothing when compared to this unitive reality. ... Everything is not only connected together, everything is also one. So I felt a wholeness with the light, a sense that all is right with me and the universe.

Jesus did stress this unity, a unity within the three persons of God, and a unity between God's children. "In that day you will know that I am in my Father, and you in me, and I in you" John 13:20 RSV. There are three distinct Persons in the one God, each distinct yet one. So too, on the other side, we will experience our unity with God, with one another, and with all creation in a totally new way.

George also discovered how one travels on the other side, "I could be anywhere instantly, really there. I tried to communicate with the people I saw. Some sensed my presence, but no one did anything about it." This fits in with the experience of many people who have a deep sense of their loved one's being right there with them in the period after death.

George saw his wife grieving for him, and his two little sons who were too young to understand what was happening. Then he found himself in his neighbour's house. They too were grieving because of his death, but they also had their own problems. A little baby boy had been born to them a few days earlier, and could not be got to stop crying. He was just crying, crying, crying, and hardly slept at all. The doctors couldn't find the problem, and had sent parents and crying baby home in the hope that the baby would eventually come out of it. But he didn't.

George believed that he 'talked' to the baby, and was able to ask him what was wrong. The baby said that his arm hurt, and George could then see that it was

---

"For we know that if the eartly tent we live in is destroyed, we have a building from God, a house not made with hands, eternal in the heavens."
2 Cor 5:1 RSV

broken. Whether George is correct in his claim that he could talk to the baby I cannot say. But he certainly discovered what the problem was. Normally a baby's arms are pliable, and so the doctors hadn't checked for a break, but broken it was. It was only when George came back into his body and told the parents that the baby's arm was broken, that the break was discovered. When this was found to be true, people listened to what George was saying about his near-death experience - and to his testimony that there is life after death.

Concerning other aspects of his near death experience, George said that now that he knew that God existed, he felt a desire to learn the Bible. On the other side there is a different way of learning. As soon as the question forms in one's intellect, the answer comes automatically. George described it as follows, "You want, you receive. Think and it comes to you."

But George was not in Heaven. He was still going through a purgatory phase. What he didn't realise is that until one is in Heaven, one's intellect is not yet perfect, and so it is possible that comes to you is wrong - because it comes through one's not yet perfected intellect.

George says, "I went back and lived in the minds of Jesus and his disciples. I heard their conversations, experienced eating, passing wine, smells, tastes - yet I had no body. I was pure consciousness. If I didn't understand what was happening, an explanation would come. But no teacher spoke. I explored the Roman Empire, Babylon, the times of Noah and Abraham. Any era you can name, I went there."

But was Noah an actual historical figure? Most Biblical experts would tend to the view that the first truly historical figure we meet in the Bible is Abraham; that the first ten chapters of the Bible is theology expressed in story form. That there was creation is a historical fact. That there were first humans is a historical fact. That somehow sin entered the world is a historical. The first then chapters of the Bible uses stories to explain these historical facts. This applies especially to the stories of Noah and the flood.

The visionary 'Anne' in her visions of Heaven, describes how the saints in Heaven meditate on the events of Christ's life on earth in order to understand them even better. I presume the same applies to the souls in the upper realms of Purgatory. So what George says is consistent with her visions, but, his intellect not yet being perfect, he may have got a few details somewhat wrong.

Just when his near death experience was getting better and better, it came to an abrupt end. After his body was in the mortuary for three days, it was taken out for the autopsy. Just when the doctor was beginning to cut into George's body

— —

"Beloved, let us love one another; for love is of God, and he who loves is born of God and knows God" 1 John 4:7 RSV

during the autopsy, George's spirit returned to his mortal body. Just imagine the shock the doctor got when the dead body he was cutting into, suddenly came alive. Imagine too how cold George felt after his body being three days in the refrigerator unit of the mortuary. He said "As they began to cut into my stomach, I felt as though some great power took hold of my neck and pushed me down. And it was so powerful that I opened my eyes and had this huge sense of pain. My body was cold and I began to shiver."

The autopsy naturally came to an abrupt end!! He was, however, to spend a full nine months in the hospital. Meanwhile he was a 'new' person. Before the incident he was an atheist. Now not merely was he a believer, but he immediately signed up to study for the priesthood in the Russian Orthodox Church, taking a PhD in the psychology of religion along the way. When he eventually got to America in 1989, he became an associate pastor at the First United Methodist Church in Nederland, Texas.

He stated, "I now believe in the God of the universe. Unlike many other people, however, I have never called God the light, because God is beyond our comprehension. God, I believe, is even more than the light, because God is also darkness. God is everything that exists, everything – and that is beyond our ability to comprehend at all." But in saying this, he contradicts the Bible which says, "God is light. In Him there is no darkness whatsoever."

George continued, "So I don't believe in the God of the Jews, or the Christians, or the Hindus, or in any one religion's idea of what God is or is not. It is all the same God, and that God showed me that the universe in which we live is a beautiful and marvellous mystery that is connected together forever and for always."

What George says here is partially correct. God is the God of the story of the Good Samaritan as told by Jesus. The Samaritan was not a disciple of Jesus. He had his own understanding of God, but seeing a man in need, he went to his assistance. Our God rewards all those who performs acts of love even when they have no realisation that they are doing them for or to Him. See Matthew 25.

God is love, and those who know God, will seek to be transformed by love and to live a life of love. The message of the Good Samaritan story is that the person who lives a life of practical love is closer to God that the religious person who fails to love. If one does not know that God is love, one does not know God! If one does not seek to live a love empowered life, one isn't a child of God.

Yet George is also incorrect in what he said. Even after one discovers that God

— —

"Then the righteous will answer him, 'Lord when did we see thee hungry and feed thee, or thirsty and give thee drink? And when did we see thee sick or in prison and visit thee? And the King will answer them, 'Truly I say to you, as you did it to one of the least of these my brethren, you did it to me.'" Matthew 25:37-40 RSV

is love and commits oneself to living love, there is still the task of discerning how to live love in complex situations. That is where one needs the teaching of Jesus to help one to see what loving involves. In Jesus alone is there the fullness of truth.

Furthermore, Jesus alone can give the power to live the love-filled life. Of course, He generously gives it to all who truly seek it, even if they don't know Him by name, but those who do know Him by name clearly have a major advantage.

Furthermore, in the New Testament alone do we find the true presentation of the God of love. Yet this God of love, revealed to us in and by Jesus, calls us to recognise goodness and love wherever we find it - just as He does.

George continued, "Anyone who has had such an experience of God, who has felt such a profound sense of connection with reality, knows that there is only one truly significant work to do in life, and that is love; to love nature, to love people, to love animals, to love creation itself, just because it is. To serve God's creation with a warm and loving hand of generosity and compassion – that is the only meaningful existence."

George also said, "Many people turn to those who have had NDEs because they sense we have the answers. But I know this is not true, at least not entirely. None of us will fully fathom the great truths of life until we finally unite with eternity at death." In this George is totally correct. He was 'dead' for three days, yet he realised that his experience was partial. Others have near death experiences lasting a few minutes or even seconds and think that they know everything.

George continues, "But occasionally we get glimpses of the answer here on earth, and that alone is enough for me. I love to ask questions and to seek answers, but I know in the end I must live the questions and the answers. But that is okay, isn't it? ..... Live the questions, and the universe will open up its eyes to you."

George died (again!) on October 12, 2004 due to heart failure - and this time remained on the other side. He was on his way to Dallas to speak on Trinity Broadcasting about his NDE when he went to meet the God he first came to know during his near death experience. George is survived by his wife Nino, his daughter Natia, and his son Greg.

Footnote

All direct quotations are from George's testimony as taken from "The Journey Home" by Phillip Berman as repeated on the internet.

— —

"Father Abraham, if someone goes to them from the dead, then will repent." Abraham replied, "If they will not listen to Moses and the prophets, neither will they be convinced even if some one should rise from the dead."
Luke 16:30 -31

The 'Diehard' Atheist

George Rodonaia was what might be termed a good atheist who never had a chance to come to know Jesus before what was in reality his after-death experience. But what about someone who rejects Jesus and becomes 'bitter'? **Dr. Howard Storm**, head of the art department at North Kentucky University, grew up in a Christian home, but rejected the faith as a teenager, and became an ardent atheist, one of those who feel a need to knock Christians. One of his secretaries was a committed Baptist. He ridiculed her for her faith. **Then a nun enrolled for his lectures**. It was like a red rag to a bull!! He was deliberately rude to her. Instead of disappearing, she made him her prayer project - to pray for his conversion.

Dr. Storm thought that people who were religious were "kidding themselves" He says, "I viewed them with contempt. I thought they believed in fairy tails because they couldn't cope with the harsh reality of life. .... I had no faith, no hope, no reliance on anyone, just survival of the fittest. ... Man was the measure of all things. I was in control of my life."

In 1985, he was leading an excursion to Paris when he suffered a ruptured duodenum (intestine). A surgeon was needed immediately, but none could be found. Nine hours later, he was still waiting in agony and felt that he could take no more. He turned to his wife, kissed her goodbye, and gave up the struggle. He was fully certain that it would be 'lights out'.

Then he found himself outside his body. A group of 'people' were waiting for him, and started taking him away with them. At first they just invited him to go, but when he refused to go with them, they became vicious, started attacking him, and then dragged him to the very entrance to hell itself. He experienced real fear.

He says, "We were in darkness over this very long period of time. I said, 'I'm not going with you any further.' They said, 'We're almost there.' They started pushing and shoving me and I fought with them and there were many of them. A wild orgy of frenzied taunting, screaming, and hitting ensured. They had very sharp, hard fingernails. My impression was also that their teeth were longer than normal. I tried to defend myself but with this huge horde of people it was impossible. What they were doing was playing with me, initially scratching and biting, punching and slapping, pushing and taunting, very vulgar.

"Then it got much worse than that. It was so obscene, I don't feel free to describe what they did. They were playing with me as a cat plays with a mouse. ... After

"Everyone who acknowledges me before men, I also will acknowledge before my Father who is in heaven; but whoever denies me before men, I also will deny before my Father who is in heaven." Matthew 10: 33 RSV

they had humiliated me to the best of their ability, I was lying on the floor of that place and I had been all kinds of ripped up and broken, outside and inside. I was devastated, having been stripped of any worth. Then I heard a voice that said, 'Pray to God.' But I thought, I don't believe in God, it's a stupid idea."

Somehow he managed to remember and say a few phrases of prayers from his childhood. This drove the 'people' around him really furious, and they tried to bully him into believing that there was not God. Seeing how angry his attempts at prayer were making them, he kept trying. Every time he used the name 'God', they were repelled. He says, "It was as if I was throwing boiling oil on them."

Eventually he was all alone, but was aware that they were still in the distance. Finding himself alone, he started thinking about his life. It was as if he needed a preliminary life-review, and to realise how bad his life had been and then to repent before he could be embraced by God's unconditional love. He says, "The bottom-line conclusion was that I had led a bad life. My god was my art career. That's what I worshipped."

"I thought of how cold-hearted and cruel and manipulative I was. I felt that where I had ended up was where I belonged, and that the people who had come and picked me up and taken me to this place were people who had lived lives like mine. We were people who hadn't loved God and hadn't loved fellow human beings. In this place there was nothing left but to tear and gnaw on one another, which was essentially what we had done on earth. I was also aware that this was just the beginning, and that it was going to get worse. Much, much worse!

"I knew the only way to survive in this place was to be crueler than the people who were around you. There was no kindness, no compassion, no hope. I had no hope of seeing the world or getting back to life but I didn't want to be part of their world. I had gone down the sewer pipe of the universe to the cesspool and was still on the top of the cesspool. A memory from my childhood came very vividly of me as a small child sitting in a Sunday school classroom singing 'Jesus loves Me' and the memory was so simple and innocent and pure, believing in something good, and that Jesus cared about me and was good and powerful.

Some people during their near death experience are reconnected to how they were loved as children. Howard was reconnected to how he had loved Jesus and been loved by Him. Now he yearned to believe in God with the same trust he had as a child. So he called out, "**Jesus, please save me.**" Then off in the darkness, he saw a tiny point of light, like a faint star in the distance. This 'star' started to come towards him with enormous speed, and to get brighter and brighter. At first Howard was frightened, thinking that is was going to run over him and crush

— —

"They are fighting constantly here. They are assaulting each other. They are molesting each other. They are shaming and humiliating each other."
From 'Anne's vision of Hell as told in "The Mist of Mercy"

44

him. Yet he couldn't stop looking at it. He says, "I couldn't take my eyes off it, because emanating from the light was more intensity and more beauty that I had ever seen before in my life. Almost immediately the light was very close. I realized then that while it was indescribably brilliant, it wasn't light at all. It was a living entity, a luminous being approximately eight feet in diameter and oval in shape. Its brilliance and intensity penetrated my body. In a very vivid and beautiful experience I slowly rose up with no effort into the light."

He then describes how he experienced being permeated by God's unconditional love. "As I was being picked up I saw all my gore blown away like dust and I was restored physically, and emotionally, I was in ecstasy and I knew this person who had come was Jesus and I knew instantly that He was very intelligent, very strong, and I knew that He was very good, and most importantly I knew that He had loved me more than any concept I had ever had of what love was. If I had taken all my experiences of love and compacted them into a moment, this experience would have exceeded that.

"And I knew that He knew absolutely everything about me. He knew my thoughts. He knew every moment of my life, even things I didn't remember. And He held me, and I cried and cried and cried out of joy, and He began to carry me directly straight up, like a helicopter. We started leaving that place. Fairly soon we were entering into a world full of light and off to the distance was a great centre of brightness. The goodness and the love and the holiness were permeating through me, and I thought to myself, 'I'm a piece of garbage. They've made a terrible mistake, because I don't belong here.' I was so ashamed.

"With that we stopped our movement and He spoke to me for the first time and He said, 'You do belong here, and we don't make mistakes'."

Soon however he was placed in the presence of three angels who reviewed his life. This for him, was to be a painful process. The angels allowed him to see the times that he had been mean to people, and to feel for how this had caused others to feel. He literally experienced how the people he hurt felt.

He says, "We watched and experienced episodes that were from the point of view of a third party. The scenes they showed me were often incidents I had forgotten. They showed effects on people's lives of which I had no previous knowledge. They reported thoughts and feelings of people I had interacted with which I had been unaware of at the time. They showed me scenes from my life that I would not have chosen and they eliminated scenes from my life that I wanted them to see. **It was a complete surprise how my life history was presented before us.** I believed that my worth was measured by my success in my chosen career. When the angels showed me how destructive this careerism was to the well being of my loved ones, I wanted to end my life review. They insisted that I needed

"If we confess our sins, he is faithful and just, and will forgive our sins and cleanse us from all unrighteousness." 1 John 1:9 RSV

to see the truth of my life and learn from it. I begged them to stop it because I was so ashamed for the ways I had failed to live lovingly and because of the grief I had caused."

Eventually the angels told him that his time hadn't yet come; that he was to go back to earth. Suddenly he found himself back in bed. A surgeon had arrived and his life was saved through an operation.

The first thing he did afterwards was send for the nun that he had been so rude to. He wanted to apologise to her, but he also wanted to tell his story to someone who might be able to understand it. He then asked her if she could believe that he had actually converted. She replied that the only thing that she couldn't understand was what had taken him so long, because ever since he had been rude to her in the classroom, she had been praying for his conversion.

Before his experience, he was an ardent atheist. After it, not merely did he become a Christian, but he retired from his well paid position as art professor and became a Methodist minister, and then went to work as a missionary in South America. But while he became a Methodist minister, he has a very Catholic understanding of the afterlife - especially of Purgatory. After all, he believes that he has been there! That is, he ended up there after first having a brush with Hell!

Evaluation of Dr. Storm's testimony

If through our own fault, we reject God in this life, then by our own choice we will begin the next life outside God's love. One's eternal spirit enters the next life with the attitudes with which it leaves this life. Yet while Dr. Storm had rejected God, and while he had been nasty to Christians, he was by no means the worst man on earth. He clearly loved his wife. He was considered a good lecturer, who took an interest in his students. **If this is how it went for him, think of how it might be for someone who is truly vicious.**

His story also gives us very real hope, that if we help our children to love Jesus when they are still children, even if they drift from the faith later, there is sill the possibility that, in those critical moments immediately after death, their love for Jesus and the prayers they said as children will come back to them. In Dr. Storm's case, he hadn't said a prayer since he was 15, and had real difficulty recalling anything. However, when he began to cry out to Jesus the evil spirits were driven away, and he began to move from darkness into the light.

Then he experienced the pure form of the Baptism in the Spirit which souls outside their bodies can experience. It involved being forced to face the full truth about his life, and then being embraced in and permeated by God's unconditional love.

— —

"God never meant us to experience the Retribution, but to be saved through our Lord Jesus Christ, who died for us so that alive or dead, we would be able to live in union with Him" 1 Thess 5:9

In his case, it was as if he had to repent of the basic wrongness of his lifestyle before he could be embraced in God's unconditional love and then taken through a more detailed life-review.

But his description of Jesus is very strange and needs analysis. He claims to have experienced 'a living entity, a luminous being approximately eight feet in diameter and oval in shape' and concludes that this was Jesus. Jesus is pure spirit, and can reveal Himself in any way that He wishes. He even comes under the form of bread and wine in the Mass. But it is more likely that this was either an emanation of the love of Jesus or quite possible a manifestation of the Holy Spirit. The way he experienced himself being embraced in God's unconditional love and then being cleansed, is totally consistent with being embraced either by Jesus or by the Holy Spirit.

His use of the word 'entity' is also a little unfortunate because of the way many New Age people use that word, but it should be remembered that the word 'entity' was not invented by the New Age no more than the word 'angel', and it isn't tied to New Age connotations.

His description of hell as a place of ongoing bullying matches perfectly with vision of hell by the visionary Anne. See pages 29-30

Comparison with St. Faustina and the Dying Sinner

Dr. Howard Storm had the experience of evil spirits awaiting his death. There is a clear comparison between what he experienced and a vision that St. Faustina had in February 1938. She was in the chapel praying when Jesus appeared to her and said, "Help me to save a certain dying sinner. Say the chaplet that I have taught you for him."

As she prayed the chaplet she saw in vision the dying man. He was truly in a very bad way. She saw that his guardian angel was powerless to help him because of the extent of his sinful life. She also saw that "a multitude of devils were waiting for his soul". Then as she prayed the chaplet, Jesus appeared, and the rays of love emanating from the heart of Jesus caused the evil spirits to depart in confusion. Then the man died in peace. (Diary 1565)

Footnote

Dr. Storm's testimony is in Michael Brown's lovely book, 'The God of Miracles' Queenship Publishing Company. A very uplifting book, and suitable to give as a present.

— —

"It is better for you to enter the kingdom of God with one eye than with two eyes be thrown into hell, where their worm does not die, and the fire is not quenched." Mark 9:47b-48 RSV

St. Don Bosco and the boy who was ten hours dead

Many remarkable things happened through the ministry of Fr. John Bosco. These included praying with a couple of people who were thought to have just died, but when they recovered, people suggested that they hadn't been dead at all. These included the godson of Marchioness Jerome Uguccioni. The little boy had stopped breathing and appeared dead. Fr. Bosco was sent for, and after he prayed with the boy, he began to breathe again, sat up and smiled.

An even more extraordinary event occurred with a boy called Charles in Turin. Charles was just 15 when he became seriously ill and died within a couple of days. Before death, he asked for Fr. John, but unfortunately Fr. John was not in Turin at the time. When Fr. John returned to Turin, Charles was already ten or eleven hours dead. The doctor had long since signed the death certificate and Charles was laid out, which then involved being sewn up in a bed sheet, and was being waked.

When Fr. John was told, he immediately declared, "The boy is not dead, just asleep."
"But the death certificate has been signed and he is being waked."
"Merely a misunderstanding!" replied Fr. John.
Being brought to the wake room, Fr. John asked everyone to leave except the boy's mother and aunt.
When the rest had left, Fr. John prayed silently for some time. Then he suddenly cried out "Charles! Rise!"
To the mother and aunt's utter shock, Charles was seen to move. Then Fr. John putting out the bedside light, tore apart the bed sheet in which Charles' body had been sewn. With that, Charles came fully around. It was just as if he was waking up from a deep sleep, but he had a strange tale to tell.

Seemingly, without the family knowing, he had got involved with bad companions. He had done some very bad things, and covered them up in Confession. Turning to Fr. John, he declared, "Only for you I would now be in hell." He said it was like he had been in a horrific nightmare. "I dreamt I was standing on the edge of a huge furnace surrounded by hordes of devils. They were about to throw me into the flames when a beautiful lady appeared and stopped them. 'There is still

---

"Dorcas died and they laid her out upstairs. ..... When Peter came, he put everyone outside, then knelt down and prayed. Then he called out, "Tabitha, rise." She opened her eyes, and when she saw Peter she sat up."
See Acts 9:36-42

hope for you, Charles, you have not yet been judged' she declared. At the moment I heard you calling me. Oh Don Bosco, what a joy to see you again! Will you please hear my Confession."

The boy's mother and aunt then left the room, while Fr. John heard the boy's Confession. Then the boy shouted out loud enough for everyone in the house to hear, "Mamma! Don Bosco has saved me."

Everyone was then allowed back into the room. However the drama was still far from over. There was general commotion and excitement for some time as Charles told the full story of what he had experienced. Some claimed afterwards that even though he was alive, his body remained deadly cold.

Then when everyone had a chance to see Charles and to hear his story, Fr. John called for silence. Then he said, "God has been kind to all of us today by showing us the importance of a good Confession."

He then turned to the boy and said, "Charles, now that the gates of Heaven lie wide open for you, would you rather go there or stay here with us?"

The boy looked away for a moment and his eyes grew moist with tears. An expectant hush fell over the room.

"Don Bosco," he said at last, "I'd rather go to Heaven."

The mourners now watched in amazement as Charles leaned back on the pillows, closed his eyes, and once again stopped breathing. Naturally this incident led to much talk and speculation. All that can be established is that the boy had been certified as dead, that he had been laid out and waked for about 10 to 12 hours, that there were many witnesses both to his brief recovery and then to his sudden departure.

Naturally we do not have the boy's first hand written description of what he actually experienced while dead. All we have is the account given by the eye witnesses, and only written down much later, of what he said when he recovered. Because of that, we do not have what might be termed 'comprehensive' accuracy, just general accuracy - so one cannot analyse the minor details. But the basic story is very similar to that of Dr. Howard Storm in its description of how Charles found himself in the company of evil spirits on his death. It is similar to that of Fr. Steven Scheier on the role of Our Lady. It is similar to that of Stanley Villavicencio on the importance of the Sacrament of Confession.

Quotations taken from the beautiful book, "Stories of Don Bosco" by Peter Lappin, Don Bosco Publications.

— —

"Let it be known to your therefore, brethren, that through this man forgiveness of sins is proclaimed to you, and by him every one that believes is freed from everything from which you could not be freed by the law of Moses." Acts 13:38-39 RSV

After 33 years of sex and drugs, he had an NDE

Marino Restrepo was born in Colombia in a small coffee-growers town. His family was one of strong Catholic faith. At age fourteen he moved to the capital of Colombia, Bogota, where he got his high school education. Quickly he rebelled against his Catholic upbringing. Then, when 17, he got involved with a group of American hippies. First two ladies, Cindy and then Donna initiated him into drugs, sex, and a whole range of New Age practices.

When he was 20, he got his then girlfriend pregnant. Her family were deeply distressed by her hippie lifestyle. Marino married her, and her family paid for them to move to Germany - partly so that they would not continue to be embarrassed by her weird lifestyle. His two sons were born in Germany. In order to get along, he cleaned up his act somewhat - had a haircut, shaved off the beard, etc, yet he continued the Bohemian lifestyle, and continued following the Beatles, and also continued his involvement with eastern religions.

After spending six years in Germany, he moved back to Colombia. His wife had got nostalgic for her roots. He was still into drugs. Eventually they separated. He moved to America. Now separated from his wife and children, his life continued on a downhill spiral - drugs, sex and drink. The gap in his life was somewhat filled when he got established as a singer. Then his wife got cancer. After some months, it was decided that it was best for the children to live with him, as her condition continued to deteriorate. Taking responsibility for the children led him to cut out some of the excesses, but not to a real change around. His life still centred around alcohol, drugs and sex. In 1992 his wife died.

Visiting Colombia on Christmas Eve, 1997, he was kidnapped by a drugs gang on behalf of the FARC rebels and taken hooded to the jungle as a hostage. They took him to the ruins of a house that were completely derelict and overgrown. He was hooded again, and thrown into one of the derelict rooms. Here he was held under the most horrendous conditions. The place was full of bats. He was lying in their excrement. The bugs from the excrement crawled all over him biting him repeatedly. He couldn't even scratch himself because his hands were tied up. The FARC were slow in coming to pick him up. Meanwhile the drugs gang ran out of food. There was nothing to eat but roots. Eventually after fifteen days, the FARC arrived. They threatened to kill his sisters one by one unless a large ransom was paid. Furthermore they told him that they planned to kill him once

---

"Those whom I love, I reprove and chasten, so be zealous and repent."
Rev 3:19 RSV

the ransom was paid. It was part of their deal with the gang that had kidnapped him - a drugs family known to him from his own town. Then he was thrown back into the derelict room with the death sentence over his head. He tried to call on the occult, but to no avail. Despite all his involvement in occultic practices, none of that was any use now - and the magic charms that he was wearing proved useless. **Finding no help, he surrendered himself to death.** Immediately he entered into some sort of deep mystical experience which was identical to a Near Death Experience, including a complete life-review.

Suddenly he began to see his previous life in a bright light. Others are shown how they were loved as children, but he was shown how his selfishness began when he was just three. He saw how he had loved a tricycle, and how he had formed an attachment to material things through his love for it. So even before the age of reason, his inner self was making wrong choices.

He also saw how he had hurt people with cruel words. One incident that he saw in great detail, occurred when he was aged 15 and staying for some months in a house in Bogota. There was a young maid in the house, and he was extremely cruel and abusive to her. He saw all that now in detail. As he now saw the full truth about this part of his life, he says, "My soul was torn apart when I saw this."

Yet another incident happened when he was in elementary school. Another child was a victim of jeering. Marino joined in and gave the child a cruel nickname which the boy was to carry with him throughout his life, hurting him deeply, and leading to others mocking him. He could now see that, as a result, the boy grew up suffering from isolation and extreme loneliness.

As well as being shown the full truth about his own life, he was also shown how sin spreads - that when one hurts a person even in a simple thing like being rude to them, that person, being upset, is then likely to be impatient or rude with someone else, and so just by one moment of rudeness or harshness, we can start a process that spreads out and out. Every word we utter has eternal significance for better or for worse. This is something many people have been shown during near death experiences - see Barbara's testimony and that of Gloria Polo.

Somewhere early on in his mystical experience, Marino had a vision of Heaven. He says, "On top of the mountain was a small but vibrantly lit-up city, filled with apparent life. ... In that instant I heard an incredible voice that transformed my very existence the moment it began speaking to me - a voice so majestic that not even a million words could describe it. ..... The voice I heard was not human. It was the voice of Our Lord. No one could speak that way. **It seemed to come from everywhere and at the same time from within me**. It filled everything around me.

"But God, who is rich in mercy, out of the great love with which he loved us, even when we were dead through our trespasses, made us alive together with Christ" Eph 2:4-5 RSV

This description of the Lord's voice as coming "from everywhere and at the same time from within me", tallies with that of other people who have had genuine Near Death Experiences. So too does Marino's experience of being embraced in God's unconditional love. He says, "I was in the hands of one from which I had nothing to fear, someone I could only love and from whom I could receive love. There was no sense of time or space even though I was observing the mountains, the lit-up city ..."

He says that Jesus appeared to him "in majestic light" that cannot be described in earthly terms, and that Jesus revealed to him the state of the world, and how people are living lives that are utterly spiritually impoverished. Yet he says that he was shown that "the devil cannot seize an incarnate soul completely. At the moment of death that soul has the opportunity to renounce sin and recognize God, saving itself even though it will remain in an alarming state of purification."

This may be true, but one must be careful as it is not an official truth affirmed by the Church. It could be said that in Marino's case, while there was the rejection of God and grave sin, yet there was also some goodness. Because of this, there was some capacity to respond to Jesus when he encountered Him. He could have escaped hell 'by the skin of his teeth'. It is true that those destined for Purgatory do have the capacity to renounce sin after death, but what about those who become truly evil?

During his mystical experience, Marino saw hell. He found himself floating over a horrible abyss. For 33 years, he had declared that there was no such place as hell, but now he saw it very clearly. He didn't want to look at it, but when we go to the other side, closing our eyes does not prevent us from seeing. In this abyss, he saw what appeared like a floating fog, but then realised that it was millions of souls. They had traces of human faces, but these had been destroyed by sin. Now many of them were demonic like.

In the context of being shown the reality of hell and evil spirits, he was also shown some of his more serious sins, including his sexual sins. He says, "I will never be able to explain the pain I felt when reliving such a scene before Heaven."
At the time, he had experienced his relationships with Donna and Cindy as 'beautiful relationships', but now he saw exactly how they appeared before God. Indeed while to his emotions, these relationships felt lovely, even then his eternal spirit knew the truth. He says, "I could see how in the midst of my most intense sinful activity (when I thought I had enjoyed the most physically), my soul was bleeding rivers of internal pain that consumed my entire being."

He also saw how through these relationships, evil spirits got a deeper grip on his life. When a person sins, it gives satan and evil spirits a foothold in that area

"The wrath of God is revealed from heaven against all ungodliness and wickedness of men who by their wickedness suppress the truth."
Romans 1:18 RSV

of a person's life. This isn't possession. It is sometimes called oppression. The evil spirits are able to intensify the compulsion to the sin or weakness. They can also begin to prompt that person. That is why one's house is far more likely to be broken into when one is in Church that when in the pub. Satan is not at all happy when you are in Church. Thieves have given satan a foothold in their lives and are open to his prompting.

Likewise satan both knows who is vulnerable to being tempted sexually or with drugs, and will target some people in particular. If satan knows that a person who is working for God, (be in a priest, sister or layperson) is vulnerable to being tempted sexually, or indeed to drink or drugs, he will raise up people to tempt that person, sometimes going to bizarre lengths. Marino says, "I recognized the work done by the enemy when he gave me infernal gifts in order to seduce others without effort and to be seduced even more easily. When we find ourselves in evil territory, the type of evil spirit that is guiding us influences our behaviour."

He also saw how himself and Cindy and Donna had brought destruction to others. He says, "Cindy and I were the cause of a lot of souls being destroyed; through us, they were initiated into LSD and a spontaneous, relaxed sexual life."

After he came back from his mystical experience, he was still a captive. Six months later, he was brought to a secluded mountain road. The four men ordered him to walk straight ahead without looking back. He expected to be shot in the back and begged God for the grace to die instantly. But no shots came. Eventually an old bus came along. He was free. What a sight he must have looked as he climbed on the bus - he hadn't had a change of clothes in six months, nor had he had a shave, while being starving much of the time, he looked like a skeleton.

After a few days recuperation, he went to a Franciscan monastery, where he was placed under the guidance of a priest. Here he went to Confession. It was a long one!! For a year, he kept his mystical experiences to himself. Then he felt led to share them, and to take on a mission in the Church seeking to lead people to conversion. His life is now devoted totally to this task.

For thirty three years, he had been addicted to drugs, drink and sex, yet after his eternal spirit had first been exorcised, and then permeated by God's love during his NDE, he was able to come back into his mortal body and live the new life. His life is a witness to how if one's eternal spirit is cleansed and permeated by God's love, one can then live the transformed life even after years of drugs, drink and sex. **If one's eternal spirit is healed, then one can live the new life.**

Footnote
Quotations from **Marino Restrepo's book "From Darkness into the Light"**. Published by Pilgrims Of Love. See www.marinorestrepo.com

— — — — — — — — — — — — — — — — — — —

"Behold, he is coming on the clouds, and everyone will see him, even those who pierced him" Rev 1:7

The Mother Who Lost All Hope

Angie Fenimore's father was overbearing, her mother, who suffered from depression, eventually left home to join a hippie commune. A few times as a child Angie was brought to Church. Then she felt very close to God, and prayed for her parents. But it isn't easy for a little child who is praying that her parents will sort themselves out, to see instead her mother go off to live in the woods with a weird hippie commune and to see her father turn to drink and to a litany of shallow sexual relationships. She stopped praying and lost touch with God; perhaps even lost the ability to trust God.

Angie then effectively had no parent caring for her, nobody to bring her to school or to church, nobody to protect her, and she also became a victim of sex abuse. This left her feeling utterly dirty, caused her to develop eating disorders and left her feeling so worthless that she believed that not even God could love her. Later, fleeing home from a mentally sick stepmother who verbally and physically abused her, she ended up abusing drugs and alcohol, and then rushed into marriage while still a teenager.

She and her husband had some good times, but there were endless rows. She felt no good, worthless, that her life had no positive purpose, and her husband's attempts to challenge her only made her feel infinitely worse. There was a 'tape' playing in her mind telling her that she was no good, and she interpreted everything in the light of that belief. She felt that she was only hurting her husband and two children, and eventually she came to believe that the greatest gift she could give them was to take her own life.

Years earlier her stepmother had had a brief near-death experience. She had claimed that she had been embraced in peace and had seen the light. Angie expected the same. She cut the veins in her wrists, and then took an overdose of pills. At first she was embraced in God's unconditional love. She says "I felt enveloped in a warm, comforting embrace that gave me a greater sense of peace and security than I had ever experienced. Could this be death. .... I knew I had longed to feel love like this all my life."

Then she experienced her whole life being replayed, even from when she was in her mother's womb. She was allowed to re-experience how her parents loved

"Come to me, all who labour and are heavy laden, and I will give you rest. Take my yoke upon you and learn from me; for I am gentle and lowly in heart, and you will find rest for your souls." Mt 11:28-28 RSV

her when she was born. This is something that often happens to people who have suffered a lot in life or who feel that they have never been loved. During their near-death experience, they are allowed to re-experience moments when they were loved. Thus Angie re-experienced how her mother had held her. She says, "I was content just to be held, ... I recognized that this was my mother nearly three decades ago. I was enthralled with her."

God was letting her see that regardless of what came later, she was loved as a wee child, and God was letting her understand her mother's weakness. She says "These first two memories - of my birth and of being cradled by my mother - were the most protracted, detailed, and emotionally coloured of all that I was shown. Through them I came to understand that my mother had cherished me just as much as I did my boys. I'd never imagined that - and so I could see her in a different way, realizing that what she'd done for us was the best she could."

Then she found herself before a large screen. She says "I was being drawn into a three-dimensional slide show of my life that played out before my eyes chronologically." During this life review, not merely did she re-experience her own feelings, but she also saw how the other people involved had felt, and how they had perceived what was happening.

In particular she was shown in vivid detail exactly what her childhood was really like. She was shown several more occasions on which she was happy, and experienced the love of her parents. She says, "As a little girl, I had felt secure in my home and in myself. I saw myself with pure, accepting eyes. My emotions were clear and intense, not muddled and conflicted. My picture of myself was dipped in the pride and love of doting parents - the exact opposite of what I had come to believe. My mother's presence, especially, brought me warmth and happiness. She was the central figure in most of the early memories."

As she experienced her life-review, she had a sense that Jesus was with her, and that He wasn't judging her, neither was he condoning. She says that the only feeling she got was, 'This is the way it is. This is the life that you lived'."

The latter part of her life flew past, but she would be brought back to it later. At this stage, it was the love in her early childhood that was focused on. It was, as if, God needed to reconnect her with the love she had experienced as a child before the healing could take place in her spirit.

She had died in despair, losing all trust in God. This may help explain what happened next. After the life-review, she found herself immersed into darkness. Even though it was dark in all directions, she could still see. This darkness enveloped her and everything else. Then in the darkness she could see a handful of teenagers. She had a sense that they too had died in total despair, many of

---

"I have come as light into the world, that whoever believes in me may not remain in darkness" John 12:46 RSV

them by suicide. She went to speak to them, and discovered that here one didn't have to use one's mouth to speak - that the words just came out.

There was so little reaction from the group that at first she thought they hadn't heard her. Then one of them looked at her, but he didn't say a word, just looked her up and down with "absolutely no expression on his face, no warmth or intelligence in his eyes." Across the way was an equally expressionless girl in her late teens. She too was just looking aimlessly ahead, and showed no sign of interest or curiosity.

Then Angie found herself being sucked even further into the darkness by some unseen force, as if a process of sorting was taking place. She ended up in a place of deep mist. This black mist which shrouded the floor, was swirling around her feet, and formed the thick, waist-high barrier that held her prisoner. This mist appeared to be formed of molecules. Angie felt that, "It had life, this darkness, some kind of intelligence that was purely negative, even evil. It sucked at me, pulling me to react and then swallowing my reaction into fear and dread. In my life I had suffered pain and despair so great that I could barely function, but the twisting anguish of this disconnection was beyond my capacity to conceive."

She says, "I knew that I was in a state of hell, but this was not the typical fire and brimstone hell that I had learned about as a young child. **The word Purgatory rose, whispered, into my mind.**" She wasn't alone for all around her were men and women of all sages. These were totally caught up in their own world, some of them mumbling to themselves, and they were surrounded with darkness."

In this place, it was possible to hear other people thinking. It was as if thoughts were being expressed aloud, yet nobody else was listening, each being too caught up in their own thoughts to listen to anyone else's. People were trying to come to terms with the truth about their lives, but this was the depths of Purgatory, the place where serious sinners end up. For them, coming to terms with the truth about their lives isn't easy. For example, one woman was trying to justify her lifestyle. Angie says, "She was justifying herself, over and over again, as if she were speaking to the ghosts of her past, trying to fix blame." Angie felt that she had been doing this for years.

Beside her was a man of about sixty. He was just sitting there utterly expressionless. She had a sense that both he and the woman had killed themselves. His clothing suggested to Angie that he lived around the time of Jesus. She wondered if it was Judas Iscariot, who had betrayed Jesus. Angie felt that she should be embarrassed for thinking such thoughts in his presence, given that here her thoughts could be heard by him. Angie herself had always tried to be helpful to people, but she says, "Now I didn't care. I felt no desire to be helpful or even polite to him or to anyone else."

— —

"The sting of death is sin" I Cor 15:56

Even with all these people around, Angie now experienced a growing sense of complete aloneness. There were people around, but nobody was making any connection with anybody else. How she now missed her children and would love to have gone home to them, but she knew that such thoughts were futile. She feared that she was going to be in this place of desolate darkness for ages and ages, and found all hope dying within her.

Then she says that she heard a voice "of awesome power ... a voice that encompassed such ferocious anger that with one word it could destroy the universe, and that also encompassed such potent and unwavering love that, like the sun, it could coax life from the earth." She adds, "I cowered at its force and at its excruciating words: **'Is this what you really want?'**

She says, "The great voice emanated from a pinpoint of light that swelled with each thunderous word until it hung like a radiant sun just beyond the black wall of mist that formed my prison. Though far more brilliant that the sun, the light soothed my eyes with its deep and pure white luminescence. ... And I knew with complete certainty that I was in the presence of God."

Within the light, she could see a Being of Light. She believes it was God the Father. She says, "He almost seemed to be made of the light. It was a light that had substance and dimension, the most beautiful, glorious substance that I have ever beheld."

Not merely was God radiating light, He was also radiating love. She had never felt herself to be worthy of God's love, but now she was experiencing it, and she immediately knew that while she was on earth, her sense of unworthiness of God's love had served as a barrier blocking it out.

Now being instilled into her was a sense of being made in His image. He appeared to her with a humanlike form, with a head, arms and legs. With this sense of being made in his image, there also came a sense that He had a special plan for her life. During all this time, she continued to be permeated by God's love. She says, "There is nothing that we are even capable of imagining that comes close to the magnitude of perfect love that this Being poured into me."

But the people around her had no sense of what was happening. They were still in the dark. Then God spoke to her again. She says, "His words were excruciating: **'Is this what you really want? This is the worst choice you could have made.'**"
"But my life is so hard," she said, still trying to justify herself.
"You think that was hard? It is nothing compared to what awaits you if you take your life," came the immediate response.

———————————————————————————

"There came a voice from above. .. On this throne above was a radiant being that looked like a human person." Ezekiel 1:25a, 26a

Then she felt another presence, Jesus. She realised that He had indeed been there all the time, but she only now became aware of His presence. He too was radiating light, and once again enveloped her in unconditional love. Angie says, "The rays of light penetrated me with incredible force, with the power of an all-consuming love. This love was as pure and potent as the Father's, but it had an entirely new dimension of pure compassion, of complete and perfect empathy. I felt that He not only understood my life and my pains exactly, as if He had actually lived my life, but that He knew everything about how to guide me through it; how my different choices could produce either more bitterness or new growth. Having thought all my life that no one could possibly understand what I had been through, I was now aware that there was one other person who truly did.

"Through this empathy ran a deep vein of sorrow. He ached, He truly grieved for the pain I had endured, but even more for my failure to seek his comfort. His greatest desire was to help me. He mourned my blindness as a mother would mourn a dead child. **Suddenly I knew that I was in the presence of the Redeemer of the world.** He spoke to me through the veil of darkness: 'Don't you understand? I have done this for you'."

As she was being permeated with His love, and realising how He had given His life for her, Angie found her spiritual eyes opened, and she began to experience this in a truly remarkable way. She says, "He had taken me into himself, subsumed my life in his, embracing my experiences, my sufferings, as his own. And so for a second I was within his body, able to see things from his point of view and to experience his self-awareness. He let me in so I could see for myself how He had taken on my burdens and how much love He bore me."

Then she knew immediately where she had gone wrong. She had doubted God's love and God's goodness. She had doubted the Scriptures because the message seemed too good to be true. She says, "To believe without seeing requires a great deal of trust. My trust had been violated so many times that I had very little to spare. And so I had clung to my pain so tightly that I was willing to end my life rather than unburden myself and act on the chance that a Saviour existed."

Now she could see that Jesus had wanted to embrace her in His love all the time, but that she had held Him at a distance. She had been afraid to trust Him. Now Jesus was pleading her case. Not that there was any conflict between Him and the Father. The Father immediately accepted the verdict of Jesus. Now too she could see that the suffering in her life didn't have to be without meaning, that it could even be turned to her good, so long as she surrendered it to Jesus; that is so long as she allowed Jesus to embrace her and her suffering.

As her life review continued, she realised that the decision to take her own life

— —

"God shows his love for us in that while we were yet sinners Christ died for us." Romans 5:8 RSV

was wrong, but she started to ask how she could have done otherwise given the circumstances of her life. Then she was shown where she had missed opportunities to receive spiritual help; how God had reached out to her through people, especially through one minister, but she hadn't responded.

Now she could see the full truth about her life, and about her actions. She says, "I was painfully aware of the suffering I had caused my family and other people because of my own weaknesses. But now I also saw that by ending my life, I was destroying the web of connections of people on earth, possibly drastically altering the lives of millions, for all of us are inseparably linked, and the negative impact of one decision has the capacity to be felt throughout the world."

She saw especially how her children would be devastated and scarred by her suicide, and how, as a result of the trauma, they would end up making choices that would lead them to miss God's plan for their lives. She was shown how much God loved her children, and how her suicide would become, for them, a block to experiencing God's love in their lives. She was also shown how her husband would be hurt, as would her sister, Tonni. But the hurting would not stop with those. It would spread out to countless others, including people she had never met.

She also saw that, had her death been permanent, she would have had to face the full truth about this, and that it wouldn't have been easy. Now however she realised that she was being given a second chance. She wondered why she was the one who experienced God's love and not the vacant husk of a man next to her. Why had she moved into the light, while he remained in darkness?

The answer came to her immediately:- it was because she was willing to believe in God. Because she was willing, then it was possible for her to respond. These others were so stuck in their disbelief, in their distrust and in their hardness of heart, that it was going to take them ages, perhaps even centuries to become open to belief. She realised now that the length she stayed in Purgatory depended on her willingness to believe and to respond.

She also found herself asking who would pay for all the damage that she had caused up to and including her suicide? Again the answer came immediately:- Jesus had already paid the debt for her. She says that she was told, "Jesus Christ had experienced all the suffering that has or ever will take place in the life of any human born on this earth. He experienced my life, he bore my sins, he accepted my grief. ...... My heart broke as I realized that I had been not only hurting my

— —

"Surely he has borne our griefs,
and carried our sorrows; .....
He was wounded for our transgressions,
he was bruised for our iniquities;
upon him was the chastisement that made us whole" Isaiah 53:4a,5 RSV.

59

family, who are beloved children of God, but also causing my Saviour, who had such all-encompassing love and compassion for me, to suffer - all because I had allowed myself to be moulded by other people's weaknesses."

She was also shown how instead of turning to the Lord for strength in her times of darkness, she had turned in wrong directions - including to the rock music that she played endlessly when depressed. She says, "Probably the most significant dark influence on me was the music I listened to. Some music may have words that seem harmless - mindless, in fact - but when these words are paired with musical combinations that have a dark spiritual form, they have power to create more darkness in the minds of those of us who hear them. ... The music I chose at that time lulled me into a stupor, preaching death and selfishness in symbolic phrases, and it crowded out the light."

She now realised that even then, deep down, she had known that this music was not good, but she had felt cut off from God, unworthy of His love, and had just given it. Instead of turning to God for comfort, she had turned to this music.

But she was also shown the good choices that she had made - like deciding to sacrifice the possibility of a career to care for her children.

After having gone through the full process of her life review, and of having her spirit cleansed and transformed, she was returned to her body . She says, "Then the powerful energy source that had transported me to the dark prison returned to liberate me. For a split second a rushing sensation engulfed me. The darkness sped past, and suddenly I was back in my body, lying on the couch."

My evaluation of Angie's testimony

There is a very strong resemblance between Angie's experience of the depths of Purgatory and the visions of Anne concerning the deeper levels of Purgatory. Anne saw the mist as a visitor, and was able to see the meaning and purpose of what took place there. Angie experienced what it is like to be a participant in the mist. She experienced the despair of those who have rejected God and caused grave hurt. She saw how hard it is for some to accept the truth about the hurt they had caused in life. For her the depths of Purgatory are truly terrifying, as indeed they are. One could debate whether when Jesus spoke of the "outer darkness" where "there will be weeping and gnashing of teeth" (Matthew 8:12; 13:42; 13:50: 22:13; 24:51; 25:30), He was referring to hell or to the depths of Purgatory. There certainly is great darkness in the depths of Purgatory. There is also great anguish there.

— —

"For God so loved the world that he gave his only Son, that whoever believes in him should not perish but have eternal life. For God sent his Son into the world, not to condemn the world, but that the world might be saved through him." John 3:16-17 RSV

Angie experienced what is it like in the depths of Purgatory as a participant. To her, the suffering there appeared "pointless, redundant, and stifling". In this she is incorrect, but it is how it appeared to her. This naturally has coloured her presentation - and prevented her seeing that Purgatory truly is a place of God's mercy; a place where one gets a 'second chance' to open one's heart to God. Even the depths of Purgatory, however horrific an experience it may be, is a place of God's mercy for great sinners, and once they open their hearts to God at all, they move forward from there - just like Angie did.

Those who enter Purgatory 'by the skin of their teeth', do find it very hard to come to terms with the truth about their lives - how they have hurt perhaps millions of people. Coming to terms with this, will be all the harder for them if they entered Purgatory with 'hearts' and 'intellects' bound in selfishness and lacking trust in God. But from Angie's testimony, we can also say that, if there is openness to Jesus in a person's heart, then they will be able to respond to Him even in the depths of Purgatory.

Meanwhile, if a loved one commits suicide, the greatest assistance we can give them is to draw closer to God instead of away from Him; draw our strength from Him and be guided by Him. A key element of Purgatory is seeing the damage we have caused - and the worst damage is spiritual and moral damage. If instead of allowing a loved one's suicide to cause us spiritual and moral damage, we draw close to God, this will be a source of very real comfort for them.

Angie's experience should not be taken as representative of all who commit suicide. For some, it may go far better, for others it may go far far worse. Some who commit suicide have always been deeply selfish people causing hurt to others, while others have lived loving lives. Some may cry out to God in repentance even as they die, others may die in complete rebellion against God.

While Angie's own experience of the depths of Purgatory appears frightening at first, remember that she was only briefly there, just as Marino Restrepo and Dr. Howard Storm were briefly at the gates of hell. I believe that had she remained dead, she would still have been permeated by God's love just as she describes, after being challenged about her serious wrong choice. Afterwards, I believe that she would have found herself in the mid to higher levels of Purgatory to pray and to intercede for those she had hurt. Yet suicide is not something to be made light of.

During her near death experience, Angie could be described as having received the full Baptism in the Spirit. First she was helped to re-experience how she had

— —

"This is the will of the one who sent me, that I should lose nothing of all that he has given me, but raise it up on the last day. For this is the will of the Father, that everyone who sees the Son and believes in him should have eternal life." John 6:39-40a RSV

been loved as a child. The manner in which she was allowed to re-experience how she had been loved as a child, serves as a reminder to us of the importance of getting in touch with how we too have been loved in life. It is so easy to allow one's bad experiences to fill one's mind. Especially if one has suffered much in life, it is important to get in touch with the moments when one has been loved, and to allow those memories to fill one's mind. This then opens one to being permeated by God's love.

After being allowed to re-experience how she had been loved as a child, Angie was shown the possible consequences of her wrong choices, followed by being directly challenged about them. Then she was utterly permeated by God's love, given remarkable insights into both the nature of God and the redemptive actions of Jesus. Then she given the second part of her life-review, focusing primarily on her wrong choices as an adult, but also her good choices.

After that she came back into her body, and was enabled to live the new life. Once again we see how, if one's spirit is transformed, then, even after being broken by the hurts of life and even after years of despair, one can come back into one's body and begin to live a transformed life. Heal a person's spirit, and then that person can move on from there leaving behind the hurts of the past.

Being a quiet person by nature, at first Angie did not publicly share her experiences, but seeing the way suicide is almost being glamorised, she felt impelled to step forward and to share her experience, praying that through her testimony, some might be protected from taking their own life.

Meanwhile her testimony is also a reminder to us of how our every word, and our every act, has its influence on others. We can bring blessing that will spread out and travel down through the generations, or we can cause a cycle of hurt that could still be impacting on people who will not be born for up to 500 years.

Footnote

All quotations are taken from Angie Fenimore's book, "Beyond the Darkness" Bantam Books. Angie does not come from a mainstream Christian Church. While this does colour how she gives her testimony, if anything, it makes her description of Purgatory more valid, especially when compared with Anne's visions. Angie is, I believe, a Mormon. I am a Catholic priest. Naturally there are some beliefs in her book with which I disagree. But clearly in Jesus, she is my sister. God is love, and His love is big enough to embrace us both.

— —

"Behold I stand at the door and knock; if anyone hears my voice and opens the door, I will come in to him and eat with him, and he with me"
Rev 3:20 RSV.

She Had Sponsored Abortions

Dr. Gloria Polo grew up believing in Jesus, but her life moved further and further from her Catholic upbringing. Then she was struck by lightning, and had two near-death experiences in quick succession. Many people who have near death experiences, speak of undergoing a life-review. Few however share in such great depth and detail as Gloria does exactly what their life-review involved.

One day as she and her nephew were sharing an umbrella, they were struck by lightning. The lightning killed her nephew instantly, and inflicted major injuries on Gloria, burning away her breasts and large areas of her side. It went right through her:- her liver was charred, her kidneys burned, so too were her lungs. She was using a copper-intrauterine device. The copper, an excellent electrical conductor, charred her insides, and pulverized her ovaries. She was left in cardiac arrest, her lifeless body jumping from the electricity that remained in it.

She says, "At that instant I found myself inside a beautiful white tunnel full of joy and peace, a happiness for which there are no human words that can describe the grandeur of the moment. The climax of the moment was immense. I was happy and joyful, nothing weighed me down. At the end of that tunnel I saw like a sun, a most beautiful light. I call it white to name a colour because no colour on earth is comparable with that most beautiful light."

Many people who have near-death experiences share about this beautiful moment as they enter the tunnel, and their experience of the light. Does that mean that they are guaranteed permanent happiness? Or that their mistakes (sins) in life don't matter? Some people like Angie Fenimore even commit suicide having heard about the beautiful light. Others use their experience of the light to campaign for issues like gay lifestyles. They would do well to read Gloria's full story.

She says, "As I was going up I realized I had died. At that instant I thought about my kids and I said 'Oh, my God, my kids! What will they say? This very busy Mom never had time for them!' That's when I saw my life truthfully and I became sad. I left home to transform the world, and I couldn't handle my kids and my home. In that instant of emptiness for my children, I looked and saw something beautiful: my flesh was not in this time or space. I saw everybody in a single instant, at the same time, both the living and the dead. I embraced my great-grandparents and my parents, who had passed away. I hugged everyone; it was a full and beautiful moment."

She had believed in reincarnation, and used to 'see' her grandfather and great-

---

"The kingdom of God is at hand; repent and believe in the gospel."
Mark 1:15 RSV

63

grandfather everywhere. But now she met them again and they hugged her. She also tried to hug the living, including her nine year old daughter. The daughter felt something and was frightened.

Now too Gloria was seeing people in a new way. Previously she had judged people by their outer appearances, but now she could see people on the inside. What a difference! Her experience was still good, beautiful; she was still full of joy, and it appeared to be getting better. Effectively she was still going through the initial experience of God's unconditional love. Just then she heard her husband's voice. He loved her and devastated by her apparent death, was crying out, 'Gloria, please don't go! Gloria, come back! The kids, Gloria, don't give up!' As she saw him, she had compassion, yet she didn't really want to go back, but Jesus encouraged her to do so. She says "I went back into my body. It was very painful to go back because sparks came out everywhere. And I saw myself fit into such a 'small thing'. Plus my flesh hurt, it was burned. It hurt a lot."

She had been a woman of the world; and describes herself as, "an intellectual, enslaved by my body, beauty, and fashion. ... I would slave to have a beautiful body: massage therapies, diets, that was my life:- an enslaving routine for the sake of a beautiful body. And I would say 'If I have beautiful breasts, I might as well show them off'. The same was true for my legs, because I thought I had great legs and breasts. But in an instant, I realised with horror how I had spent my life taking care of my body. But now, there was no body and no breasts; just some horrible holes. In particular my left breast had practically vanished. My legs were the worst: empty gaps with no flesh, completely charred and blackened."

Then while under anaesthesia, she came out of her body again. First she was worrying about her legs. Then she realised that she had more serious things to worry about:- how she had lived her life. She had once heard a priest say that neither hell nor the devil existed. Believing this, she had started telling everybody that there is no hell and no devil, and soon she was telling them that there is no God either. It sounded a cool thing to say to her college friends.

Now however, just like Dr. Howard Storm, she saw demons waiting for her to die. She says that "at first sight they looked normal, but with a look of hatred on their faces, a horrible look." She had a realisation that she 'owed' them; that because of her many sins they had a claim on her and were now coming for her.
She was utterly scared. First she tried to get back into her body, but couldn't. Then she tried to make a run for it, hoping to find a hiding place. She entered a series of tunnels. First there was light, but that grew weaker and weaker, and eventually she was in sheer pitch darkness. She says, "the darkest darkness on earth is like noontime sunlight compared to it. That darkness causes pain, horror,

"One cannot love both the things of this world and the Father. Craving possessions, lusting for all sorts of things, boasting of what one does or owns is not of the Father." 1 Jn 2:15-16

and shame. And it smells very bad."

Then she felt herself being sucked down through a hole, being sucked into what was either hell or the very depths of Purgatory. She says that "it was a horrifying moment. My atheism fell to the wayside. I started clamouring for the souls in Purgatory to help me out of there. As I was shouting I felt intense pain because I realized that thousands and thousands of people are there, many of them young people. Very painfully, I heard the gnashing of teeth, horrible screams and moans that shook me to the core. It took me several years to assimilate this because I would cry every time that I remembered their suffering."

She started to protest her innocence, screaming 'Who made this mistake? I've never stolen, I've never killed, I gave food to the poor. What am I doing here? I went to Mass on Sundays. **I'm a Catholic, please, I'm a Catholic, take me out of here!'"**

While she was screaming about being a Catholic she saw a tiny light. Then up some 'stairs', she saw her Dad, who had died five years before. There was faint light where he was. Higher up she saw her Mom in plenty of light, praying. The sight of them made her very happy. She says, "I started yelling 'Daddy, Mommy, please take me out of here, I beg you, take me out of here!'

Her father most likely was still in the deeper levels of Purgatory, grieving for his many serious sins and the terrible impact these had on his entire family including Gloria. Now he could see how they had impacted on his daughter, leading to her developing wrong attitudes. She says, "My Dad started crying, holding his head with his two hands and shaking, and saying, 'My daughter! My daughter!'"

Her Mom, who was surrounded in light, was either in the upper realms of Purgatory or in Heaven. While her father was powerless other than to cry, her mother was praying, clearly interceding for her. But, Gloria says, "I noticed that they could not take me out of there, and that my pain was compounded noticing they were sharing that pain with me there.

"So I started screaming again, 'Please, take me out of here, I'm a Catholic! Who made this mistake? Please, take me out of here!' As I was shouting this second time, a voice was heard, a sweet voice, a voice that made my soul shake. Everything was inundated with love and peace and all those creatures ran away in horror. And there was peace for me when that precious voice called out to me: **'All right, if you are a Catholic, tell me the commandments of God's law.'**

She says, "I knew there were ten, but nothing beyond that. What was I going to do? My Mom always talked to me about the first commandment of love."
Her fear somewhat abated, Gloria now thought she could bluff her way. She

— —

"The sons of the kingdom will be thrown into the outer darkness; there men will weep and gnash their teeth" Matthew 8:12 RSV.

started to say, "Love God above all and your neighbour as yourself."
"Very well, but have you loved them?" she was quickly asked.
She said 'I have, I have, I have!'
But the voice came again with a resounding 'No!' Gloria say that this was worse than being hit by the lightning.
"No, you haven't loved your Lord above all things, and much less your neighbour as yourself. You made a god for yourself! You would prostrate yourself before God when you were poor, when you wanted to go to college! Back then you prayed for whole hours, begging your Lord to pull you out of poverty and to allow you to get a degree and to become someone. Whenever you were in need and wanted money, you would say a rosary. Lord, please send me some money! That was your relationship with your Lord!"

Gloria says, "I had an 'ATM' relationship with the Lord, I have to admit. I grabbed the rosary, and expected money in return, that was my relationship with Him. Now I was shown how, as soon as I got my degree and made a name for myself, the Lord became too small for me and I started thinking myself better. Nor was I ever thankful for the help the Lord had given me."

She was then shown how she had even turned to astrology, believing in the stars.
She was also shown how when a sorcerer called to her dentist's office, she had accepted the charms 'to scare away bad energies'. She was shown that even when younger, when she thought she loved the Lord, she didn't really walk in His ways.

She says, "I used to criticize everyone. I was now shown how I was full of envy and always ungrateful. I never recognized my parents' love and selfless effort, to see me through college, to raise me. As soon as I got a college degree, even they became too little for me. I even felt ashamed of my Mom, because of her simplicity, humility, and poverty.

"I was shown too how I failed as a wife, complaining day in and day out. My husband would say 'good morning' and I would respond 'What is good about it? I was likewise with the children. ... I now saw that I had a heart of stone. It was terrible, devastating. I was in total chaos."

She was shown her lack of practical love for others, and that whatever help she gave had strings attached. She was told "You had a god, and that god was money! Because of it you have sunk into the abyss and you distanced yourself from your Lord." This at first appeared ironic, as they had lost their money, but that didn't mean that she didn't love it. Then she was taken through each of the ten commandments. On the second commandment, she saw how as a little girl,

— —

Then you will begin to say, "We ate and drank in your presence, and you taught in our streets" Luke 13:26 RSV.

she had become an liar to escape her mother's severe punishments. Knowing how much her mother loved Jesus, Gloria would say, when telling a barefaced lie, **"Mom, I swear to God...."** If her mother still did not believe her, she would add, **"Mom, if I'm lying to you, let a lightning bolt strike me!"** Well it did strike her with devastating effects!!

"On keeping holy the Lord's Day, she was shown how she would spend up to five hours a day looking after her body, but she hadn't even ten minutes for the Lord. If she said the Rosary, it was rushed through during the commercials on TV. She was also shown how as a teenager, if she didn't feel like going to Mass, she'd say, "But Mom, God is everywhere, why do I need to go there?"

She says, "Instead of caring for my soul, I took care of my body. ... I used to say that I would never go to Confession to those old men who were far worse than me." This insulated her from facing the truth about her life, and facilitated her passage towards depravity. As an adult, she still went to Mass for social reasons, yet she would mock the Blessed Sacrament saying things like, "Why call the Host 'the Blessed Sacrament'? Can you imagine God being alive in a piece of bread? Priests should put some caramel spread on that wafer to make it tasty!"

She says, "I would criticize priests constantly. Ever since we were little, I remember criticism against priests being present in my family. My Dad used to say that those guys were womanizers and much better off than we were, and we would repeat that." Now Jesus challenged her on that. She says, "The Lord showed me that each time I criticized priests, the demons would get attached to me."

On the fourth commandment, she was shown how she would belittle her parents because they could not give her everything her friends had. When she got educated, she was ashamed of her mother. Later in life, she did pay their doctors' bills, but then she felt that she had the right to manipulate them afterwards; that she could step all over them.

In his younger days, her father sadly was not merely a womaniser, but boasted of it even to her mother. In his eyes this made him a real man. No wonder he was crying in Purgatory!! When growing up, Gloria could see how her mother covered her tears when her father was boasting of the other women. Very understandably Gloria rebelled, and became full of anger and resentment. She says, "That resentment led me to my spiritual death. I became embittered by the way my Dad humiliated my Mom in front of everyone. I rebelled and I told my Mom I would never be like her. ... When I grew up, I told my Dad, 'Mind you, I'll never, ever, let a man humiliate me the same way you humiliate my Mom.'"

Gloria was right for standing up against her father's outrageous behaviour. It was

---

"By this we may be sure that we know him, if we keep his commandments. He who says 'I know him' but disobeys his commandments is a liar, and the truth is not in him" 1 John 2:3-4 RSV.

67

the way that it turned her bitter that was the problem. She also tried to get her mother to divorce him but her Mom would tell her: "No, honey, of course I'm hurt, but if I leave him, who is going to pray for his salvation? I'm the only one who can pray so he will be saved because the hurt and suffering he causes me, I raise to unite to the pain of Christ on the Cross. Every day I tell the Lord, 'This pain is nothing compared to your Cross, so please save my husband and children!'"

Gloria couldn't understand that. Instead she became full of rage, and in the process, started defending abortion, cohabitation, and divorce, and speaking out in favour of 'an eye for an eye and a tooth for a tooth'. Her rage led to Gloria supporting both 'liberated sex' and abortion. This in turn led to worse. Thus when they came to the Fifth Commandment, Jesus showed her how money empowered her to pay for several abortions. She says, "I saw it in the book of life, and it hurt me deeply when I saw a fourteen-year old girl aborting because I had taught her. When one's soul is poisoned, nothing good remains. Everyone that comes close to you is also spoiled."

Because she had a 'glamorous' home, her nieces and nephews spent a lot of time there. She says, "I talked to them about fashion, glamour, how to show their bodies, and so on. I corrupted them. I corrupted minors, that was a horrible sin, compounding abortion. I would tell them not to be innocent. I'd say, 'Your mothers talk to you about virginity and chastity because they're outdated. Your mothers talk about what the Pope says, but the Pope is outdated.'

"I taught these girls that they were to enjoy their bodies. I taught them the 'perfect woman' method. Then the 14 year old, my nephew's girlfriend, came to my office one day (I saw this again in the book of life) and in tears told me, 'Gloria, I'm just a baby and I'm pregnant!' I scolded her and told her 'Didn't I teach you about contraception?' She replied 'Yes, but it didn't work'!"

Gloria's solution was to give her the money for an abortion. In fact she sponsored several abortions. Now she was shown the full terrible significance of abortion; that each abortion is like a holocaust offered to Satan, and how it hurts and grieves the Lord. She says, "In the book of life I saw how our soul is formed the moment the sperm and the egg unite. A beautiful spark is formed, a light beaming from the sun of God the Father. As soon as the womb of a mother is impregnated, it lights up with the brightness of that soul. When there is an abortion, that soul screams and moans in pain even if it has no eyes or flesh. When it is being murdered, that cry is heard and heaven shakes, and an equally strong cry is heard in hell, but this time of joy."

Gloria says, "After those abortions, I had no more sense of sinfulness. For me

— —

"Whoever causes one of these little ones who believe in me to sin, it would be better for him to have a great millstone fastened round his neck and to be drowned in the depth of the sea" Mt 18:6 RSV.

everything was okay." Nor was it just those abortions. Now she also saw how the intrauterine device had worked. She says, "I painfully saw how many little babies had been created, with the cry of that baby being torn away from the hands of his Father God. No wonder I was always sour and ill-tempered, with a grim face, frustrated with everyone and very depressed. I had become a baby-killing machine!"

"That sank me deeper into the abyss. Then how about every person I disliked, hated, or simply couldn't put up with? I was being a murderer there too, because people don't only die from a gunshot. It's enough to hate them."

On the Sixth Commandment, she had only had one man, her husband, her entire life. But now she saw how she had dressed, inciting men to look at her and have impure thoughts. Furthermore she had encouraged women to be unfaithful to their husbands, had advised against forgiveness and encouraged divorce.

On the Seventh Commandment, regarding not stealing, Jesus showed her that while food was being wasted in her house, the rest of the world was going hungry. He said: "I was hungry and look what you did with what I gave you and how you would squander it. I was cold and see how you became enslaved to fashion and appearance, wasting lots of money in treatments to look thinner."

She was also shown how she stole when she gossiped. She says, "It would have been easier to steal money from someone, because at least I could have returned it, but not so a person's reputation. I also stole from my children the grace of having a mother at home, tender and loving, and not the mother out in the world leaving them with the TV, the computer, or the video games for baby-sitters. To clean my conscience, I would buy them brand-name clothes."

"I felt ashamed because in the Book of Life you get to see everything like in a movie. I saw my children saying 'Let's hope Mom doesn't come home soon, because she is always complaining.' How sad it is for a three year old boy and a slightly older girl to say that. I stole their mother from them! I stole the peace I was supposed to give in my home. I didn't teach them to love God. I didn't teach them to love their fellowman.

"My sins of the word were terrible! I saw how much I had hurt with my tongue. Whenever I gossiped, whenever I made fun, whenever I gave anyone a nickname, how much did that person hurt. How much did that nickname hurt. I could give someone with a weight problem an inferiority complex by just calling her fat.

"I was shown how so much of my sinning came from covetousness. I always thought I would be happy if only I had lots of money, and it became an obsession.

"Depart from me, you cursed, into the eternal fire prepared for the devil and his angels; for I was hungry and you gave me no food, I was thirsty and you gave me no drink .... Truly I say to you, as you did it not to one of the least of these, you did it not to me." Matthew 25:41-42,45

69

Yet the worst moment for my soul was when I had the most money. I even thought of killing myself. With so much money, I was alone, empty, sour, frustrated."

After the ten commandments, Gloria was shown the book of life. She says, "My book of life started at conception, when my parents' cells united. Almost immediately there was a spark, a beautiful explosion and a soul was formed.

"I saw all sorts of things from my life, like how I would tell someone 'You look beautiful in that dress, it looks great on you', but inside I would be thinking, 'What a disgusting outfit and she thinks herself the queen!' In the Book of Life, it would show up exactly as I had thought about it, both my words to her and the inside of my soul. All my lies were uncovered.

"Once a woman gave me back too much change. I noticed her mistake in the car, heading to my office. I muttered, 'That stupid woman gave me back 4,500 pesos too much and now I have to go back!' There was a huge traffic jam so I decided not to turn back. After all, why was she so stupid! I confessed it in Confession, but didn't return the money. The Lord showed me how she suffered and went hungry for a couple days. Because of me, her two little ones hungered. That's how the Lord shows these things. It shows how someone suffered from something I did.

"The Lord asked me: 'What was the point in your owning two condos, houses, and office buildings? You thought yourself a successful professional. You couldn't even bring the dust off one of the bricks here. And what did you do with the talents I gave you?'
"Talents? I thought. I had forgotten I had a soul so I could hardly remember that I had talents, that I was meant to be the merciful hands of God. Much less that all the good I didn't do, hurt the Lord.

"The Lord kept on asking me about my lack of love and charity. That's when He told me about my spiritual death. I was alive, but dead. ... I could see my soul on the outside, smelling well, with good clothes on; but on the inside there was stench. I had been living deep in the abyss. No wonder I was so depressed and sour!"

Jesus also told her: "Your spiritual death began when you stopped hurting for your brothers! When you saw media coverage on murders, abductions, refugee situations, and with your tongue you said, 'Poor people, how sad', but you didn't really hurt for them. You felt nothing in your heart. Sin made your heart into a heart of stone. You can imagine my deep sorrow when my book closed."

Her sorrow was all the greater as she realised how Jesus had tried again and again to reach out to her. Right to the end, He had been giving her chance after chance.

— —

"You say, I am rich, I have prospered, and I need nothing; not knowing that you are wretched, pitiable, poor, blind and naked." Rev 3:17 RSV

She says, "Out of my free will, I chose my father, and my father was not God. I chose satan, he was my father. When that book closed I noticed I was heading down into a pit with a door at its bottom. And as I'm heading there, I started calling out to all the saints begging them to save me. I thought I could ask for help from Saint Isadora or Saint Francis of Assisi. When I ran out of saints, the same silence remained. I felt great emptiness and hurt.

"Everyone back on earth was probably thinking I had died a saint, but look where was I headed!! I lifted my eyes and they met the eyes of my Mom. With intense pain I cried out to her, 'Mommy, how ashamed I am! I was condemned, Mommy! Where I'm going I'll never get to see you again! At that moment, they granted her a beautiful grace. She was still but her fingers moved and pointed upward. A couple of very painful scales fell from my eyes, that spiritual blindness. Then I saw a beautiful moment, when one of my patients told me: 'Doctor, you are very materialistic but some day, when you find yourself in imminent danger, ask Jesus Christ to cover you with His Blood, because He will never abandon you. He paid the price of blood for you.'

"I started to cry: **'Jesus Christ, Lord, have compassion on me! Forgive me, Lord, give me a second chance!'** That was the most beautiful moment. I have no words to describe that moment. He came and pulled me out of that pit. When He picked me up, all those creatures threw themselves on the ground. He picked me up and He pulled me onto that flat part and told me with all His love: 'You will go back, you will have a second chance.'"

Then she was shown that it wasn't her family's prayer that saved her. She was shown instead a poor peasant who lived up in the hills. He had bought some processed cane. It was wrapped for him in the previous day's newspaper. Her accident was the front page news. They even had a picture of her, all burned. Seeing this, the poor peasant fell to his knees in prayer for her, promising to cross Colombia to the shrine of Our Lord in Buga if she was saved. She says "The Lord told me, 'That is love for your fellowman.'

"Then He told me: 'You will go back, but you won't repeat this 1000 times. You will repeat it 1000 times 1000. And woe to those who don't change their ways despite having heard you, because they will be judged much more severely.

Gloria adds, "When you will get your Book of Life opened in front of you, when you die, you will see that moment just as I saw it. Then you will see yourself just as you are. You will see even your thoughts in the presence of God, and the most beautiful part, with the Lord in front of each one of us, once again, 'begging' us to convert and to become a new creation with Him, since we cannot do it without Him."

— —

"Go, make disciples of all nations. .... Teach them to observe everything that I have taught you, and behold, I will be with you" Matthew 28:19a, 20.

71

My Evaluation of Gloria's Testimony

Both Gloria Polo and Angie Fenimore were first embraced by the Light and experienced God's unconditional love, but then they were faced with the stark truth about their lives and the possible eternal consequences. This is a most important point, for some people come back saying things like, "I saw the light", "There is nothing better than death," "There is no sin and no judgement" (See page 76ff).

In our life-review, we will see the full truth about our lives, including exactly how people were hurt by our words and actions, and how that may have created a cycle of hurting spreading out to other people or spreading down through the generations. We will also see how we responded to God's love and to the opportunities that He gave us in this life. The truth of our lives has to be faced, nor can our eternal spirit be 'born again' without facing the truth. One may have initial experiences of God's love, either in this life or in the next, but after that the full truth about one's life has to be faced. One cannot live the transformed life here on earth without facing the full truth about one's life, nor can one enter Heaven without first having faced it.

Gloria during her near death experienced faced the truth about her life the hard way. For her it was almost the equivalent of an exorcism as her eternal spirit was being cleansed of bitterness, selfishness and the lust for things of this world, just as in the case of Marino Restrepo, it was almost the equivalent of an exorcism as he was faced with the truth about his attachment to material things, about his hurtful treatment of people, and then about his addiction to drink, drugs, and sex.

But in both cases, after their eternal spirits had been exorcised and then embraced in God's love, they were able to come back into their mortal bodies and live the transformed life. If the eternal spirit is transformed, then the person is transformed. On the other hand, if one becomes addicted, or selfish, or lustful, so too does the one's eternal spirit.

If you desire to go to Heaven the moment you die, or even to the upper realms of Purgatory, then take a crash course in the truth about your life and your personhood. Face what needs to be faced and do so now.

Footnote

All quotations from Gloria Polo are taken from gloriapolo.neuevangelisierung.org/ indexeng.htmls See also www.apostolat.org/gloriapoloCOM/contactoeng.html (Or just go to Google and call up Gloria Polo.)

— —

"Enter by the narrow gate, for that gate is wide and the way is easy, that leads to destruction, and those who enter by it are many. For the gate is narrow and the way is hard, that leads to life, and those who find it are few." Mt. 7:13-14 RSV

Did Jesus have an out-of-body experience?

The temptations of Jesus as described in Matthew and Luke's Gospel's are often treated almost as an embarrassment. People take it that they did not happen in the manner described by Matthew and Luke on the basis of a belief that they could not have happened like this. It is claimed that Matthew and Luke are using symbolic language to say that Jesus faced the normal human temptations:- turning stones into bread as a symbol of the temptation to materialism; jumping off the temple as a symbol of the temptation to exhibitionism; and then being offered the kingdoms of the world as a symbol of the temptation to pursue power for the sake of power. This symbolism is certainly there, but that does not mean that the temptations were not a real experience - in the form of an out-of-body experience.

It is quite possible that Jesus had an out-of-body experience following his forty days of extreme fasting and of living in the desert under harsh circumstances. Remember that it was after being semi-starved and being held under very harsh circumstances that Marino Restrepo had his out-of-body experience. Marino makes no claim to his experience having been a near-death experience, yet his out-of-body experience was identical to many near-death experiences.

Remember also that Jesus was truly man, and that it is clearly not altogether uncommon for a person to have a near-death or out-of-body experience. Likewise it is not uncommon for a person to encounter satanic forces during near-death or out-of-body experiences. So it is almost to be expected that Jesus, in his total sharing of the human condition, would have had an out-of-body experience. Likewise, because He had taken the sin of the world upon Himself, it is logical that He would have encountered satan.

The first temptation of Jesus occurred while He was still either in his body or closely connected to His body, as it occurred while he was experiencing hunger, and satan tempted Him to turn the loaves into bread. "The devil said to him, 'If you are the Son of God command this stone to become bread.' And Jesus answered him, It is written, 'Man shall not live by bread alone'." Luke 4:4 RSV

But then "the devil took him up, and showed him all the kingdoms of the world in a moment of time and said to him, 'To you I will give all this authority and their glory; for it has been delivered to me, and I give it to whom I will. If you, then, will worship me, it shall all be yours.' And Jesus answered him, 'It is written, 'You shall worship the Lord your God, and him only shall you serve.'"

— —

Jesus came and said to them, "All authority in heaven and earth has been given to me" Mt 28:18 RSV

Now that is the description of an out-of-body experience. In Luke's Gospel, there is the detail that he showed Him "all the kingdoms of the world in a moment of time". Being showed all the kingdoms of the world in a moment of time is something that happens during near-death and out-of-body experiences. In Matthew's Gospel, there is the detail that satan took him "to a very high mountain" and showed him all the kingdoms of the world. This too is an out-of-body experience. One cannot see all the kingdoms of the world from any earthly mountain, so it had to have been a mountain in the realm of the spirit. Many people in their out-of-body experiences, or near-death experience, or visions, speak of seeing a mountain or being on a mountain.

Then satan "took him to Jerusalem, and set him on the pinnacle of the temple, and said to him, 'If you are the Son of God, throw yourself down from here, for it is written, 'He will give his angels charge of you, to guard you,' and 'On their hands they will bear you up, lest you strike your foot against a stone.'" And Jesus answered him, 'It is said you shall not tempt the Lord your God.'" Luke 4:9-12 RSV.

This one is more complicated. How could satan have taken Jesus to Jerusalem and to the pinnacle of the temple, if it was not an out-of-body experience? Yet the temptation makes more sense if Jesus is in his body, since when out of the body, one could easily move down from the pinnacle of the temple to the ground. Both Matthew and Luke were writing many years later, and were dependent on their sources for the details of what actually happened, so some inaccuracies in the details are inevitable. But overall, if He was actually taken by satan to Jerusalem and placed on the pinnacle of the temple, the odds are very much in favour of it being an out-of-body experience.

In Luke this is listed as the third temptation, but as the second in Matthew. Either order would be consistent with an out-of-body sequence of experiences. Some people's experiences start close to their own body, with a consciousness of the needs of the body (hunger in the case of Jesus), then they move further away but are still in the same region (Jerusalem in the case of Jesus), and then move further away still. Others start close to their bodies, then move a distance away, and then are back in the general region of their body (See Barbara Harris Whitfield's story).

After the temptations, "angels came and ministered to him" Mt. 3:11 RSV. This too is totally consistent with an out-of-body experience. During near-death experiences, after satan is resisted if this is necessary, and then driven away, one begins to be ministered to. In the case of many who have near-death experiences, this ministering comes from Jesus Himself, or from Our Lady. But in the case of Jesus, and with Our Lady still very much alive, it is totally normal that it was the angels who ministered to Him.

It should also be noted that Jesus, while without sin, took upon his shoulders, the sin of the world. He had to step into the world of sin and condemnation to rescue us from this world of sin and condemnation. This would have applied also if He had an out-of-body experience. Instead of finding Himself in the realm of God's love, He would have found Himself in the realm where satan had power. This once again is consistent with the temptations of Jesus taking place during an out-of-body experience.

This also should alert us to what can sometimes happen when a person, who has attached himself to false gods or who has rejected God's love, has a near-death experience. Remember that Jesus' out-of-body experience was a 'benign' one. He was brought to the 'holy city' and placed on the parapet of the temple. He was brought to a high mountain and shown the splendour of the universe. He had no 'horror stories' to tell. It could have been described as a magnificent experience, but it was the work of satan. Satan knew that there was nothing to be gained by trying to drag Jesus off to hell in the manner described by Gloria Polo, or by physically attacking him in the manner described by Dr. Howard Storm.

Instead satan set out to tempt Jesus and to mislead Jesus. So too, where people have attached themselves to false gods (evil spirits) or rejected love, they may find themselves in satan's realm and they too may be shown all the kingdoms of the universe and its glory. It may be a 'beautiful experience' - but it may all be courtesy of satan.

In resisting the misleading and tempting presentation from satan, Jesus each time used Scripture to challenge satan. In doing so, He established for us a basic principle:- if someone comes along claiming to have had a wonderful spiritual experience, but if it contradicts Scripture, then it is not of God, but could well be of satan. This is a most important principle in evaluating near-death experiences.

In the next two chapters, I will analyse the near-death experiences of David Oakford and of Barbara Harris Whitfield. David Oakford, like Jesus, was shown the kingdoms of the world, and I will be suggesting that what he experienced is not consistent with the teaching of Jesus, and that one has to question its origins. I will be suggesting that Barbara's near-death experience on the other hand is compatible with Jesus and His teaching, but that, because of her background, she has interpreted it in ways that are not compatible with the teaching of Jesus.

— —

"In this the love of God was made manifest among us, that God sent his only Son into the world, so that we might live through him. In this is love, not that we loved God but that he loved us and sent his Son to be an expiation for our sins. Beloved, if God so loved us, we also ought to love one another." 1 John 4:9-11 RSV

75

David's NDE:- Was it from God or from satan?

David Oakford's young life was pretty messed up. During a party in 1979, when aged 20, he overdosed on drugs, and while in a coma, he had what he claims was a near-death experience. His story is told in Kevin Williams' book **"Nothing Better Than Death"**. It is a rather sad title for a book that contains the testimony of a person who overdosed on drugs. **The title of the book should immediately alert one to the fact that there is something wrong here.** It is only true that there is "nothing better than death" if one is walking with Jesus. But one has only to read Dr. Howard Storm's, Angie Fenimore's and Gloria Polo's testimonies to know that there is nothing worse than death if one dies in sin.

You may find it strange that I include sections of David Oakford's story in this book, but I think it is right to give our readers some guidance on his type of story.

He says that after his drugs overdose, the next thing he knew was that he was travelling north in his friend's car; that he passed the family home and saw his parents sitting in the porch; and that he could see the roots of the trees going right down into the ground.

He says that when he returned to the house, his friends had music blaring; that he tried to turn it down but couldn't turn the knob; that he tried to pull out the plug but couldn't; that he ran around the house calling his friends, but they could no longer hear him; that he tried to get away from the noise by going into the bathroom, but the noise was still tearing at him, and that he tried to get back into his body but couldn't.

David's account so far is totally consistent with him having either a dream or a drug induced psychedelic trip. People often dream about what is annoying them. For example, people regularly have weird dreams involving wanting to go to the loo, and then wake up to realise that they do need to go. Furthermore, when one leaves one's mortal body, one doesn't need a car for travel!!

But back to his story. He says that he then asked God to help him. He adds that he did believe in God, but was angry with Him because of his "crappy life" . When he called out to God, he says, "I saw a beautiful being standing there. .... He looked both female and male and was young. ... He had this glow about him."

"Nothing unclean shall enter Heaven, nor any one who practices abomination or falsehood, but only those who are written in the Lamb's book of life." Rev 21:27

He told David 'I am here to help you' without his mouth moving. This 'being' then called David by another name. David told him that he must have the wrong guy; that that was not his name. The 'being' then told him that he, David, was in reality "a great master" only he had forgotten who he really was.

He then told him that he could go anywhere he wished, so they headed off to the pyramids of Egypt, then to the United States, and then to the Far East. As they travelled David could see "energy emanating" from most things, especially the plant and animal life. It was strongest where there were no humans, but humans also had energy.

He says that he was shown people with the "higher energy levels" and some of them actually talked to the 'being' he was with. He also saw "dark souls" These he says "were earthbound spirits who refuse to go to the light." The 'being' then told him that spirits are able to measure a human's level of spiritual advancement by the energy the human gives off, and that David's would eventually grow to match that of the 'being' so long as David chose to evolve his soul.

The 'being' told him that there are "beings of higher vibration" living on earth, but they are "part of earth itself". These "beings" look after "the plant life, the mineral life and the water-borne life". The 'being' then told him that the proper name for planet earth is "Gaia". The 'being' told him that Gaia has its own energy and that Gaia is really a true living being."

David then asked to be taken into space, so off they went. From space he could see Gaia. It was beautiful and he felt a deep love for it. His 'being' told him that of all the planets Gaia is "the most unique" because it was specially created for humans to live on forever. Humans only die because they have "fallen away from the balance of nature".

They then travelled past all the planets in our solar system. He says that he saw spirits and great cities on every planet. The 'being' told him that these other planets are where spirits prepare and practise for the various times they are reincarnated on Gaia; that Gaia is the ultimate experience for a soul. The 'being' then explained to David how we pick our parents before we are conceived.

The 'being' then said, "Jesus was a master God sent to earth to teach humans how to act toward each other and find their way back to the path of harmony with each other as well as with Gaia. I was told that Jesus is the being that is entrusted by God to ensure that souls evolve."

David was further told that Jesus had higher "vibrations" than anyone else, and that he held the highest favour with God because he was "the best example of what humans need to do". David says that he then got to see the 'being' he calls

— —

"Salvation belongs to our God who sits upon the throne, and to the Lamb"
Revelation 7:10 RSV.

Jesus. He says, "I saw his light. Jesus' light was the purest I have ever seen." He was then told that "loving one another" is what is required for there to be peace and harmony on Gaia.

Then he was shown the whole solar system all at once in full colour. He could see from Pluto to the sun. He says, "I felt very blessed and very important. ... There I floated, a being that went out of his way to inflict pain on other souls, yet I was never asked about what I had done."

They then came back to a city in the clouds near Gaia. From here he could see spirits coming and going from Gaia. Some of the ones coming back from Gaia were broken by their experiences there just like he, David, had been, and were coming back to be renewed before their next reincarnation.

Then he was taken to a room where spirits were waiting to interview him and to do his life-evaluation. First he was shown his parents before he was born, the type of personalities that they had. Then the 'beings' asked him why he had chosen those parents to be born to, and he was able to tell them.

He says, " I saw myself being born from an observer standpoint as well as having the actual experience." Then he was shown his entire life in this manner, being able to see it as an observer, and yet able to experience it as he then experienced it, and also able to experience the feelings of the people his actions had affected. He says, " I saw both the positive and the negative things I had done as they had truly happened, nothing was left out or presented inaccurately. ...."

"I felt all of my emotions and the emotions of the souls I had hurt as well as loved. From all of this I learned that it matters deeply what choices I make on Gaia. ... I learned just how powerful we humans are and how we can affect each other in positive and negative ways. It was amazing to see how my innocent actions had such a powerful effect on souls that I had no idea I was affecting. ...."

"I could see how I became what I had become on Gaia and why I became that way. .. I saw the reasons for all of my actions and understood why I did what I had done. There was a place for all of my positive and negative actions. There was no action that was necessarily wrong, but there were actions I took that did not enhance positive growth."

Afterwards the beings questioned him about his life, and about how he could have made better choices. They then told him that he still had much work to do on Gaia, and suggested that he should return now, that the work had to be done either now or later. They told him that he had "great potential to affect other souls", and that what he had experienced so far was a preparation for the work that he had to do.

"Every spirit which does not confess Jesus is not of God. This is the spirit of antichrist, of which you have heard that it was coming, and now it is in the world already." 1 John 4:2b-3 RSV

When he came back into his body he believed that his experience was merely "a really vivid drug induced 'trip', but, he says, that when he evolved more, he realised the gift that he had been given.

Evaluation of David Oakford's Experience

It is possible that David merely had a 'psychedelic trip', but it seems more likely that it was an NDE. **If so, which was it courtesy of God or of satan?**

People's near-death experiences will always be coloured by their own beliefs. Also we find imperfections in the teaching that most people claim to have received during near-death experiences. This is because, until final entry into Heaven, one's intellect remains imperfect, and it is through one's intellect that one receives the teachings. As George Rodonaia described it, "Think and it comes to you". Thus finding incorrect teachings in a person's near-death experience is totally natural. It is quite possible that David Oakford merely misinterpreted a relatively brief genuine experience of God's unconditional love.

Yet in David's testimony we find a multitude of serious errors, including the three most serious errors that one finds in New Age teaching,

1. That Jesus wasn't really God but merely an advanced spirit or, as David calls him, a 'master'. How satan would love to have people believe that!!

2. That Jesus wasn't truly the Saviour. In fact according to David (and the New Age) man does not need a Saviour. Some people may be really messing up their lives, but while that isn't good, don't worry since eventually everybody will evolve to their destiny as a higher spirit. Again how satan would love to have people believe that!!

3. We can make wrong choices, but there is no such thing as sin, so neither is there any need for repentance for sin. Yes, our actions may be impacting negatively on the people around us, and if we are to evolve, we should do something about that, but ultimately that is okay too. Again how satan would love to have people believe that!!

Jesus started his ministry with the message of repentance. There is no other way to salvation but through the repentance of sin. Contrast this with what David says, "There was no action that was necessarily wrong, but there were actions I took that did not enhance positive growth."

One of satan's tricks is flattery. David was told he was "a great master" - despite his messed up life.

There are many things in David's story that appear 'positive'. David felt good during his brief experience. He speaks about love and about caring for the earth.

— — — — — — — — — — — — — — — — — — — —

"You will die in your sins unless you believe I am he." John 8:24 RSV

After his recovery, he cleaned up his act, and started to live as a 'master' but satan knows that people will not follow him (satan) unless he can convince them that they are choosing good. It would be very helpful to satan's cause if he can convince people that Jesus was merely a "master" (just like David!), not either God or Saviour; and if he can convince people that "there is no action that is necessarily wrong"; in other words no such thing as sin.

David says, "He told me Jesus was a master God sent to earth to teach humans how to act toward each other and find their way back to the path of harmony with each other as well as with Gaia. I was told that Jesus is the being that is entrusted by God to ensure that souls evolve."

Jesus was indeed the master and is called the master by Himself:- "You have one master, the Christ" Mt. 23:10 RSV. That David recognises Him as master is a start, but Jesus was far more that merely a master. He was also both God and Saviour. Either He was both God and Saviour or everything that He said was bunkum. If He was not both God and Saviour, then He was not "the way, the truth and the life"; nor was He "the bread of life"; nor could He turn bread and wine into His body and blood; nor was He our Redeemer. Furthermore if the teachings received by David Oakford are correct, then Jesus was wrong about sin and its consequences; and wrong about Hell; and wrong about satan and evil spirits. Furthermore if there is no sin, then Jesus was totally wrong about His own death:- if there is no sin, then His death was not needed for our salvation, and if it was not needed for our salvation, then it had no special meaning. **But how could Jesus have been a 'master' and still have been wrong about so many things?** It is just not possible. So Jesus could not have been merely a 'master'. Either He was Our Lord and Saviour or He was a fake.

David Oakford's experience, and the teachings he claimed to have received during it, are not consistent with Scripture. They are however consistent with what we find in a certain brand of New Age teachings - which very often have also been received from "spirit guides". Those who are leading this trend of thinking, (though it must be stressed that David Oakford may not share their views), claim things like, "There is no sin ..... The atonement is the final lesson man need learn, for it teaches him that, never having sinned, he has no need of salvation."

This is the ultimate perversion. It is very literally turning the cross of Jesus upside down. They deny the existence of sin. They deny the need for redemption. They deny the need for a Saviour. They even make statements like a "slain Christ has no meaning"; and "The journey to the cross should be the last useless journey"; and "Do not make the pathetic error of clinging to the old rugged cross".

Yet let us not forget that God is love. Jesus is indeed the one and only Saviour,

— —

Jesus said to him, "I am the way, and the truth and the life; no one comes to the Father, but by me" John 14:6 RSV.

but in the great judgement scene of Matthew 25:31-46, Jesus Himself declared people righteous, not on the basis of their accepting Him as Saviour or their understanding of God, but on the basis of practical love. That too is the message of the story of the Good Samaritan. The Good Samaritan had not accepted Jesus as his Saviour. He had an imperfect theology, but he was prepared to go to the assistance of his neighbour. Where New Age people, who through no fault of their own have an imperfect understanding of God and of the role of Jesus in salvation, start living a life of practical love, then they too join the 'righteous'. God is love. All love comes from God. We can have authentic dialogue with any person who gets a glimpse of the fact that God is love and of the fact that we are called to put love first, love of God and love of one's neighbour; dialogue on what it means to say that God is love, and dialogue on what living love involves in the practical situations of everyday life.

Does that mean that knowing Jesus as one's Saviour is not important? By no means!! **To know Jesus as Saviour is to know the truth, and to become open to the power.** I walked into a Prayer Meeting in Dublin after years of an inner emptiness that was so intense that it was like as if there was a bottomless hole in my chest. I was also struggling with suicidal desires. As I left that meeting, suddenly and unexpectedly, I was touched by the power and presence of Jesus. I experienced the love of God coming into my heart. This experience of the love of God filling my heart was followed by the experience of Jesus coming alive in my heart. My experience does not compare with the experience of being permeated by God's love that many people have had during their near death experiences, yet it was clearly a taste of being permeated by God's love.

I know that Jesus is Lord and Saviour, because He has saved me in more ways than one. I know that He is "the bread of life" because every day since late 1972, I have experienced Him to be "the bread of life" for me! I know that He is the way, the truth and the life, because I, utterly unworthy servant that I am, have been given the great privilege of experiencing the truth of these realities.

As I continue to walk with Him, every word He ever said makes more and more sense. But the most important teaching of Jesus is that God is love. God absolutely and utterly is love. If you desire to be a child of God, then seek to be transformed by Love, live love, and affirm love wherever you find it - just as Jesus did.

Footnote

All quotations from David Oakford's NDE are taken from www.near-death.com

— —

Jesus said to her, "I am the resurrection and the life; he who believes in me, though he die, yet shall he live, and whoever lives and believes in me shall never die." John 11:25 RSV

Barbara had been the victim of ongoing abuse

All near death experiences are partial. People are given an incomplete taste of the other side. They can only interpret what they experience using their existing intellect. They are limited also by their existing belief system. Take the case of Barbara Harris Whitfield - one of the big names where Near Death Experiences are concerned, but from a New Age background.

Barbara had a horrific childhood. Her mother was a very sick woman emotionally and mentally. For example her mother's feet grew slightly. It was upsetting her that her feet no longer fitted into her many shoes. Her psychiatrist told her that she had a choice:- get new shoes or have her toes shortened. She had her toes shortened!! It was a typical of the person she was. She was also very abusive to her daughter, Barbara. The only way Barbara could cope with the ongoing abuse was by numbing her mind. She cried out to God asking Him to heal her mother, but not seeing her many prayers answered, she concluded that there couldn't be a God. So, even while a child, she became an atheist.

Barbara herself was born with a severe curvature of her spine called scoliosis. In 1975, at the age of 32, she needed extremely painful back treatment, called spinal fusion. After the surgery she was placed in a bed that revolved like a Ferris wheel. Then two days after surgery, a serious infection set in, and she came close to dying, having the first of her two near-death experience in the process. The way she interprets her experience isn't consistent with the teaching of Jesus, but I will let her tell her story and then evaluate it.

First she found herself out of her body, and had an experience of looking down at her body in the strange bed. She says, "I was out of pain. I felt calm - incredibly peaceful - in a way I had never felt before. ..... Next, I was in total blackness. I don't know how I got there. I was floating in darkness with a gentle sense of movement. I knew I was moving away from this life. I had left this life behind.

Then she felt herself being embraced by her grandmother. She says, "She was pulling me close to her in a wonderful embrace. She had been dead for fourteen years, and I had never before thought of her existing beyond her death." Barbara had believed there was no afterlife. Now she was experiencing it first hand. As she realised this, and was held in her grandmother's embrace, she says, "I felt like I released a load of toxic pain. And as I experienced that release, there was

"We too believe, and so we speak, knowing that he who raised the Lord Jesus will raise us also with Jesus and bring us with you into his presence."
2 Cor 4:14 RSV

a sudden replay of every scene my grandmother and I had shared during our nineteen years together in this life. It wasn't just my memories of her - it was also her memories of me. And our memories became one. I could feel and see and sense exactly what she was feeling, seeing and sensing. And I knew she was getting the same thing from my memories. It was both of us together, replaying everything that we meant to each other. It was wonderful."

Barbara gives the example of one day when she was just three or four. Herself and her grandmother ('Bubbie') were in the kitchen; her grandmother letting her join in the cooking. It was a most happy memory, full of love and caring. Towards the end of the scene, Barbara says, "I watched her take a lemon and cut it in half. She rubbed a lemon half on my hands and then wiped them with her already stained and wet apron. Then she looked at me with such love in her eyes and said, 'Don't move. Bubbie will be right back.' She came back with her hairbrush and brushed my hair for what seemed like a very long time. It felt so good. Then she made me long curls, twisting each lock of my hair around her fingers. When she was finished, and she lifted me down to the floor, I ran into her bedroom and looked in the mirror. I looked just like Shirley Temple."

After their memories had been played out, Barbara moved on, now so happy to be away from the thirty two years of pain on earth. She found herself in what she later called a tunnel. It started off totally black, then she became aware of "energy churning through the blackness." She says "As I watched the energy move, shades of gray to almost white separated from the churning. Out of the darkness Light was coming, and the Light was moving way ahead of me. The Light and I were moving in the same direction, but it was far, far ahead."

Then suddenly her first near-death experience ended and she was back in her body in the hospital ward. A week later, things went wrong again, and Barbara had a second near-death experience. This time she experienced her life-review in greater detail. Some people see their life-review on a screen, others in a book, but Barbara saw hers in a whole series of bubbles, each bubble containing a scene of her life. She says, "Looking down and off to the right, I saw myself in a bubble - in the circle bed - crying. Then I looked up and to the left, and I saw my one-year-old self in another bubble - face down in my crib - crying just as hard."

Eventually she decided that she didn't "want to be the thirty-two-year-old Barbara anymore" and that she would go to her one-year-old self. As she did

---

What the Bible says about the energy coming from God

St. Paul uses the Greek word **'energountos'** to say that **"God energises all things"** Ephesians 1:11. The more usual word is **'dunamis',** (from which we get the words dynamic and dynamite) to speak of God's power at work in us. St. Paul speaks of **"the immeasurable greatness of his power in us who believe"** Eph 1:19.

so, she was embraced in God's unconditional love. She says, "I felt as though I released myself from this lifetime. As I did, I became aware of an energy that was wrapping itself around me and going through me, permeating me, holding up every molecule of my being."

"It was not an old man with a long white beard. It took me a long time to use the word 'God'. In fact, I never used any word until I saw the movie Star Wars and heard about 'The Force'. By then, I was already reading quantum physics, trying to figure out how I could explain what had permeated me and was me . . . and you . . . and all of us. Now it was here, and it was holding me. It felt incredible.

"There are no words in English to explain the kind of love God emanates. God was totally accepting of everything we reviewed in my life. In every scene of my life review, I could feel again what I had felt at various times in my life. And I could feel everything everyone else felt as a consequence of my actions. Some of it felt good and some of it felt awful. .... The information came in, and then love neutralized my judgments against myself. In other words, as we relived my life, God never judged me. God held me and kept me together. .... No matter how I judged myself in each interaction, being held by God was the bigger interaction. God interjected love into everything, every feeling, every bit of information about absolutely everything that went on, so that everything was all right. There was no good and no bad. There was only me and my loved ones from this life trying to be, or just trying to survive. ... I - we at this point, for we are one, a very sacred one - God and I were merging into one sacred person."

Barbara then was taken through her entire life. As she witnessed each scene, she found herself saying "No wonder, no wonder." She adds, "I now believe my 'no wonders meant 'No wonder you are the way you are now. Look what was done to you when you were a little girl'."

She saw again how dependent on drugs her mother had been, and how abusive she had been to her. She also saw how her father was seldom there, and that when he was there, finding himself helpless to cope, he would just close the windows so that the neighbours wouldn't hear her mother ranting, and then he would go out to talk to the neighbours. But it wasn't really her mother's fault either. She says, "Just as I had felt everything my grandmother had felt, I now felt my mother's pain and neglect from her childhood. She wasn't trying to be mean. She didn't know how to be loving or kind. She didn't know how to love. She didn't understand what life is really all about. And she was still angry from her own childhood."

Barbara saw again all her mother's operations. She had had twenty six operations before Barbara left home, twenty five of them were elective. She had two spinal

---

Jesus looked up and said to her, "Woman, where are they? Has no one condemned you? She said, "No one, Lord." And Jesus said, "Neither do I condemn you; go, and do not sin again." John 8:4-11 RSV

fusions on her neck, two or three on her lumbar spine, while both knees, both elbows and one wrist were also operated on.

Barbara saw again how lonely she herself felt the times when her mother was in hospital. Then, she says, "I watched her abuse me when she was home. I could now feel that she abused me because she hated herself. I saw myself down on my knees by the side of my bed, praying for a doctor to help my mother. What I didn't realize as a child, but was understanding in the life review, was that she didn't want anyone to help her. She thought her job in life was to have doctors and be a patient. ... I saw how I had given up 'myself' in order to survive. I forgot that I was a child. I became my mother's mother."

She says that she suddenly knew that the same had happened to her mother; that her mother too as a child, had given up on herself to look after her father. She says, "As children, she and I both became anything and everything others needed. .... I also saw my mother's soul, how painful her life was, how lost she was. And I saw my father, and how he put blinders on himself to avoid his grief over my mother's pain and to survive. In my life review I saw they were good people caught in helplessness. I saw their beauty, their humanity and their needs that had gone unattended to in their own childhoods. I loved them and understood them. We may have been trapped, but we were still souls connected in our dance of life by an energy source that had created us."

Barbara then experienced the sense of unity with all things and all people that there is on the other side, but concludes from this that "we don't end at our skin. We are all in this big churning mass of consciousness. We are each a part of this consciousness we call God." (See my footnote.)

Barbara in her life-review, also saw when she married and had her own children, and how she was now on the verge of "repeating the cycle of abuse and trauma" that she herself had experienced as a child. She says, "I was on prescription drugs. I was in the hospital. I was becoming like my mother."

She says "I felt God's memories of these scenes through God's eyes just as I had through my grandmother's eyes. I could sense God's divine intelligence and it was astonishing. God loves us and wants us to learn and wake up to our real selves - to what is important. I realized that God wants us to know that we only experience real pain if we die without living first. And the way to live is to give love to ourselves and to others. We are here to learn never to withhold our love. But only when we heal enough to be real can we understand and give love the way love was meant to be." Barbara then saw how hard she had been on herself, and says, "I realized that the only big mistake I had made in my life of thirty-two years was that I had never learned to love myself."

———————————————————————————————

"There are three things that last, faith, hope and love; and the greatest of these is love." I Cor 13:13

85

Before Barbara came back into her body this time, she visited the nurse's station, and heard her case being discussed. After her first near-death-experience, the nurses tried to convince her that she had been hallucinating. This time, she was able to tell them exactly what they had said to one another and also what they were doing down in the nurses station! It was no longer possible for them to dismiss what she had to say about her near death experience as a hallucination!

On coming back into her body, she was able to feel her memories in a new way. As a child she had numbed her feelings to cope with the pain of the abuse. This is called psychic numbing. Many abused children do it to cope. It means that they are able to remember the events without feeling the feelings. But the feelings have been buried deep within them, and will either come out in the form of illness or in the form of psychiatric problems. Furthermore one will not be able to love in the normal way until one can feel again in the normal way. After her near-death experience Barbara was again able to feel the feelings she had blotted out as a child. It was painful, but it is the only way to healing.

She says, "In my life review I also saw the beginnings of abuse in the way I was reacting to my children. For me it wasn't just a choice of numbness or healing. I needed to break the chain of abuse. I needed to save my children from what I had been through. .... I learned in my life review that the only thing that is real is love, and the only way to share love is by being real. Being real happens when we acknowledge our feelings and continually share our truth. When we feel our feelings and are real, we share our truth out of love. Then our relationship with God and our self is healthy."

Evaluating Barbara's Experience

Barbara's near-death-experience is compatible with the Bible, but some of the ways in which she interprets her experience is not compatible with the Bible.

She was an abused child, a victim. As a wee child, she cried out to God to heal her mother, but when her mother did not get better, it was easier for her young mind to conclude that there was no such thing as God, than to believe that there was a God but that He wasn't listening to her prayers. She already felt that her mother didn't love her, and had questions about whether her father loved her. How could she possibly have coped with the thought that God didn't love her either? Yet God loved her everyday of her life, and ached to enfold her in His love. Her cry for help was answered - but not for many years.

When she had her near-death experiences, she first experienced the darkness. This is a very common experience for those who have not known Jesus, who is the Light. But she was very open to being brought to the light so she moved quickly

— —

"You are precious in my eyes and honoured and I love you" Isaiah 43:4 RSV

from the darkness. Then God allowed her to re-experience how she had been loved as a child by her grandmother. Barbara and her grandmother relived what for Barbara were simple childhood experiences of being loved by her grandmother. Where a person has been a victim of abuse, God often allows them to re-experience and to connect with those moments when they were loved, before embracing them in His love. Angie Fenimore experienced this in an even bigger way during her near death experience. This is a reminder to us of the importance of getting in touch with the love that we have experienced. It is easy to remember the hurts, and indeed to allow the memories of hurt to dominate one's thinking, but if one desires healing, then rekindle the memories of being loved.

There is a unity between people on the other side that goes way beyond what we can experience here in our mortal bodies. Barbara has misinterpreted this, thinking that we all blend into one - a very understandable mistake. In fact we retain our own personhood, yet being now pure spirit, we will have this tremendous sense of unity with everyone else, and a whole new way of communication. We will literally know what others are thinking.

Having first allowed her to re-experience moments when she was loved as a child, God then embraced her in His love. We can see here her somewhat childish image of God:- "It was not an old man with a long white beard." She also says that it even took her a long time to use the word "God".

What she experienced was Baptism in the Spirit. She speaks of being 'permeated' by God's energy. One of the three secular meanings of the word 'baptism' before it came to be used as a religious word, was for the dying of clothes. If the dye went right through the clothes, it was 'baptised'. So too, in Baptism in the Spirit, we are meant to be permeated through and through by love and by the healing, cleansing and delivering power of the Holy Spirit. That is what Barbara experienced. Her eternal spirit was penetrated and permeated by love and by the healing, cleansing and delivering power of the Holy Spirit. Unfortunately there was no one to tell her what had happened. Nor indeed that it was the Holy Spirit that she experienced - no wonder she speaks of energy and of being permeated. Of course, where the Holy Spirit is, Jesus is not far away.

We are called to a life of deep unity with Jesus and with the Holy Spirit in this life. In the next life, we will, if we go to Heaven or even to the upper realms of Purgatory, experience a tremendous sense of unity with Them. We will have this union with God, yet we will retain our own personhood. We will indeed be like on to God. God is at once one, yet three distinct persons, Father, Son and Holy Spirit. Becoming like on to God, we too will be deeply united with everyone else, yet still totally distinct. How could Barbara, without a Christian background, have been able to understand this? Instead she thinks that we will merge into a

---

"In that day you will know that I am in my Father, and you in me, and I in you." John 13:20 RSV

87

consciousness that is God. Once again this is a very understandable error given her background.

She was a victim. Any mistakes she had made in life were possibly totally understandable. She had cried out to God for help as a child, and even though to protect her own sanity, she had concluded that God didn't exist, yet there was within her a real openness to God. Thus she could move so quickly into His presence and into His love. Thus also her life-review was a further experience of being embraced by God's love, even if some of her past mistakes were to cause her real pain. But from this she states, "There was no good and no bad."

Here she is on the verge of serious error - the fundamental New Age error that there is no sin. There are people who, through their own fault and their own selfishness, have rejected God. There are people who, through their own fault and their own selfishness, have caused great hurt to others. There are people who, through their own fault and their own selfishness, have invited evil powers into their lives. The life-review for them will be a totally different experience. They discover that there most certainly is sin. See the stories of Dr. Howard Storm, Gloria Polo, Marino Restrepo, Fr. Steven Scheier, and Angie Fenimore.

Yet God is truly compassionate. There is the truly moving scene in Barbara's near-death experience during which she sees the truth about her mother's sickness, and comes to understand her and to forgive her. **But those who walk in a very close relationship with Jesus are sometimes gifted with this insight without the need for a near-death experience.** Take Lee Ezell. Lee had a horrific childhood. But as she forgave her father, she began to see him as God sees him. She says, "The man I saw as my father was not the real person. In some way that I didn't really understand, he was sick. It was the booze that had changed him. Underneath was a man who wanted to love his daughters, but his thinking had become distorted." That is the insight that was granted to an eighteen year old girl who was penniless, homeless and pregnant as a result of rape without any need for a near-death-experience!! See Lee's story on page 106.

Back to Barbara:- she thought that she visited Heaven during her hear-death experience. In fact she was in the upper realms of Purgatory. The visionary Anne tells us that the upper realms of Purgatory are a very happy and comfortable place, a place of God's love and mercy; and that she (Anne) would be very happy to spend time there. In the upper realms of Purgatory, souls help one another to reflect on the truth about their lives. The description Barbara gives of her encounter with her grandmother is totally consistent with the work that is done in the upper realms of Purgatory. It would appear most likely that her grandmother was still a temporary resident there - interceding for her family.

———————————————————————————————

"Nothing can come between us and the love of Christ, no matter what trials or troubles we now face" Romans 8:35.

The fact that Barbara had difficulty recognising and naming God is further indication that she was in Purgatory. She experienced herself being grasped in God's love rather than seeing God. God remained for her almost an impersonal force, possibly because it was primarily the Holy Spirit she experienced. There were limitations to her experience of the light. She wasn't embraced by the Heavenly music. She only met her grandmother. She was still coming to terms with the truth about her life. All these elements are consistent with Barbara being in the upper realms of Purgatory.

Furthermore we do not know what she might have experienced had she remained in Purgatory after her life-review. In Angie Fenimore's case, first she experienced the love and acceptance of Jesus during her life-review, but after her life-review, she found herself in the depths of Purgatory. First one experiences the life-review, then one experiences what results from the life review. This is a most important point to remember when evaluating near-death experiences.

Many people's near-death experience do not last long enough to experience what comes after the life-review. One views one's life-review with the same intellect and conscience with which one left the earth. But what if one's conscience and intellect are not yet sufficiently tuned to God to be able to recognise the truth about one's life, to recognise the extent to which one rejected God and rejected love, and to recognise the extent to which one caused hurt to others? Then one could end up, after one's life-review, a bit like the man who, after committing adultery, says, "It felt good, so it can't be all that wrong." That, I would suggest, is why some people come back after their life-review and declare "There was no good and no bad" while others come back and declare "I saw how terrible my sins were." Some spirits are sensitive enough to see the full truth about their lives. Others are not. The real test is what comes after the life-review. So while it looks as if Barbara was destined for the upper realms of Purgatory, it is possible that she could have been in for a rude awakening.

In my own case, without leaving my body, I had the tremendous experience of the love of God in 1972. I experienced myself as being loved by God to the depths of my being; and that sense of being loved by God and of Jesus living in my heart has remained with me. But it took me many years to face the full truth about my life:- to recognise the ways in which I was still outside God's will and indeed hurting others; to let go of my own hurts and bitterness; to take the steps to come into healing; and to even basically align my life to God. So too in the upper realms of Purgatory, one experiences the love of God, but one may still have much work to do.

Meanwhile Barbara's sharing of the healing of her eternal spirit that took place

— —

"God's love has been poured into our hearts through the Holy Spirit that has been given to us." Romans 5:5 RSV

during her life-review shows us that we need healing to the depths of our being. After her near-death experiences, she was able to start over in life, despite all the abuse she had suffered as a child. Once again we see that if one's spirit is permeated by God's love, then one can come back into one's mortal body and be a new person. Heal the spirit, and the person is, at least, on the way to being healed.

Barbara experienced much healing, but she did not return to earth a perfect soul. She still does not know Jesus. She has however grasped that God is love, and committed herself to an ongoing life of caring love, and indeed has been putting that into practice to the best of her ability. She has embraced forgiveness, has seen the importance of understanding other people's failures and of letting go of judgementalism. She has also seen the importance of coming to understand oneself, and of breaking the cycle of abusing that was being passed down through the generations in her family.

As Jesus once said of a person, she is not far from the Kingdom of God; yet she has misinterpreted some of her experiences, and there is at least the potential that she could go seriously astray if she continues down the New Age route. I say the potential because she displayed such openness to God's love during her near-death experiences, and has such a commitment to living that life of love, that I cannot see her ending up too far wrong. Indeed it is quite possible that she will point many New Age people in the general right direction. God loves them too, and will be with any of them whose hearts are open to Him, especially those who are not personally to blame for their erroneous beliefs.

Yet how wonderful it would be if Barbara came to truly know Jesus - I mean the real Jesus, Son of God, our Saviour. Then her experience of unity with God could be lived at a whole new level.

Meanwhile the motto on the front page of her website speaks volumes,

"If people can look into each other's eyes
With love and truth in their hearts,
Anything is possible."

Footnote
All quotations from Barbara's NDE are taken from her website
www.cbwhit.com/barbarahome.htm

_ _

"Beloved, let us love one another; for love is of God, and he who loves is born of God and knows God. He who does not love does not know God; for God is love." 1 John 4:7-8 RSV

First she had an NDE, then she became a Catholic

Linnie Smith was a Pentecostal Christian with a deep love for Jesus. In December 1994, she was seriously ill. Doctors had failed to diagnose her serious gall bladder condition, and kept turning her away from hospital every time she presented, despite her being in serious pain. Eventually she could take no more.

She says, "I had no more strength to keep me inside my body. I knew I was dying, that I couldn't do any more to keep 'me' in there. All I had was my faith. As I was lying there in my room, I began to tell the Lord how much I loved Him, how very much I loved Him, and when that happened the room suddenly filled with the sounds of music, bells, birds, voices, and instruments. It was the most beautiful music I ever heard. It was so harmonic. I know now why churches have bells!   As that music filled my room, a foggy mist rolled in, and as it did, I got further and further from myself.

"In the blink of an eye, I was in a closed-like tunnel, but not dark. The end was not far away and it was bathed like everyone says, in a light brighter than the sun but with no yellow:- pure white light, and transparent and translucent at the same time, radiating out. There are no earthly words for it because you can't find it on earth.

"As a kid I used to go outside and want a cloud to come down so I could ride it and now I thought, 'Yes, I got my cloud!' That's how He cares about us. He remembered it. It was a cloud-like tunnel revolving clockwise around me. Light hit the side of the tunnel and burst into pastel colours that were alive and sparkling. If the colours could have giggled, they would have – they were full of life. Everything there was full of life.

"Something drew my eyes to the light at the end of the tunnel and there was Jesus. He was light. He was full of light and His Hands were out to receive me. There were all these shades of lighter white in His Light (in and around Him) but with no dark - more like a prism. There were different shades but no darkness! An artist couldn't do this. He is light. It became whiter than white. There was so much light coming out of Him that you couldn't see Him. His arms were outstretched and I knew I was home and I was ecstatic!"

But just then, the phone next to Linnie's bed rang and she was suddenly back in

---

Thanks to the resurrection of Jesus, we have the guarantee of an everlasting inheritance in Heaven that can never be spoiled or soiled or taken from us. 1 Peter 1:4

her room. That too happened in a 'blink'. The fog, the mist, was still there, and there was still the sound of music, but Linnie had snapped back into her body. It was a friend calling to make sure Linnie was okay – which she was, more than ever before in her life, more than anyone could know.

Later that year, in another near-death experience, Linnie found herself in the tunnel again, and again with Jesus. She says, "The tunnel experience repeated exactly."

Then, six months later, in June of 1995, she had surgery but it did little to relieve her distress. Two Christians friends started to pray over her. She says, "They were praying and it was like someone put a straw into my head and suddenly I was on this green grassy hill and I could feel each blade of grass under my feet and my feet were transparent and translucent with light emanating from them, a soft light. The grass was holding me up and each blade was giving me life. The blades didn't bend under my weight.

"I looked at all the flowers. You know how a rose looks when it is at its peak? Everything there was at a vibrant peak of perfection. Heaven is full of life and all about life. And there were the bells, the birds, the music. There were lots of hills. No shadows. The sky was like sapphire azure blue and it was alive!"

Then she saw bright white letters, the words of a prayer, scroll before her like a news ticker. They were the words being prayed by her friends who were interceding - and they arched in front of Linnie, bounced back, caught her up, and thrust her back into her body. She says, "Our prayers pierce the clouds. They are seen and heard in Heaven. It was amazing!"

Like Don Piper, she had loved Jesus and lived a love centred life. There was no need for any life-reviews. She was able to go straight to the gates of Heaven. She would love to have stayed there, but came back with a mission to witness to Jesus in a new way. "I grieved for years that I was sent back," she says.

At the time of the experiences, she was Pentecostal. After her experience however, she wanted to know more. Having been given a taste of Heaven, she wanted to imitate the saints here on earth. She wanted to live a life of total preparation for Heaven. She felt led to read the saints life stories - including that of St. Therese of Lisieux. Soon she had also turned to St. Faustina and the Divine Mercy.

She started reaching out to people of every denomination. She formed a Prayer Group that was half Catholic, half Protestant, and prayed the Divine Mercy Chaplet. She was so regularly perusing books in the local Catholic Bookstore, that when a job vacancy arose there, so got the job. It being a Catholic Bookstore with

---

"You have come to Mount Zion and the city of the living God, the heavenly Jerusalem where millions of angels are gathered for the Festival" Hebrews 12:22

Catholic customers, she felt it right to take a crash course on Catholic teaching so as to be best able to assist those who came. This led her on another journey. In 1998, she became a Catholic. It is not that she rejected what she learned in the Pentecostal Church. Far from it. She says, "Their worship and praise was like singing with the angels." She tried to bring that with her, and to impart this spirit of singing to her new friends in Catholicism - not an easy task!!!!

For Linnie what she loves most in the Catholic Church is the Mass. She says, "At Mass, Heaven meets the earth. There are actual angels." She now sees those. Her mystical visions concerning what happens in the Mass bear some similarity to what was seen in Knock, Ireland in 1879 when the visionaries saw the angels circling the Mass altar.

She also has developed other mystical inclinations. She believes we are in special times. Christ is the Prince of peace. It's time, she advises, for all of us to love - urgently. She says that the phrase "Judgement is Mine" (God's) so resounded in her heart, it was like as if it was written on it after her return.

Another key message she received is, "Only I, God, can see the heart. You are to love and help others on their path and journey."

Editor's Footnote Re Catholic Church

Jesus founded just one Church which He called 'My Church'. Today there are over 30,000 Christian denominations and ecclesial communities. This clearly isn't the will of Him who prayed so hard, 'May they all be one'. Some Catholics have asked me, "Why don't all those who meet Jesus during their near death-experiences join the Catholic Church?"

The answer is simple. When we cross to the other side, there will no longer be different Churches. The prayer of Jesus at the Last Supper, "May they all be one" will at last be answered. We will not be tested on whether we are Catholic or Protestant or Baptist, but on whether we have loved Jesus and loved our neighbour.

Of course, if we are personally responsible for causing or fermenting divisions between Christians, or, if through our own fault, we lead people away from the Church Jesus founded, or, through our own fault, lead people from the Church in which they can best be spiritually nourished, then it will be part of our life review.

Furthermore Jesus is trying to reach out to all people regardless of which Christian denomination they belong to. Indeed he is also seeking to reach out to all who believe in God, and indeed to all people. Those who have near-death experiences come back with a mission to reach people within their own faith tradition.

Editor's Footnote Re Linnie Smith

All quotations from Linnie Smith are taken from the **"Spirit Daily"** website.

— —

"May they all be one. Even as you, Father, are in me and I am in you, may they also be so united in us, that the world will recognise that it was you who sent me." John 17:21

Evaluating Near Death Experiences

When I was about 14, I went up one Sunday to receive Communion. When the person in front of me stood up after receiving, I immediately knelt into her place. After I knelt, the priest had to go the full length of the rails and then come back again before I could receive. I began to feel weak. I was too embarrassed to get up from the altar rails without receiving. Eventually I fainted. The next thing I remember is looking down on the men who were carrying me out of the Church just as we neared the back door. Then outside, I heard one of the men say, "He is taking a long time to come round." After that I went blank again, then gradually came round, and was looking up at the men upon whom I had previously been looking down.

At the time I made nothing of it, but the memory has very clearly stayed in my mind to this day - far far clearer than most memories from that period of my life. Out-of-body experiences and near-death experiences do take place. Yet it is important to be careful in assessing what people claim to have experienced.

1. All near death experiences are but partial experiences of life on the other side. Some mistake what is partial for the total reality.

2. We bring our belief system with us when we die. Our existing belief system will be the starting point for how we interpret what we experience on the other side - unless it becomes totally clear that it was wrong.

3. Those who through their own fault both rejected God in this life and sinned seriously, are vulnerable to coming under the influence of evil spirits on their death - spirits which may masquerade as angels of light.

4. Those who have near death experiences testify that there is a different way of learning on the other side. As soon as the question forms in one's intellect, the answer also forms. Thus George Rodonaia says, "Think and it comes to you." But during a near death experience, one has not yet become a totally transformed spirit. One's way of thinking has yet to be perfected, and it is liable to be greatly influenced by one's preconceptions. Thus one should be doubly careful in assessing those who claim to have received all sorts of teaching on the other side. For example Dr. Richard Eby clearly

---

"Beloved, do not believe every spirit, but test the spirits to see whether they are of God; for many false prophets have gone out into the world."
1 John 4:1 RSV

had a genuine near death experience. As a result he retired from his position as medical professor and obstetrician to become a minister. **But amongst the great amount of teaching he claimed to have received during his NDE was that he would not die again before the Second Coming of Jesus.** He died on December 2nd 2002 - and this time remained dead!

5. People may not always correctly present what they actually experienced, but may add to it or omit parts that don't suit them.

6. Some, like Gloria Polo and Angie Fenimore, are given an initial experience of the light and of God's love before they have to face the truth about the sin in their lives. Had Gloria Polo's near death experience ended after the first phase, she could so easily have come back, as some do, and said, "I saw the light. Have no fear. Carry on sinning. It doesn't matter." But during the second phase of her NDE, she discovered that it certainly did matter.

7. Human nature is still human nature even after near-death experiences. There will still be temptations - including the temptation to believe that one now has special powers. An occasional person may start claiming psychic powers and acting as a medium.

So one should be both prudent and cautious when evaluating the claims of any individual concerning out-of-body or near-death-experiences, That near-death experiences are real and not just some form of dream can be seen from what happens when blind people have such experiences. Vicki Umipeg was blind from birth. Yet while she was having a near death experience, she was able to see clearly, and later described everything she had seen in detail.

The Further Dimension

There are also countless people who have profound experiences of God's love while still in their mortal bodies. For the proper understanding both of God's love and of how the human person can be embraced by God's love, it is important to include a review of these as well.

Studying near-death experiences can help us to see how God ministers healing, transformation and deliverance to one's eternal spirit, and so the role of the healing of one's eternal spirit in all spiritual healings and authentic experiences of God's love. Studying those who have life-transforming spiritual experiences while still in the body, helps us to understand the relationship between our eternal spirit and our mortal bodies, and how even our mortal bodies can be immersed in God's love. For the study of spiritual experiences while still in the body, the proper place to start is with Jesus and the New Testament - His baptism, His transfiguration, Pentecost, the conversion of St. Paul etc.

— —

"And he was transfigured before them, and his face shone like the sun, and his garments became white as light. And behold, there appeared to them Moses and Elijah, talking with him." Mt 17:2 RSV

Don't Risk Hell

Dr. Howard Storm had the experience of evil spirits waiting for his death and of them then bringing him to the very gates of hell. Marino Restrepo believes that if he had died at the time of his near-death experience that he would have been eternally lost - though he is probably incorrect in this, but he may have had much to face in Purgatory. Fr. Steven Scheier heard himself being judged and condemned to Hell, though I believe that, even if he had died, he would still have received the reprieve, though he too may have had much to face in Purgatory. Angie Fenimore visited the very depths of Purgatory, and felt that some of the souls around her were actually in Hell. She was, of course, incorrect in this, but who, after having read her testimony, would want to end in the very depths of Purgatory? Gloria Polo, very like Dr. Howard Storm, also had the experience of evil spirits waiting for her death and of them then bringing her eternal spirit to the very gates of Hell.

Dr. Howard Storm had rejected God and was rude to Christians, but there are bigger sinners around. Marino Restrepo had drifted far from God and was living a messed-up life, but there are more vicious sinners around. Angie Fenimore had dwelt in despair and attempted to take her own life, losing sight of the damage that this would do to her husband and children, but there are greater sinners around. Gloria Polo had committed very grave sins, yet there are more vicious sinners around. Fr. Steven Scheier was more interested in what people thought of himself than in witnessing to God, had little prayer in his life and was compromising in different ways, yet there are far greater sinners around - including amongst us priests and religious.

Each of them found themselves in different ways, facing the reality of either eternal damnation or the depths of Purgatory, and would likely have spent time, possibly much time, in the depths of Purgatory. Both Dr. Howard Storm and Gloria Polo had the terrifying experience of discovering that evil spirits had been waiting for their deaths; waiting to take their souls of Hell.

There are serious consequences both to rejecting God and to immoral living! If we, through our own fault, reject God in this life, we will begin the next life, by our own choice outside God's kingdom. If we choose selfishness in this life, we will, by our own choice, begin the next life in the desolation and darkness that selfishness creates, and we will, at best, have to go through a major and difficult process of transformation before we can enter the land of light and love. If we choose to become vicious and cruel in this life, we will begin the next life amongst

---

This is the judgement, that the light has come into the world, and men loved darkness rather than light, because their deeds were evil. John 3:19 RSV

those who are vicious and cruel - and who will be vicious and cruel to us. Those who, through their own fault, become bullies in this life will find themselves at the hands of even greater bullies; those who, through their own fault, terrorise people in this life will discover what terror really is in the next life.

People like to think that there is no such place as hell, or that, if it does exist, next to nobody goes there. Yet Jesus was very clear about the risk of hell. Indeed He developed a whole set of totally original images to warn people of what hell is like, using the image of the fire and the worms at the horrible smoky smelly city dump outside Jerusalem to drive home His message; and He developed yet another set of totally original images to emphasise the absolute importance of breaking with sin. "If your right hand or your foot causes you to sin, cut it off. Better to enter Heaven without a limb, than to keep your full body but end in hell." Mk 18:8. To suggest that either hell does not exist, or that nobody goes there is to overrule the clear and distinctive teaching given by Jesus. It is also to ignore both the testimony of many people who have had near-death experiences, and also many people who have had visions or apparitions.

But what must one do to avoid hell?

After a miraculous event at the jail where Paul and Silas were being held prisoner, the jailer asked, **"What must I do to be saved?** And they said, 'Believe in the Lord Jesus and you and your household will be saved'." Acts 16:30-31

Open your heart to Jesus, and start walking with Him, and you will be saved. You can do that right now. Right now you can "repent of your sins and believe the Gospel" Mk 1:15b. Just sincerely pray,
"Lord Jesus, I am a sinner and I am sorry. I repent of all my sins, and accept You as my Lord and Saviour. Help me to take the steps necessary to grow in my relationship with You."

Pray that prayer sincerely, and unless you become totally perverse, you will be 'saved'; that is you will escape Hell. But if you continue to be selfish and to bring hurt into the lives of others, especially moral or spiritual hurt, then you will still have much to face when you die. It could still be better for you to have a millstone tied around your neck and to be thrown into the depths of the sea.

However if you pray the above prayer sincerely, and then start seeking to live by the teaching of Jesus, you will become more and more open to Him. You will initially have struggles. Some, because of their history, will have great struggles. Breaking free from a compulsion or from an addiction or from an immoral

— —

And I heard a loud voice in heaven, saying, "Now the salvation and the power and the kingdom of our God and the authority of his Christ have come, for the accuser of our brethren has been thrown down, who accuses them day and night before our God." Rev 12:10 RSV

emotional attachment is far from easy. Likewise breaking free from anger and bitterness is far from easy. I suggest the following steps for starters.

1. Repeat regularly the prayer of the sinner, **"Lord be merciful to me a sinner"**. This is a special prayer given by Jesus himself for sinners. (See Luke 18:13).

2. Trust in God's mercy. Jesus said that the sinner who prayed that prayer went home at rights with God. Do not let satan beat you up with guilt.

3. Continue to confess your sins, (preferably finding a regular confessor to whom you go to Confession face to face).

4. Make a list of all people you have harmed, especially those you have harmed spiritually or morally, and start doing what is in your power to make it up to them - even if the only way open to you is by praying for them regularly.

5. If you have a deep compulsion, addiction or attachment, accept that you will have to feel the pain for a period. Try to find other ways of occupying yourself.

6. Take reasonable steps to become open to the power of Jesus to set you free. See the 25 steps for healing on page 119

Keep on doing that, and you will quickly move up through the ranks in terms of what you will have to face when you come before Jesus and have to face the full truth about your life.

The coming chapters are about so living that one will be able to go to Heaven the very moment one dies. Indeed they go further than that. They offer a vision of how ordinary people could live in such union with Jesus in this life, that not merely will they go to Heaven the moment they die, but from Heaven, they will be able to continue to bring blessing on earth; in other words, sections of this book offer a vision of how the ordinary person could become a living saint.

But do not become disillusioned if you feel that you are not yet ready to meet all the requirements for becoming a living saint. Satan would absolutely love it if you became disillusioned. The Bible describes him as the accuser of God's people, "who accuses them day and night before our God" Rev 12:10. If he cannot get you any other way, he will try to convince you that you are no good. He will tell you that you are full of sin; that you are only a hypocrite; that you are never going to be any better; that you have no place in the Christian community;

"We know that our old self was crucified with him so that the sinful body might be destroyed, and we might no longer be enslaved to sin."
Romans 6:6 RSV

that you mustn't really be sorry for your sins since you keep falling into the same sins again and again.

St. Paul clearly faced ongoing struggles in his own life. He wrote, "I do not understand my own actions. For I do not do what I want but I do the very thing I hate. ..... I can will what is right, but I cannot do it. For I do not do the good I want, but the evil I do not want is what I do. Now if I do what I do not want, it is no longer I that do it, but sin which dwells within me." Romans 7:15-20 RSV

We have an eternal spirit. This eternal spirit is conjoined with our mortal bodies by what is sometimes called the spiritual soul. This is described in much greater detail later in the book.

In the early stages of the spiritual life, our eternal spirit comes to know Jesus and desires to walk with him, but both our eternal spirit and our spiritual soul still need much transformation, including healing, cleansing and deliverance, before one can easily walk with Jesus. This is particularly true if one has had severe problems. That the healing, cleansing and deliverance needs to start right in our eternal spirit can be clearly seen from the testimony of Barbara Harris Whitfield, who gives a moving account of how her eternal spirit was penetrated and permeated by God's love, leading to a major transformation at the centre of her being. This, in turn, enabled her to start living in a new way. Likewise Marino Restrepo was able to leave behind thirty three years of drugs, drink and sex after his eternal spirit was cleansed during his near-death experience.

One of the three secular meanings of the word 'baptism', before it came to be used as a religious word, was for the dying of clothes in the garment industry. A garment was 'baptised' if the dye penetrated right through it; in other words if it wasn't just painted on one side. So too for us, both our eternal spirit and our spiritual soul needs to be dyed through and through by the healing, cleansing and delivering power of the Holy Spirit.

This is a two way process:- it is part grace and can sometimes come as pure gift, but very often we have to take the steps to open ourselves to this grace; that is to open ourselves to the healing, cleansing and delivering power of the Holy Spirit. Along the way we struggle, and for some, the struggle is great. Realising that he is losing his grip on your life, satan will be very angry and desperate. First he will go to great lengths to put temptation into your path and to play on your weaknesses. If you are a Christian leader, expect the bizarre and the unbelievable in the lengths to which satan will go in order to tempt you, and in the lengths to which he will go to destroy you. I have seen this first hand.

If he cannot succeed in that, his next effort will be to convince you that God could never love you, given your human weakness. He will try to convince you that

"I am writing to you, little children, because your sins are forgiven for his sake" John 2:12 RSV.

99

you are a hypocrite; that you do not belong in the Christian community, that it is useless for you to keep trying etc.

Faced with this dual attack, St. Paul asks, "Who will deliver me?" He immediately answers 'Jesus Christ is the one who can set me free'. See Romans 7:22-8:1. Jesus sets us free in two ways:- by the forgiveness of our sins while we struggle, and then by delivering us from the compulsion to sin. If you have invited Jesus into your heart, and if you are seeking to walk with Him, then your eternal spirit is already "in Christ Jesus". St Paul affirms, "There is therefore now no condemnation for those who are in Christ Jesus." Romans 8:1

The crucial point for St. Paul is what is in your mind and your heart. If you really desire to do what is right, but still fall, then there is no condemnation - you are to trust Jesus totally. You are to trust that Jesus loves you totally and completely even as you are. You are to trust that if you died at this moment, your spirit would be penetrated and permeated by God's love in a way similar to that of Barbara Harris Whitfield; that the healing and cleansing that you long for, would be yours very quickly. That is what St. Paul means by "no condemnation". It means total unconditional love. It means being cleansed of guilt, being cleansed of thinking that you are no good, being cleansed of looking upon yourself as a hypocrite, being cleansed of beating yourself up. "No condemnation" literally means no condemnation!

But if, in your mind and heart, you have decided to go on sinning, or are condoning your sin, then you are still under condemnation. St. Paul wrote, "To decide to go on sinning means death, but if your thoughts and desires are guided by the Holy Spirit, then you will find life and peace. For the mind that chooses sin is hostile to God. It cannot be guided by God, and it cannot please God. If you are in the Spirit, then you will renounce sinful ways, that is if the Spirit of God really lives in you. If the Spirit of Christ does not live in you, then you do not belong to him. But if you do belong to Christ, then even though you still struggle with sinful human nature, your eternal spirit is alive by God's free gift." Romans 8:6-10

The first step is for one's spirit to come to a living relationship with Jesus. The second step is for one's intellect to decide in favour of the Christian way of life.

For most, and especially for those who through their own fault have either rejected Jesus or caused serious hurt to others, repentance of sin needs to take place at a very early stage. Once that has happened, and so long as one is taking reasonable steps to overcome one's weaknesses, one is not to come under condemnation. Instead one is to trust Jesus, and when one falls, one is to trust Him even more.

Jesus promised St. Faustina that the sinner who trusts in Him will make real

---

"Come, O Blessed of my Father, inherit the kingdom prepared for you from the foundation of the world" Mt 25:34 RSV.

spiritual progress. "I desire trust from my creatures. Encourage souls to place great trust in My fathomless mercy. Let the weak, sinful soul have no fear to approach Me, for even if it had more sins than there are grains of sand in the world, all would be drowned in the unmeasurable depths of My mercy." Diary 1059.

Keep trusting Jesus and you will make progress. Keep trusting Jesus and doing your best to walk with Him, and not merely do you not have to fear Hell, neither do you have to fear the depths of Purgatory. Remember too that Purgatory is a place or state of God's mercy, a place or state where souls are safe, and where one's eternal salvation is assured. The visionary 'Anne' assures us that that she would be very happy to spend time in the upper realms of Purgatory. Barbara Harris Whitfield believes that she was in Heaven and that she met her grandmother in Heaven. But I strongly believe that it was the upper realms of Purgatory that she was in. But Barbara was so happy and felt so loved that she thinks that she was actually in Heaven.

So the upper realms of Purgatory are not to be feared. I would suggest however, that just like every footballer dreams of being a star, that you should dream of so living that you will be able to go to Heaven the very moment you die. It is God's wish and plan for you. Continue to dream about it and it will become possible. Indeed dream even greater things than that. Dream of so living that not merely will you be able to go straight to Heaven the moment you die, but that you will be so open to God, that you will be able to spend your time in Heaven doing good upon earth. The later chapters in this book will show you the way.

Better still, not merely will God be able to work through you in Heaven, but He will begin to do so here on earth. God would absolutely love to bring blessings into the world through you, and He would absolutely delight in pouring His love into your eternal spirit, and helping you to take the steps necessary to be able to live the transformed life. The title of one of my little booklets is, "The World's Most Amazing Experience - To have Jesus come ALIVE within you." That truly is the most amazing experience open to the human person.

"The hour is coming when all who are in the tombs will hear his voice and come forth, those who have done good to the resurrection of life, and those who have done evil to the resurrection of judgment." John 5:29 -30 RSV

He Didn't Know Jesus

Fr. Joe Bill was a busy priest, teaching, involved in parish work, and in founding an orphanage. Then, in 1976 he collapsed with a major heart attack, and remained in a coma, literally on death's door, for three days. He suffered a second major heart attack while still in the coma. The doctors warned everyone to prepare for the worst, but on the third day he opened his eyes.

His condition however was still critical. His heart was badly damaged and another heart attack was considered highly likely. Absolute rest was ordered:- no movement, no talking, total quiet. For 45 days, he lay on the flat of his back, then limited movement was allowed. But the prognosis was still bad. He was told that his only hope was an extremely quiet life. Two things in particular were forbidden:- to climb steps and to preach. Effectively he was advised to use the rest of his time in this world to prepare for the next world. At 46 years of age!

Friends invited him to a Charismatic Retreat. Previously he wouldn't have been caught dead at such an event. It is amazing, however, how attitudes can change when one is actually faced with death. He went, albeit with many reservations. During the retreat there was considerable emphasis on healing. "Jesus is here and Jesus is God, and Jesus desires to continue His ministry of healing even now", they were told.

On the final day of the retreat, the bishop who was leading the retreat issued an invitation, **"Those who are sick, please step forward and we will pray with you."** Fr. Joe Bill joined those who went forward for prayer, and was prayed with by the bishop and a priest. He felt nothing, absolutely nothing while being prayed with. He did however have a vision or mental picture of Jesus standing in front of him and felt that Jesus was touching him. At that moment he believed that Jesus was healing him, but there was no outward sign to confirm this.

The next day he visited his doctor for tests. The doctor was amazed at his recovery, couldn't explain the extent of it, even asked him had he got some special medication from somewhere. Fr. Bill said to him, "The God who created my heart has renewed my heart." The doctor however didn't believe in miracles. Instead he arranged for a fresh set of tests after five days. The results were the same - there was no sign of Fr. Bill ever having had a heart attack.

Fr. Bill then went to his Superior and told him that he wished to devote his life to a ministry of preaching. The superior, however, had been told by the doctors that preaching was banned, and replied, "If you start preaching, you will die." Fr. Bill

---

"To have God do His own work through us, even once, is better than a lifetime of human striving." Watchman Nee

assured him that Jesus had healed him completely from the heart attack. "I have been healed by Jesus Christ and now I want to go preach this Jesus Christ."

The Superior still wasn't convinced, so Fr. Bill insisted on climbing a local mountain as proof of his new well being. With the evidence of that before him, the superior gave both his blessing and his approval for Fr. Bill's preaching mission. From then on, Fr. Bill toured the world, giving one retreat after another, without ever taking a break, until his death in April 2008, aged 80.

But the most remarkable healing Fr. Bill received at that retreat was not of his heart. **The most remarkable healing, he himself said, was that he truly met Jesus for the first time in his life - and he a priest for over twenty years.**

He said "Before my heart attack, I believed in Jesus, but it was all in my head. I believed in Jesus but I didn't have a living relationship with Him. I was preaching about Jesus, yet I didn't really know Him. I was doing all sorts of things for Jesus, serving Him in whatever way I could, yet I didn't really know Him."

He often compared it to a bar of chocolate. "One can know everything that there is to know about a bar of chocolate, but if one hasn't eaten a bar, it remains just head knowledge. .... It is the same with Jesus. Unless you actually experience a living relationship with Jesus, belief in Him remains just head knowledge. By contrast, people in the early Church really expected to come into a direct personal experience of Jesus."

I know what Fr. Bill was talking about. Before my spiritual experience in 1972, I believed in Jesus, believed that He died for us, believed that He was in the Sacred Host, and believed that He answered prayer. I believed all these things, yet I felt so empty that it felt as if I had a bottomless hole in my chest, and I was also suffering suicidal desires. I had not experienced Jesus as the bread of life. I had not experienced Him coming alive in my heart. Then one night in 1972, after being prayed over, Jesus came alive in my heart and what a difference that makes. Not merely has Jesus brought enormous happiness into my life, but I have not had a suicidal thought since that moment in 1972.

Fr Bill used to say, "God made man with a heart for love. We are made to love and we can only be satisfied by the experience of infinite love. We will not be satisfied by loving anything in this world, nor will we even be satisfied by human love, though it is a sharing in divine love. Human love is limited, finite. We can only be truly satisfied by the experience of infinite love, of God's love.

"We were created for love, but even marital love, while sharing in the Divine love, is yet not capable of totally satisfying. Only a deep experience of God's love can make us totally happy."

"Whoever does the will of my Father in heaven is my brother, and sister, and mother" Mt 12:50 RSV

Did you ever notice that when religious surveys are carried out, people are asked, "Do you believe that God exists?" I have yet to see a survey in which people were asked, "Do you know God?" Or asked "Is Jesus living in your heart?" or asked "Do you have a living relationship with God?" These are the questions that need to be asked. Nor should it be left to those conducting secular surveys to do the asking. These are the questions that need to be asked regularly in our Churches; need to be asked of every person.

One of the real tragedies within the Catholic Church, indeed the Catholic Church's greatest weakness, is that we have countless people who believe in God, and who often indeed seek to 'serve' God, but yet have not been introduced to a living relationship with Jesus Christ. Our failure to provide successful ongoing programmes to help people come to a living relationship with Jesus and to have Him come alive in their hearts is a real scandal. It is also causing us to lose members in two directions.

Many are drifting from the Church. Some of these are drifting because they are closing their hearts to God, but others are drifting from the Church without ever getting a real opportunity to enter a living relationship with Jesus. That is a terrible indictment of the Catholic Church; absolute shame on us!!

Believing that God exists will not put new energy into your heart. Believing that Jesus died and rose again 2,000 years ago will not put new energy into your heart. Neither will believing that Jesus is God. You will only have new energy in your heart if Jesus comes alive in it.

Again believing in God will not give you the strength to live the Christian life. Believing that Jesus died and rose again 2,000 years ago will not give you the strength to live the Christian life. Neither will believing that Jesus is God give you the strength to live the Christian life. The strength to live the Christian life comes from Jesus coming alive in your heart, and then leading you, by His power and that of the Holy Spirit, into inner transformation.

Without that, being told that you have to live the Christian life can appear like a burden:- rules and regulations to be kept to keep a God-up-there happy. Is it any wonder that the Church does not appear attractive to those who have never had a realistic chance of coming to a living relationship with Jesus?

Others are leaving the Catholic Church to join communities that offer programmes that help people come to a living relationship with Jesus. Of course, some of those who join other groups do so out of rebellion, but some join other Churches because, for the first time, they are helped to a living relationship with Jesus.

─ ─

"People need to recognize that implanted within them is a deep thirst for God. They need to be given opportunities to drink from the wells of his infinite love. ... Without God, ... our lives are ultimately empty."
Pope Benedict 16:4:08

That again is a terrible indictment of the Catholic Church; absolute shame on us!! Any section or subsection of the Catholic Church that fails to provide its members with ongoing meaningful opportunities to come to a living relationship with Jesus, and to have Him come alive in their hearts, leading on to a life of inner transformation, is a branch that bears no fruit.

I also believe that this was a contributory factor to the scandals that the Church has had to face - and sadly a factor that has not been properly addressed. People, with the best of intentions, set out to serve a God-up-there out of their own strength. It is very difficult to serve God, if Jesus is not living in one's heart; and if one has problems, it is very difficult to overcome them without His transforming power. As St Paul put it, all the law can do is show that we are sinners. It has no power to deliver us from our sinful compulsions. Those who sought to keep the law, believed in God-up-there, but belief in God-up-there cannot transform one's life.

But how does one come into this living relationship with Jesus? The first and most necessary step is becoming aware that it is possible. People cannot become open to it unless they are told about it, and unless they are also told something of what happens when Jesus is coming alive in one's heart and the difference that it makes.

Jesus is with us continuously. As soon as we invite Him to live in our hearts, He does so, **but there is a need for this to be experienced by us.** Coming into the experience of Jesus living within us may come about in a number of ways. It may be a gradual process that develops as one learns to spend time with Jesus in prayer, or there may be a special experience at some spiritual event. It is extremely common for those who seek Jesus to have at least one significant spiritual experience during their lifetime, during which their own inner spirit is brought to life or touched in some way by God's love.

Spiritual experiences usually happen where there is an expectant faith. In the early Church, where adult Baptism was common, people were helped to become open to it at their baptism. They spent two years preparing for Baptism, and went forward for it with heightened expectations. We too need to take part in events where there are heightened expectations of coming to a living relationship with Jesus.

"However well of Christ you talk and preach,
Unless He lives within, He is beyond your reach."
Angelus Silesius

She trusted Jesus in desperate circumstances

If you were a teenager, pregnant as a result of rape, put out by your mother, and effectively penniless and homeless, would you be able to trust Jesus?

Yet that is exactly what happened in the case of Lee Ezell. Lee's father, a violent alcoholic, had a basement dungeon where he kept his booze and his pornography. After a session in the basement, he would rampage through the house beating whoever he got his hands on. He had even fashioned a cat-o-nine tails by fixing pieces of leather straps to a broom handle. Three times Lee had called the police for help. They only came once and then didn't want to know - it was an area with a very bad name. At 17, after another rampage by her father, she declared "I'm getting out of here!" She phoned a married sister in California who promised to take them in. With great reluctance, Lee's mother, herself also an alcoholic, agreed to go and to bring the two younger girls.

Although only 17, Lee had already come to a living relationship with Jesus. She was able to talk all her problems over with God. She says, "I was talking to God in a real way for the first time. I now had a relationship with God, not a religion. I no longer had to wait for church to pray. I could talk with Him on the subway, or in school, or while lying in bed at night. God wasn't changing my external circumstances, but He was making some internal changes in me."

On arriving in California, both her mother and herself found work and, together with the two younger girls, they rented a two bedroomed apartment. Lee had been determined to remain a virgin until marriage. One day she spoke about this to her two female workmates. Sadly and very ironically, later that very day, she had the terrible misfortune to be raped by a male workmate. After the rape, she couldn't bear to tell anyone - especially not her mother. She says, "I was lonely, guilty, dirty, full of fear. It had been a long time since I had known that helpless feeling of being controlled physically by a man."

Feeling that she could trust no one, her first response was to tell herself to "Tough it out. ..... You have been through worse than this." But rape isn't something that is easy to tough out. Next she turned to God, **"Why me God?"** she cried again and again. Yet God was her source of strength. Reading the Bible, she was deeply struck by the sentence, **"Commit your cause to the Lord, trust in Him and He will act on your behalf." Ps 37:5.** What she needed was to turn this experience over to God. "Commit it to God's care". The verse promised that He

----

"Entrust your worries to the Lord, and He will look after you" Psalm 55:22.

would take care of it from there and make everything work out. Yet she couldn't stop crying. On the one hand she was committing it to God. On the other hand, she was in tears and crying out, "Why me, God?"

She then read about what St. Paul suffered, "Five times I received from the Jews thirty nine lashes. Three times I was beaten with rods, once I was stoned, three times I was shipwrecked, a night and a day I have spent in the deep, ..." (2 Cor 11:25.) It was obvious that Paul, for all his godliness, didn't escape problems. Lee says, "The clear answer to my question 'Why me, God?' was 'Why not you, Lee? Why should you be exempt? Why should anyone be exempt?'"

Despite his problems, Paul had written, "We are afflicted in every way, but not crushed; perplexed, but not despairing; persecuted, but not forsaken; struck down, but not destroyed" 2 Cor 4:8. As Lee meditated on this, she asked herself, "Well, who am I to get special treatment?" She asked God to give her the strength He gave St. Paul; and to fill the void in her life. **Her new prayer became, "Lord, help me endure this pain."** But just when she had succeeded in trusting the Lord with the rape, she discovered that she was pregnant as a result of it. She says, "Feelings of utter despair surged up with the persistent thought, 'This can't be happening. It's not possible! How can I, an unwanted child, be pregnant with an unwanted child?'"

She further cried out, "God, You're all I have right now. But I thought that when I committed this rape to you, that would be the end of its effect on me." But she also knew that she needed Jesus now even more than ever; needed Him indeed if she was going to survive. Her prayer became "God, how much more can I take? Please help me. Take my life. I have nothing left. I surrender it totally to You. .. I'm not asking You to make my life rosy. Just help me get through this mess. I'll accept the results, whatever they are, but I can't go on without You in control."

Turning to the Bible she found the verse,
"Trust in the Lord with all your heart, and do not rely on your own insight.
In all your ways acknowledge him, and he will make straight your paths."
Proverbs 3:5-6

These words gave her strength. She decided to take them literally:- that she would trust Him rather than racking her own brain in this situation, and that she would acknowledge Him in all her ways, trusting that somehow He would make her paths straight. But she was in for yet another major shock. She knew she had to tell her mother. But she only got as far as telling her that she was pregnant when her mother interrupted, "No! No! Good God, Lee, how could you do this

— —

"The graces of my mercy are drawn by means of one vessel only, and that is - trust. The more a soul trusts, the more it will receive. Souls that trust boundlessly are a great comfort to me, because I pour all the treasures of my graces into them." Jesus to St. Faustina, Diary 1578

to me? This is too much. I can't handle it. You'll have to leave. I can't have your sisters seeing this. How could you do this to them? No, you'll have to get out. You'll have to take care of this yourself."

Lee thought of an abortion but quickly ruled it out. It seemed "such a permanent answer to a temporary problem." Her married sister gave her the address of relatives of her husband who lived near Los Angeles, who were willing to allow her to stay in return for doing housework. And so, with just 100 dollars in her pocket, she set out on another long journey.

That night she stayed at a seedy motel. She says, "Despair surfaced and drained my strength. I felt empty, deserted, and isolated. There was no one to support me, no one to confide in except God. It seemed logical to talk to Him aloud, as if he were my friend sitting in the chair opposite my bed. I didn't try to make my prayer sound holy. I just expressed my thoughts and feelings as they surfaced."

Her night long prayer included "I have no family, no home, and practically no money. Is this your idea of punishing me? Maybe I was wrong to tear my family away from my father. .... Look, God, You could have prevented this. .... And now I feel robbed. I saved my virginity for this? Do you realise I'm only 18 years old? I'm too young for all this responsibility."

Then turning to the Bible she read, "Forgive us our debts, as we forgive our debtors. ...... For if you forgive others their trespasses, your heavenly Father will also forgive you; but if you do not forgive others their trespasses, neither will your Father forgive your trespasses" Mt 6:14 -15. Suddenly she realised that she needed to forgive those who had hurt her:- her mother first, then her father.

As she thought of how her father had hurt her and as she decided to forgive him, she began to receive a remarkable spiritual insight. "The man I saw as my father was not the real person. In some way that I didn't really understand, he was sick. It was the booze that had changed him. Underneath was a man who wanted to love his daughters, but his thinking had become distorted." What an insight for an eighteen year old who was homeless and pregnant as a result of rape!!

There were others too who had hurt her, like various teachers. Then there was the rapist. But how could she forgive him given the level of the hurt and that her life was in utter chaos because of him. Yet after much wrestling and meditating on Christ's sufferings, she reached the stage of being able to pray, "I forgive him Lord, not because I feel like it but because you have told me to do so."

Then there was her anger against God. She knew that she had to forgive Him too for not preventing the rape or the pregnancy and not giving her any warning.

— —

"If you forgive men their trespasses, your heavenly Father also will forgive you; but if you do not forgive men their trespasses, neither will your Father forgive your trespasses" Mt 6:14-15 RSV

"Lord I admit I was wrong for holding You responsible for my circumstances. You never promised that I would be free from pain. I realize that I've been angry at You for not coming to my rescue, for not preventing this. I want to hold tight to You from now on." Finally she had to forgive herself.

All night she wrestled with herself - and with God - as she struggled to forgive those who had hurt her, and to hand herself over to God's care. By the time the dawn was creeping in, she was feeling a marvellous new freedom, able to forgive and to understand her family, and free of anger and of the desire to retaliate. Jesus was now closer to her than ever before. She says, "How ironic that the life growing inside me was actually the agent bringing me to a birth in my spiritual walk with God!"

The future was filled with uncertainty, yet she says, "I was very aware that I was no longer travelling alone." God was with her. "Just the essentials, Lord" she prayed. "I don't need any luxuries. Just food and shelter. Your love has already been extravagant." It was lucky that that was her attitude. Her connections turned out to be two elderly men, heavy cigar smokers, living in squalid conditions, who looked upon her as their new free housekeeper.

Soon she managed to get a job but, more important, she got involved with committed Christians, and joined a Prayer Group. Her spiritual growth continued. In her epic spiritual journey, Lee now added another plank:- thanksgiving. Every time she turned to the Bible, verses about thanksgiving were leaping out at her. She started to thank Jesus that He had been with her all the time; that He was working all things for her good. She thanked Him for the Prayer Group, the lovely people she was meeting, her good job, etc.

But even as she continued her thanksgiving in bed one evening, the bedroom door burst open and in came one of the old gentlemen - clearly intent on one thing only! As he climbed up one side of the bed, she shouted at him, then scrambled out the other side. The commotion drew the attention of his brother. The ensuing argument between the brothers, gave her time to phone a lady from the Prayer Meeting that she lovingly called Mom Croft. Mom Croft was there within minutes, realised immediately what was happening, and whisked her straight to her own home. The Crofts made her fully welcome to stay with them for the time being. For the first time in her life she was in a truly safe place.

Meanwhile as she felt her unborn baby moving within her, she found herself reading Psalm 139: "You made all the delicate, inner parts of my body, and knit them together in my mother's womb. ... Your workmanship is marvellous. ... You were there while I was being formed in utter seclusion! You saw me before I was born and scheduled each day of my life before I began to breathe."

— —

"You may for a short time suffer all sorts of trials, so that when Jesus comes, your faith will have been tested like gold" 1 Peter 1:6.

She says "Those words powerfully reminded me that this baby was not a mistake. This was not an 'illegitimate child'. Yes, there had been an illegitimate and illegal act. But the life inside me was now in the hands of God. And there were no illegitimate births when it was God who created life. God made all human life legitimate, regardless of the circumstances surrounding conception."

She also read in the Old Testament of how Joseph had been sold into slavery by his jealous brothers, and of how he made a new life for himself in Egypt, rose to leadership, and then he was the one to help his brothers when they fell on hard times. Joseph told his brothers, **"You intended to harm me, but God intended it for good to accomplish what is now being done."**

What an example for an eighteen year old to follow! She says, "Rather than decipher who was to blame for my circumstances, I needed to recognize that God had a plan. There was a purpose in my pain." She goes on, "Earlier I had questioned God and asked, 'Why me?' God had answered. 'Why not you?' and I had realised that no one was exempt from problems. Now my question was, **'Lord do You trust me with this?'** ...

"He had decided that He could trust me with this problem. ... I decided that if God felt He could trust me with this pregnancy, then I needed to believe it would all work into His plan for my life, for my benefit rather than my destruction. .. I needed to consider myself a trustee rather than a victim, and trust God with the outcome." What an insight for an eighteen year old in her circumstances!!

By now she had decided that it was best for the baby to have it adopted, as she just wasn't in a position to give it a proper home. There was one thing that Lee was determined about:- she wanted above all for her daughter to be raised by committed Christians. Just being told that the parents would be Catholic or Protestant wasn't enough, as many who are Catholic or Protestant in name have no real relationship with God. But when it came to filling in the adoption forms, she hit a snag. She was told that it wasn't possible to specify that it be Christians who truly believed. She replied, "In that case, I'm not signing the form. I cannot put this baby up for grabs. I'm going to do everything I can."

But the adoption agency was unwilling to bend the rules. Eventually, faced with a brick wall, she meditated on how the mother of Moses entrusted her baby to God and how God miraculously intervened. Now she too could only leave it to God to protect the spiritual welfare of her child. So when a baby girl, Julie, was born she gave her up for adoption. Often later, when she found herself yearning for her daughter, she re-entrusted her to God.

She found herself drawing great comfort from the poem, **'The Weaver'**

— —

"We have shown that we are servants of God by the way we have endured troubles, hardships, calamities, beatings, imprisonments, riots, hard work, sleepless nights and hunger." 2 Cor 6:40

"My life is but a weaving between my Lord and me;
I cannot choose the colours he worketh steadily.
Oft times He weaveth sorrow, and I in foolish pride
Forget He sees the upper, and I the underside.

Not till the loom is silent, and the shuttles cease to fly,
Shall God unroll the canvas and explain the reason why.
The dark threads are as needful in the weaver's skilful hand
As the threads of gold and silver in the pattern He has planned." Anonymous.

Given her remarkable trust in God and her remarkable walk with Him, it was inevitable that she would quickly emerge as a Christian leader. Soon she was a recognised Christian speaker, and eventually had her own radio slot. Eventually also she married a widower who had two daughters by his first marriage, but was unable to have more children. How ironic, she thought, that she had given away one daughter and was now gaining two. Life continued with plenty of fresh challenges. Meanwhile Lee continued to grow spiritually and became an extremely successful Christian and Pro-Life speaker.

Then in Dec. 1984 there was a dramatic development. Her daughter, Julie, managed to make contact with her. What a reunion it turned out to be. Guess Julie's reason for contacting her birth mother!! **She wanted to be sure that her birth mother had a living relationship with Jesus!!** Julie had been raised in a truly Christian home, and was now actively involved in both Christian and Pro-Life work also.

What a joy for both to discover that each had a vibrant relationship with Jesus. Meanwhile Julie had asked about her father and the circumstances of her birth. So some years later, Lee and her husband gently broke the news to Julie and her Christian husband of the circumstances under which she had been conceived. Julie's husband, Bob, replied, "Lee, I would like to thank you for not aborting Julie. That might have been the most convenient thing to do. I just can't imagine living my life without her, and our baby."

It took Julie a couple of days to sort out her feelings. Then she said, "I finally decided that God was the One who wanted me to be born. ... Yes, that's it. The Bible has convinced me that I wasn't an accident, that God intended for me to live for a purpose."

Meanwhile Lee Ezell's own life has gone from strength to strength. Her radio programme "Reflections" is heard throughout the United States. She had appeared on many nationally televised talk shows, and has her own ministry known as Ezell Communications. Julie has also emerged as a powerful Christian leader in her own right. She has established 'Fortress International', a special association to

---

"Those who trust in the Lord are like Mount Zion, which cannot be shaken or destroyed." Ps 125:1

help those who become pregnant through rape or incest, and to help the children of rape and incest. **It all came about because one young teenage girl, faced with the most difficult of circumstances, asked Jesus into her life, and decided that she would take Him at His word, trust Him and walk with Him.**

Lessons From Lee Ezell's Life

1. We need a living relationship with Jesus - not just to know about God, but to actually know Jesus and be able to talk with Him.

2. God does have a special plan for each of our lives. If we start cooperating with Him, He will lead us into it.

3. The key to finding God's plan for our lives and to coming into many other blessing is learning to trust God:- to commit our lives to Him, and then to go on trusting Him regardless of the crosses that come our way.   I consider Ps 37:5, **"Commit your cause to the Lord, trust in Him and He will act on your behalf"** so important that I would encourage you to write it out, and post it up where you will see it every day.

4. The importance of forgiveness. God is love. God desires to permeate us with His love. If we hold bitterness, He still loves us, but our unforgiveness is a block to being permeated with His love.

5. Difficulties are a part of life. Whatever we suffer, there are people who have suffered worse, and yet proved victorious by learning to walk with Jesus.

6. God the Father trusted His Son, Jesus, with THE cross. It can revolutionise our thinking if we realise that He is trusting us with our crosses. These crosses then become united to the cross of Jesus, and thereby a source of blessing.

7. Develop the spirit of thankfulness. It opens us further to God's blessings, and also to the power of God to bring blessing out of the bad things that happen to us.

Footnotes

A. Lee Ezell's book, **"The Missing Piece"** is one of my favourites - a truly beautiful book. It is easily amongst the best ten books I've ever read. Published by Servant Publications.   All quotations from Lee Ezell are from her book "The Missing Piece". She has since written more books.

B. Re seeking God's plan for your life, see also my booklet, **"God Has A Plan For You"**;   for more on trusting Jesus, see my booklet, **"Confession - a journey into healing, self-discovery and God's love."**

— —

"Commit your cause to the Lord, trust in Him and He will act on your behalf" Ps 37:5

Given 2 Months To Live
- 38 Years Ago

In 1969, Fr. Tomislav Ivancic had cancer. Eventually he was told that he had just a further two months to live. He was sent home to die. He was only twenty eight, just three years ordained. He was devastated by the news of his impending death. He says, "I felt totally alone. Neither medicine nor friends could help me. I felt lost, desperate. I promised God that I would pray for two hours every day and that I would fast for three days a week, that is that I wouldn't eat anything Wednesday, Friday and Saturday. I even promised to walk barefoot from Zagreb to the nearest Shrine of Our Lady, 50 kilometres away, if God restored my health. I promised all that but nothing happened. Heaven was silent."

As he continued to struggle emotionally and spiritually against the death sentence that had been passed on him, one day he picked up his New Testament. It opened at Mark's Gospel. A passage in it really lit up.
"If you want to be my disciple, renounce yourself, then pick up your cross and follow me. Whoever wants to save his life will lose it. Whoever loses his life for my sake will save it." Mt 16:24-25

He says, "The passage really hit me between the two eyes. I still remember the scene very clearly. The passage stayed with me, and I kept taking in its implications. Instead of fighting for my life, I was going to have to surrender it to God. Around 10.00 pm, I said, 'Jesus I'm now ready to die. I accept my sickness, cancer. I'm ready to die.'

He adds, "I said that deeply convinced that death was just around the corner. Suddenly I felt the greatest joy in my life. I had a sense of complete freedom. I had a sense that Jesus was just across the threshold, that soon we would embrace. I felt I had just to cross the threshold and that then I'd be there with Jesus. I was so happy."

Fr. Tomislav continues, "Shortly afterwards I went to Rome. There my friends treated me as if I was already dead. They were sad for me and I was sad with them! I felt sorry for them because they were afraid of death, and I was free of the fear of death. It is something unbelievable beautiful to surrender one's life to God, into His hands. Then I waited. The two months passed. Death did not come. Then three months and I was still alive. Then after five months, I had gained 10 lbs. I was supposed to be dead, but here I was beginning to put on weight.

"If we live, we live to the Lord, and if we die, we die to the Lord; so then, whether we live or whether we die, we are the Lord's" Romans 10:8 RSV

"I was a theologian. I already had my doctorate. I knew all the theory, but I was convinced that if I gave my life to God that He would take it, that He could hardly wait. Before this I had always been afraid that if I gave my life to God, I was ruined, that He would take away the fun, the joy. That is what I thought. This time I finally experienced the truth of the Gospel - that surrendering one's life to God leads to joy."

Instead of dying, Fr. Tomislav was restored to complete health. Thirty eight years later, in 2007, I attended the Priests' Retreat given by him in Medjugorje where he gave the above testimony. But his dramatic recovery from cancer was merely the prologue to what God was going to do in his life, for Fr. Tomislav has gone on to develop a process for the healing of one's spiritual soul which he calls Hagiotherapy - the healing of the holy. He correctly points out that there are depths to the human person which psychiatry cannot reach. We have an eternal spirit. This is conjoined to the body through a whole nucleus of cells and components which he calls the spiritual soul. This is the area that Hagiotherapy sets out to treat. Hagiotherapy has proved so popular and successful that it has now spread to many countries in central Europe. It is revolutionising people's understanding of our nature as spiritual embodied beings.

While some people need the assistance of a trained Hagiotherapist to unravel the complications in their spirit and their spiritual soul, the vast majority can have Jesus as their Hagiotherapist if they are prepared to take the simple practical steps outlined in this book. The question is:- are you prepared to take those steps? **"Do you want to be healed?" Jesus asked one man.**

Footnotes

1. When we surrender ourselves to God, our spirit becomes tuned into God. Things are then as they should be. There is an intimate union between our spirit and Jesus. There is also a harmony between our eternal spirit and our mortal bodies. Sometimes this allows a spectacular work of grace to occur within us. Sometimes, in turn, this leads to a dramatic miracle like the way Fr. Tomislav was healed from terminal cancer.

2. Fr. Tomislav shares how a Bible passage lit up for him. What happens when a Bible sentence "lights us" is that a moment of special grace is occurring in our eternal spirit. In that special moment of grace, our eternal spirit 'knows' that this is God's word for the situation. That is what causes the 'lighting up' effect.

3. For further details on Hagiotherapy, see Fr. Tomislav Ivancic's book, "Diagnosing the soul and Hagiotherapy" (Grafacommerce, Salzburg) which is available in Medjugorje.

— —

"A thief comes to steal and destroy; I have come that you might have life, the very fullness of life" John 10:10

How Our Eternal Spirit Conjoins Our Mortal Body

At the centre of our being is our eternal spirit. Our eternal spirit is united with our mortal body by means of our spiritual soul. This spiritual soul is complex, and has several cells or components.

One set of components is centred around our personhood, and includes our heart, our personality, our character, our ambitions and our sexuality.

A second set of components centres around our intellect and includes our conscience, will, memories, religious thought, creativity, culture, and how we see and hear (perceive).

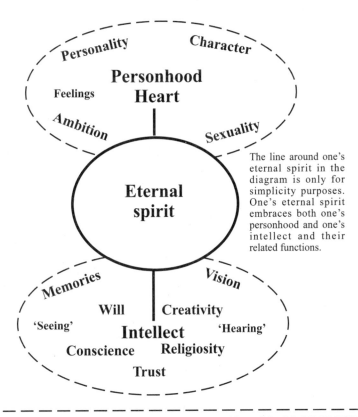

The line around one's eternal spirit in the diagram is only for simplicity purposes. One's eternal spirit embraces both one's personhood and one's intellect and their related functions.

Jesus cried again with a loud voice and yielded up his spirit, Mt 27:50 RSV

When one's eternal spirit leaves one's mortal body, one will still have the same intellect, but one's intellect will then be pure spirit. The essence of one's intellect is not mortal but spirit. It lives on when one's mortal body dies, yet it is conjoined to one's mortal body here on earth through one's brain cells.

So too with one's capacity to see, to hear, to smell, to feel and to taste. Here on earth, while in one's mortal body, one's eyes are essential for seeing. In reality one's eyes are the bodily organs through which one's spirit sees while conjoined to one's body.

One's attitudes while on earth will still be one's attitudes immediately after one leaves one's mortal body. So too will be the understanding of life and the faith beliefs that one has come to. One's intellect starts life in the spirit world at exactly the stage of development that it has finished life in this world.

One's eternal spirit is so conjoined to one's mortal body that it develops with one's mortal bodies and it is impacted upon by what happens in one's mortal body. What one does, how one lives, what one thinks, all that becomes incorporated into one's eternal spirit. As a result one's eternal spirit can become sick in a whole host of ways. This may happen if one is the victim of circumstances. Then one may end up making mistakes that are not really one's fault. In the case of Barbara Harris Whitfield due to the hurts she had experienced and her own resultant wrong choices, her eternal spirit needed to be permeated by God's love; that is by the healing, cleansing and delivering power of the Holy Spirit. When her eternal spirit had been permeated by God's healing love, then she was able to come back into her body, and to turn over a completely new leaf. **So heal one's eternal spirit, and then one's spiritual soul will respond.**

But sometimes it is through one's own wrong choices that one's spirit is poisoned, and then, unlike when one is a victim of hurts, one's spirit cuts itself off from God's love. Die like this, and one begins the next life outside God's love. Then one finds oneself in a frightening place, but there may still be hope. One is brought face to face with the consequences of one's actions. If there is enough openness to love or to God, one may still repent and be rescued, but not without suffering. If rescued, one then is permeated by God's love, and helped to face the full truth about one's life. Then one's spirit, having been purified by this process, is able to come back into one's body, and one is enabled to live the transformed life. See the testimony of Marino Restrepo who was addicted to drink, drugs and sex for thirty three years. Once his eternal spirit was delivered, cleansed and healed during his out-of-body experience, he was able to live the new life. So even with a person who was addicted to drugs, drink and sex for thirty three years, heal and cleanse the spirit, and the new life is possible. From this, we see that the

"Repent, and be baptized every one of you in the name of Jesus Christ for the forgiveness of your sins; and you shall receive the gift of the Holy Spirit." Acts 2:37-38 RSV

healing of our eternal spirit is first priority. The challenge for us is to become open to this while still in our mortal bodies.

One's eternal spirit needs a deep experience of God's love - just like happened for Jesus on the occasion of His baptism. In the early Church, the Baptism of Jesus was seen as the model for all baptisms. They spent two years preparing for Baptism:- two years having their expectations developed, that they too would have a profound experience of God's love and come into a living relationship with Jesus on the occasion of their baptisms. Being baptised as infants, we couldn't expect anything. However where children are lucky, they are raised by parents who help them become open to this profound experience of God's love and this living relationship with Jesus as they grow up, but sadly, many committed parents, do not have this type of relationship with Jesus themselves. Not having it themselves they cannot pass it on to their children.

For adults, the nearest that we have to what happened in the early Church is the "Life in the Spirit Seminars," at the end of which people are prayed with for Baptism in the Spirit. But however you come into it, you need to experience God's love in your heart, and a sense of Jesus living within you. The good news is that Jesus really wants this for you too - so your quest is to become open to what He desires to do in your heart and in your eternal spirit. Sometimes this, or at least part of this, comes by pure gift from God through some form of religious experience. But even where there is religious experience, it needs to be followed by taking the steps to grow in one's relationship with Jesus and to become open to the healing.

Sometimes there can be medical or emotional factors that make it harder for us to become open to the experience of the flow of God's love into our hearts. It would have been very difficult for Barbara Harris Whitfield, without a major miracle, to have become open to this while still in her mortal body, because of what she calls the 'psychic numbing' deep within her. The part of her inner being where one experiences a sense of being loved, had been numbed. This is quite common for those who have suffered childhood abuse. For other people, depression can be a major inhibiting factor to the experience of God's love.

Then there are spiritual factors. In Barbara Harris Whitfield's case, she was a victim of circumstances, and while she had made mistakes, there was little blame attaching to her. What she needed above all was to experience love, and the assurance of being totally loved. But Marino Restrepo's case was very different. He had made serious wrong choices through his own fault, and he had brought hurt into many lives through his own fault. His life review was very different to

---

"And when he came up out of the water, immediately he saw the heavens opened and the Spirit descending upon him like a dove; and a voice came from heaven, "Thou art my beloved Son; and with thee I am well pleased." Mark 1:10-11 RSV

that of Barbara. He found himself at the gates of Hell. Then he was faced with the full terrible consequences of his lifestyle. He had to face the truth about his life, including how he had rejected God, stepped outside God's plan for his life, and how through his own fault, he had brought hurt into the lives of countless people. What his spirit required and experienced almost amounted to a form of exorcism, delivering him from his wrong attitudes and compulsions.

Essentially the same process as happened in the case of Marino Restrepo also happened for Gloria Polo, Dr. Howard Storm, Fr. Steven Scheier, and to a lesser extent Angie Fenimore, though in her case it was the depths of Purgatory she visited and not the gates of Hell.

Serious sin has consequences for one's eternal spirit in this life and in the next. Whether it is during a near-death experience or while still in one's body, the process for the purification and healing of one's spirit is still the same:- one first has to face the truth about one's lifestyle and then repent. The only remedy for serious culpable sin is repentance. After repentance, there will also be need for a process of healing, cleansing and deliverance. This involves seeking to be embraced by God's love and to draw one's strength from him. This further involves learning to walk with Jesus - including learning to take the steps to help us to become open to His healing power, and then gradually learning to face the truth about the hurt that one has caused, and to do something about it. Even where a person has a deep spiritual experience, it needs to be followed by a process of healing and growth involving the above steps.

Regardless of whether the damage to one's eternal spirit was caused by being a victim of circumstances or through one's own sin, there will also be resultant damage to one's spiritual soul, whether it be in one's heart, one's inner personhood, one's sexuality, one's character, one's intellect, one's conscience, one's will, one's religious sensor, one's capacity for trust or wherever. This damage will block the flow of God's love in one's life until one's receives the grace to open it to His love and His light.

The challenge for us is to identify where there is damage, how it may have originated, and then to take the steps to become open to such healing, cleansing and deliverance as is necessary. But for that we first need a living relationship with Jesus, and then to learn to start walking with Him.

— —

"And I saw the dead, great and small, standing before the throne, and books were opened. Also another book was opened, which is the book of life. And the dead were judged by what was written in the books, by what they had done." Rev 20:12 RSV

24 Steps Towards Healing

We have an eternal spirit that will live on when our mortal bodies die. This eternal spirit is our very core, the centre of our being, the most important part of who we are. Our most important task in life is the development of our eternal spirit. There are four main elements to the development of one's eternal spirit:

A. Come to a living relationship with Jesus and to an experience of God's love.
B. Grow in one's capacity for self-giving love.
C. Identifying where one needs inner healing, deliverance or transformation, and take the steps to come into it.
D. Find the strength to cope with and rise above difficulties. In the process one's eternal spirit is strengthened and purified.

If you are to achieve those, the following steps are very important. These steps will lead you into enormous healing, and prepare you for direct entry to Heaven.

1. Pursue a living relationship with Jesus

Your eternal spirit absolutely needs a living relationship with Jesus. There will be something missing in your life until Jesus comes alive in your heart. Your eternal spirit only truly comes alive within you, when you have this relationship with Jesus, and when you begin to be empowered by the Holy Spirit; that is when you begin to experience what Jesus called 'baptism in the Spirit'. There is nothing more important in life than becoming open to this, so keep seeking it until it becomes a lived reality for you. Start by talking directly to Jesus in every situation. Find people who already know Jesus in this way and start associating with them. (There is much more on this step elsewhere in this book.)

2. Develop the practice of ongoing self-observation

Commit yourself to developing a capacity for self-observation. Reflect regularly on your motivation, your desires, your compulsive tendencies. Instead of hiding this away as a dark secret, start sharing about your inner self in appropriate settings:- in Confession; with your spouse if possible; with good friends; in prayer groups etc. **If one does not develop this dual capacity for self-observation and for sharing the truth about one's inner self, one will not grow spiritually, nor will one break free of one's compulsive tendencies.**

Ask the Holy Spirit to help you get in touch with what is happening in your heart. Seek to become aware of anything selfish or irrational in your thinking or in your motivation. Seek to become aware of how you relate to others, and of how others

"Be renewed in mind and spirit, and put on the new nature which is God's own likeness by becoming truly righteous" Eph 4:23, 24.

may experience you. Reflect on your speech patterns, your body language, and your activity. If something is causing you to relate in a negative way to others, identify it, and start bringing it to the Lord for healing, both opening it to the healing light of Jesus in Confession, and also bringing it to the Lord during your daily prayer time using the special method of prayer outlined below in step 4.

If you get things wrong or make a mistake, ask yourself what led you to do so. If you make a similar mistake twice, then do some soul searching. Have the humility to admit your mistakes - both to the person involved and in Confession.

3. Find appropriate ways of challenging oneself

Coming into the healing power of Jesus does not happen by chance. Neither does living a love-centred life happen by chance. It requires a real miracle of grace, one that requires your cooperation. There is a part of your inner self, the part that is selfish by nature, that has to be effectively challenged if you are to become a true child of God. Having identified those parts of one's inner self that are selfish, compulsive or that require healing, the next step is to find appropriate ways of challenging oneself. Being totally honest in Confession is one way - see step 5. Developing healing methods of prayer meditation is another - see step 4.

Other steps are also needed. Living by Gospel teaching is not easy, but if you settle for anything less, you will not become the person you are called to be. In coming into inner healing, we Catholics are at a major disadvantage, because we haven't learned how to use key Bible passages to challenge ourselves, to motivate us, and to nourish our faith. "The word of God is the sword of the Spirit" Eph 6:17. If you desire for God to touch you and to heal you, then His word in the New Testament to minister to your eternal spirit.

Find Scripture verses that challenge you where you are vulnerable to falling short, and ones that encourage you to greater heights. Perhaps put an occasional Scripture verse in a key position - I have one on the base of the computer on which I am writing this book. Try to read a least a paragraph of the New Testament each day, and underline the verses that speak to you. If you are a Catholic you will have an initial psychological resistance to this. But if you are able to read, and yet do not begin to read even small sections of the New Testament, then there will always be a lack in your relationship with Jesus, nor will you ever reach the heights to which He calls you.

4. Develop healing methods of prayer

Jesus loves you. He wants you to be penetrated and permeated by His love. He wants to draw you into an ever deeper union with Himself. He sees where you

"No one can serve two masters; for either he will hate the one and love the other, or he will be devoted to the one and despise the other. You cannot serve God and mammon (your own compulsive desires)." Mt 6:24

have been hurt by life and desires to heal you. He sees where you have developed compulsions and negative ways of responding and desires to set you free. He sees how you settle for the ways of the world, and wishes to challenge you to live as a child of the light. He sees where you are afraid, and desires to walk with you, giving you strength. He sees where you settle for second best, and wants you to seek the best. He sees what troubles you and desires to teach you how to trust Him. He has special plans for you and desires to lead you into them.

Day by day, you can gradually become open to all this through prayer meditation. I speak from personal experience. Back around 1988, I developed a method of prayer that really works for me, and which I use daily. Since I published an outline of it in the little booklet, **"A Shower of Blessings"**, thousands of people have been helped by it. It is based on the following principles,

1. Identify the areas where you need to be touched by the Lord in any of the ways mentioned above and write them out - just one item on each page.

2. Then for each area that needs healing or deliverance or challenging, find a Scripture verse that will speak right into the situation, and write that down on the appropriate page.

3. Jesus has already won for you the right to the blessing in question. He wants it for you. So compose and write down a brief prayer of thanks to Jesus that this particular blessing is already there for you.

4. Each day during your prayer time, first hold before the Lord the needs that you have written down, one at a time. Then allow each Scripture verse to speak to you. "The word of God is the sword of the Spirit" Eph 6:17. Then, using the prayer that you have written, thank the Lord that you are going to be blessed in this way.

5. Continue to keep personal inventory, seeking to get in touch with what is really happening in your mind and heart, and learning to use the above process to bring the issues that arise to the Lord for healing.

Pray like this, and you will no longer just be saying prayers. You will be allowing Jesus to heal you, to mould you and lift you up during your prayer time.

If you use my booklet "A Shower of Blessings" it is very important that you make this way of praying your own by writing in notes on the different pages. For example, on the page seeking to be delivered from worry, write down in a word or two, what is a source of worry for you at this time. Likewise on the other pages, write in your own notes, and even add in extra pages as you seek God's blessing in the areas of life that are important to you.

"The word of God is living and active, sharper than any two-edged sword. It can pierce right to where our spirit joins our mortal body, and expose our inner thoughts and motivations." Hebrew 4:12

5. Turn Confession into a Sacrament of Healing

Confession is the number one source of miracles in my own life. This, however, has only happened since I have chosen a regular Confessor with whom I am totally honest, going to Confession face to face. If you wish to turn the Sacrament of Confession into an ongoing series of miracles for you, then,

1. Start going to Confession at least monthly and go face to face.

2. Find a regular confessor with whom you can be totally honest - if that isn't possible, limit yourself to two or three priests, again priests to whom you can go face to face and be totally honest. (If no priest is available, start taking these steps with your spouse, of if it can't be your spouse, find a faith friend with whom you are in no way emotionally involved.)

3. Find the courage to open the inner areas of your being, especially any area that causes you shame, but without being long-winded. This is the same courage a person needs in talking to their doctor about personal matters.

4. Leaving aside all old lists of sins, ask the Lord to show you any way in which you are failing to live as His child in thought, word of deed.

5. Except where there are grave sins when all of them need to be confessed, select the two or three areas that most need to be opened to the healing power of the Lord at this time and briefly confess these. Then in your next Confession, you can either focus again on these or select others.

Take these steps and you will be opening your inner self to the healing light of Christ. Not merely will the healing light of Christ touch you during the actual sacrament, but you will also find that during the month, your inner self will remain open to the light of Christ. You will often experience healing the very moment you say to yourself, "This is something I have to tell Fr. X."

Having a regular confessor or spiritual director has the added benefit of placing oneself under authority. Do nothing that could have major implications without first opening your plans, at least briefly, to your confessor. This especially applies in all dispute situations. In opening your plans to your confessor you are opening them to the light of Christ.

(For a fuller treatment of Confession, see my booklet "Confession a journey into healing, self-discovery and God's love.)

6. Don't let your past destroy your future

Angie Fenimore had a voice in her head telling her that she was no good. Gloria Polo allowed her father's outrageous conduct to colour her attitude to men, sex and marriage. Identify any negative voices in your mind telling you that you are no good, or that you can't do this or that. You are God's creation, and He did not create you worthless, so come against the negative voices using the healing

"Confess your sins to one another, and pray for one another, that you may be healed" James 5:16 RSV

method of prayer, (step 4). Identify also any way your attitude to life may have been coloured by someone's bad behaviour, and again decide that you are not going to be warped by another person's bad behaviour. Open it to the healing light of Christ in the sacrament of Confession.

7. Decide to live through the pain

If you have developed serious problems, there is no soft way to healing. If one is deeply emotionally involved in a 'wrong' relationship, one needs to be prepared to live for months with the deep pain of separation, but one will be set free if one is prepared to live through the pain. Likewise if one has become deeply sexually aroused, either through taking a relationship too far or through looking at pornographic films or books, the desire in one's mind can be like a searing pain, but once again, one will be set free if one is prepared to live through the pain. Pornography itself can be most compulsive. Breaking the compulsion involves being willing to live through the pain. Likewise with anger and bitterness, one may have to live for days, weeks or even months with frustration in one's heart or annoying thoughts in one's mind, but one will be set free if one is prepared to live through the pain. The same applies to a variety of compulsions and addictions, including alcoholism, drug addiction, and eating disorders.

Indeed very often these arise in the first place because one is trying to escape from or to numb the pain that is in one's heart. This inner pain can ultimately only be taken away by one's working through it and coming into inner healing. This can best be achieved in the context of coming to a living relationship with Jesus. One can alleviate the pain to some extent by finding other things to occupy one's mind, but one cannot take it away completely. Where in response to the pain in one's heart, one has become addicted to drink or drugs, or one has developed an eating disorder, one will need specialised help, but one still needs to be willing to live with the pain. Indeed then there are two pains:- the original pain in one's heart, and the pain of separation from one's addiction or compulsion.

8. Make a decision to stop hiding your problems

There are various ways of hiding one's problem. They include going to Confession to some priest who does not know you if you have something to tell that you find embarrassing or have relapsed into an old problem. Likewise one may seek to hide one's problem or one's relapse from one's spouse, or from friends who are trying to help, or from the support group. **You will not be delivered from your problem as long as you hide your relapses.** Instead you will keep saying to yourself, "Just one more time." Every time you fall and hide your fall, the

Every one who does evil hates the light, and does not come to the light, lest his deeds should be exposed. But he who does what is true comes to the light, that it may be clearly seen that his deeds have been wrought in God.
John 3:20-21 RSV

darkness within you will become greater; deep down you will feel more and more worthless; and satan will get more and more control in your life. If you desire healing, then get honest and keep coming to the light.

9. Be embraced by Love

"God is love." God absolutely is love. Love is His very essence. Satan is the opposite to love. He is bitterness, selfishness and hatred.

God loves us first, and desires to pour His love into our hearts. But we are in a world where there is a clash between love and hatred, between self-giving and selfishness, between reconciliation and bitterness, between light and darkness. Every time we decide for love over hatred, for self-giving over selfishness, for forgiveness over bitterness, for walking in the light over darkness, a victory for God's kingdom is taking place within us, and this allows healing to take place. But every time we allow hatred to replace our love, selfishness to replace our self-giving, bitterness to replace reconciliation, darkness to replace light, there is a victory for satan taking place within us, the capacity for God's love to flow through us is reduced, our eternal spirit is ruptured from its eternal destiny, and damage is done to our spiritual soul. Decide then to open your heart to Love, and to live this in a practical way. Be prepared to persevere through whatever pain is involved in breaking free from anger and bitterness, so as to live this life of love.

10. Walk in the Light

"God is light. There is no darkness in Him whatsoever" 1 Jn 1:6. We walk in the light by learning to share the truth about our inner selves in appropriate ways and by making decisions that are consistent with walking in the light. In life we meet with many dark situations. Somebody hurts us badly. Our mind starts obsessing with the hurt, going over and over how unreasonable the other person's actions were. In human terms, we may feel totally justified in taking certain actions in relation to the person. Even a committed Christian, seeking as best he can to follow Gospel principles, may feel fully justified in taking strong measures.

But if one asks oneself:- "Is this walking in the light?" one may see things in a whole new 'light'. Allow into your mind's eye, an image of being before the great eternal Light and the great eternal Love. Become aware of yourself being embraced by the Light and the Love. Then hold the situation and your planned response before this Light. It is amazing the difference this can make. One will often find oneself letting go of issues that one was determined to pursue. One realises that certain ways of living and behaving are not of the Lord. The reason for this is, that even with the very best of intentions, and even with seeking and

---

"God is light. There is no darkness in Him at all. If we say that we are in union with God while we are living in darkness, we are lying." 1 John 1:6

124

desiring to 'put on the mind of Christ', as long as we remain in our mortal bodies, there will be 'scar tissue' in our minds and hearts, remnants of darkness:- some remnants inherited as a result of original sin; some remnants the result of the ways in which we have been hurt; and some remnants arising from our own past wrong attitudes and wrong ways of thinking. To counteract these remnants of darkness, one needs to commit oneself to walking in the light and to being open to the light. In the process, very real healing can take place in one's intellect as God's light is allowed to permeate it.

11. Start drawing strength from Jesus

Jesus is with you at all times. By learning to depend on His power, you will be enabled to do many things that are impossible by your own power, including overcoming your inhibitions and being delivered from your nervousness.

One way of depending on His power is to become aware of Him going before you. **Allow into your mind's eye some sense of Jesus being above you and before you, lifting you up and giving your strength.** I usually speak of allowing an image of Jesus into one's mind's eye, but the image does not have to have a human face or specific details:- just a sense that He is there, and that He is going to give you the strength for the situation you face. Again this is something that has really worked for me. And, in the process of drawing my strength from Jesus, I have also become ever more deeply united with Him. Learn to draw strength from Jesus in this way, and He will enable you to first rise above, and then to be gradually healed of your fears, inhibitions and nervousness,

12. Take appropriate practical steps

There is a saying, "It is a smart person who flees temptation and does not leave a forwarding address." Breaking free of an inappropriate relationship or of a compulsion or an addiction does demand that one takes appropriate steps to reduce the temptation. If, for example, one has had an inappropriate relationship, avoid situations that will rekindle one's passions. If one has an affair with a work colleague and is still 'in love' with that person, try to find a new job. If one is in any way vulnerable to watching pornography, then do not have a sex channel available on your TV. If that means getting rid of your satellite dish, then so be it. Likewise with your internet connection. If you are vulnerable to watching pornography on the internet, better that your internet connection should go than that you be enslaved to pornography, though if you are honest with your confessor, and your spouse or whoever you live with, perhaps you could have your computer in an open place where you won't be tempted.
Likewise with drink and all other compulsions and addictions, there are practical steps that one needs to take if one has a problem and desires to break it..

"The fruit of the Spirit is love, joy, peace, patience, kindness, goodness, faithfulness, gentleness, self-control." Galatians 5:22 RSV

13. Make a decision to work towards forgiveness.

Satan is the one who is behind all hurting. He is the one who inspired the person who hurt you. As long as the hurt remains unhealed, satan's knife is stuck in your heart. Even while this is so, God loves you and desires to pour His love into your eternal spirit, but its capacity to flow through you is limited as long as satan's knife is stuck in your heart. I speak from personal experience. Even after my experience of God's love in 1972, I still had much bitterness. Jesus still loved me and was with me in a very special way. But I could not heal until I dealt with the bitterness; neither could I grow spiritually; neither could I possibly become what Jesus desires for all of us to become:- His living presence in the world. But for many people coming to forgiveness isn't easy.

If you have been deeply hurt, cry your anger out to Jesus. Tell Him exactly how you feel. Find appropriate ways to share your hurt and anger with others, but always with a desire to be able to let go of it, and to be able to forgive those who hurt you. This is absolutely necessary for your own healing, and for experiencing the power of the Lord in your own life.

Make a list of all the people who have hurt you. Bring your hurt and your anger to the Lord, and then, having opened it up to the Lord, set yourself the target of forgiving them. Meditate on Scripture verses that challenge us to forgive, like, "Unless you forgive others for the hurts they have caused to you, neither will your Heavenly Father forgive you for the hurts that you have caused to others" Mt 6:14. Allow this verse to challenge your eternal spirit. Remind yourself that God is love, whereas satan is bitterness and hatred. Remind yourself that satan has his knife in your heart as long as your hold the bitterness. Ask Jesus to help you to see that those who hurt you are themselves in need of God's mercy, and that sometimes it is their sickness that has caused them to hurt you. In your daily prayer time, hold them before the Lord, asking Jesus to bless them, even if part of you is still feeling hurt and is still angry with them.

14. Decide to trust Jesus

It is easy to pray, "Jesus I trust in You." It is far harder to actually do it. Part of our inner self doesn't trust Him to look after us. Another part of our inner self will often tell us that there is a better way than God's way in the different situations we face in life. We are often a bit like the student who prays for God's help and then cheats in his exams. St. Paul calls those parts of our inner being that are in rebellion against God or that draw us in the wrong direction, the 'old self'.

You have a choice to make:- who is going to be your master? Will you choose what is good for your eternal spirit and walk in the ways of the Lord or will you yield to the impulses and desires of your old self? Walking with Jesus may lead

"Be kind to one another, tenderhearted, forgiving one another, as God in Christ forgave you." Eph 4:32 RSV

to pain, and to struggle with your old self. But every day you walk with Jesus, healing takes place in your inner spirit and in your spiritual soul, whereas every time you give in to the cravings of your old self, damage is done to your eternal spirit. So, **"Commit your cause to the Lord, trust in Him and He will act on your behalf"** Ps 37:5. Make that promise your own and live by it. Identify any tendency to not trust Jesus, any tendency to worry or be afraid, and make it part of your prayer project to be healed and delivered from worry and fear. Trusting Jesus also means trusting that His way is always best, so it involves a commitment to living by His teaching. If you have erected barriers around your heart to protect it, identify them, and trust Jesus enough to bring them to Him in Confession, with a view to letting go of them.

15. Reach Out To Others

Stop thinking of what others should be doing for you, and ask God to show you what you should be doing for others. A famous nun says that every time she felt depressed, she looked for someone who was even more depressed than herself and sought to reach out to him or her. When we reach out to others, we take the focus off ourselves and our own problems. There is, of course, a time for giving full attention to one's own problems. One's own pain needs to be acknowledged, not repressed. But having acknowledged one's pain, then seek to reach out to others, or find something else to turn your attention to. In reaching out to others, God's love can begin to flow through you, and as it flows through you, it heals you first. Reaching out to others and seeing their needs will help you to take your mind off your own struggles and enable you to see things in proportion.

Become aware that every person you meet has an eternal spirit:- the person who serves you in the shop, the repair man who visits your house, the person cleaning the street, every member of your family, every person you meet. Allow yourself to see them as an eternal spirit, and to appreciate the wonder of it. Become aware also that Jesus lives in their spirit if they have asked him into their lives or if they are living a love-centred life. Then they are a living tabernacle of His presence, and so to be treated with the same reverence with which we treat the Sacred Host. If they have yet to become open to Jesus living within them, Jesus desires for you to be a bearer of His presence and of His love to them.

16. Cultivate Appreciation and Understanding

Become aware of the goodness of the people around you. Take time to appreciate their goodness, their love, their willingness to help, their dedication. Think of times that they may give of themselves beyond the call of duty, sometimes to the last ounce of their energy. Become aware, too, of how well some people

— —

"By this we know what love is:- He gave His life for us. So we ought to live our lives for one another" I John 3:16 .

are coping with their crosses. Become aware that some of those who fail and do bad things, may be trying their best. Become aware of how they may have been hurt by life, and how mentally and emotionally, they may be giving all they have got. Become aware that for some people, it may be their sickness that is causing their problems, and that while it is right to be firm with them, this needs to be done with compassion. Appreciating the goodness of others, and having compassion for them, aligns your spirit to Jesus and to how He sees people - and lowers your blood pressure!!

17. Decide to break the cycle of hurting

Identify any cycle of hurting that may have come down to you through your family tree. Decide that you want it to stop with you, and that you will take the steps to come into healing. If it has already got passed on to your children, decide now to seek healing for yourself first and also to do what is in your power to lead your family into healing. Likewise if a cycle of hurting has come down through the family tree of your spouse, seek to become a minister of God's healing love to both your spouse and your children.

Become aware of other hurts that you may have experienced, like being mistreated in school or being bullied or in some way abused. That too is part of a cycle of hurting that is like a satanic wave spreading out in the present generations, and then spreading down through the generations. Decide that you are not going to be part of that satanic wave of hurting; that you are going to take the steps to come into healing and to lead others into healing.

18. Seek to make amends for the hurt you have caused

Make a list of all the people you have hurt directly or indirectly. This includes those you have hurt by giving bad example, or by discouraging them, or by leading them into moral or spiritual danger, or by failing to give them the spiritual and moral help that you should have given them. It also includes all the people that they may hurt as a result of you hurting them. If one hurts a person spiritually or morally, they may hurt their children, who in turn may hurt their own children, and one could have started a cycle of hurting that will still be continuing in five hundred years time. Recognising the truth about this is part of seeing the truth about one's life. **If you have caused hurt to others, the truth needs to be faced, and it will be faced either in this life or the next.** It is in seeing the full truth about our lives that we realise the importance of seeking total healing. Set yourself the target of doing what is in your power to repair the hurt that you have caused, though being careful not to hurt others in the process. Pray regularly for those you have hurt - and indeed for those who have hurt you.

"He who says he is in the light and hates his brother is in the darkness still. He who loves his brother abides in the light, and in it there is no cause for stumbling. 1 John 2:9-10 RSV

19. Accept your lot in life

Bad things may have happened to you which were not God's original will. But now that they have happened, they must be accepted. Before you can move forward from where you now are, you need to accept where you now are. The Bible promises, **"God works all things for the good for those who love Him"** Rom 8:28. Allow that verse to minister healing and hope to your eternal spirit.

However you came to be the way you are, with whatever wounds or limitations that you may perceive yourself as having, if you surrender yourself totally into God's hands and start walking with Jesus, He will turn every wound and every limitation into a source of blessing for your eternal spirit. Identify anything about yourself that you don't like, and surrender it to God. Include anything that causes you a sense of shame or embarrassment, or causes you to feel inferior. Include also anything that causes you to struggle morally or spiritually.

Jesus loves you just as you are with all your wounds and limitations. You cannot be someone else, nor can Jesus lead you into the special plan He has for your life until you totally accept who you are now. Become aware of any jealousy or envy or self-pity and renounce it. Then, using the steps in the prayer for healing process, seek to come into healing and deliverance. Embrace your own weaknesses even as you desire for Jesus to set your free. Embrace your limitations, even as you trust that Jesus desires to bring real blessings into the world through you. Accept the bad things that have happened in your life, realising that as you allow Jesus to come alive within you, His love will embrace all these things, and then they become an extension of His cross, and in the process your eternal spirit will thrive. As you accept your lot in life, there will be a harmonising between your spirit and the Holy Spirit. This in turn will minister calm and healing to your inner being. It will also allow the Holy Spirit to begin to lead you forward into God's special plan for you, a plan that is exactly tailor made for you.

20. Accept that you will face problems

Problems are inevitable. Accept that this is the way life is. Decide that whatever life throws at you, that you will still trust Jesus. Every time you overcome a problem and survive through a crisis with trust in your heart, you grow closer to Jesus, you are better prepared for Heaven, your spirit within you is developing, and you are becoming a stronger person.

Jesus is with you and within you, and is willing to embrace your sufferings and problems with you. Draw strength from Him. Decide to see every problem as a challenge that Jesus is trusting you with. Be prepared to suffer the pain and the upset that comes with the problem, while at the same time taking reasonable steps

---

"I will restore to you the years which the swarming locust has eaten."
Joel 2:29 RSV

to let go of the upset or to distract yourself from it. Every time you successfully handle a problem God's way, give thanks, because you are now a stronger person.

21. Give thanks in every situation

No matter what has gone wrong, or what bad things are being done, God is still God, and God will minister blessing to you if you bring your troubles to Him. In your darkest hour, allow Jesus who is within you, to embrace your inner being and to be conjoined with you in facing whatever has to be faced. Then, as a sign of your trust in Him, start giving thanks to Him. This will allow His love to come alive in your eternal spirit, protecting your spirit from satanic hurt. Then your spirit in turn will strengthen you from within. Praise and thanksgiving tunes one's spirit into the continuous spirit of praise in Heaven, and allows Jesus to come alive in one's heart and to start ministering healing to one's spiritual soul.

22. Singing opens us to healing

One very important way of nourishing one's spirit is spiritual singing that comes from the heart. Singing is a major feature of Heaven. Our eternal spirit has a special love for singing. I am as near to tone deaf as one can get, but that does not stop me from joining in the singing when there are good strong voices around me. Hymns of praise, sung from the heart, allow one's eternal spirits to express itself and to come alive. This leaves one more open to the working of the Holy Spirit, and can often lead to healing. Singing in tongues can be especially helpful for letting one's inner spirit come alive and for becoming open to the Holy Spirit.

23. Get on with living

When feeling down it is important to get on with living. Find simple practical work that you can do, and do it. Be prepared to tolerate imperfection in yourself, and to move forward, lovingly accepting that, for the moment, this is the way you are, and that God loves you as you are. In GROW they have a slogan for able bodied people, "No matter how bad you feel you can still put your right foot in front of your left." So don't lie down and mope. Find something that you can do and do it. This gives one's mind the chance to begin to heal.

24. Make a decision to stick with the process

Dealing with the 'old self' is a lifetime process. In particular, if over many years one has built up negative ways of living, one will not break them overnight. Make a definite decision that you will stick with your journey towards healing, and do so especially through times of struggle. If you feel that you are not making

---

"Rejoice in so far as you share Christ's sufferings, that you may also rejoice and be glad when his glory is revealed" 1 Peter 4:13. RSV

progress, check how well you are practising the various steps. There is always a way forward, but it may take you some time to find it. Perseverance is absolutely essential for spiritual growth. Persevere especially in

1. Seeking to grow in your relationship with Jesus
2. Setting real time aside for prayer and for the development of your eternal spirit.
3. The practise of self-observation and of sharing the truth about what is happening within you.

These are steps that no one else can take for you.

25. Be prepared to seek help if necessary

If you take the above twenty four steps towards healing, and still have a destructive compulsion that you can't break, then seek help.   Some compulsions and addictions are so deeply rooted that they require the help of a support group - people who will know and understand one's problem, who will be able to assist in practical ways, and indeed who know enough about the problem, to be able to challenge one if necessary.   Other compulsions require deliverance ministry, while yet others spring from medical factors that require medical assistance, while other problems require specialised counselling.

Also ask Jesus to be your Hagiotherapist. If you have been using the healing methods of prayer (step 4) over a prolonged period, and there is some area of your life in which you are still not making progress, ask the Holy Spirit to show you if there is something deeper that needs healing first. For example, I had been praying for years for the gift of self-control in the area of patience, without success, and then I discovered that what I needed first was the healing of my 'inner fuse', the part of one's inner self that 'snaps' when one becomes impatient; so I started inviting Jesus to permeate my 'inner fuse' with His love and to minister healing to it, and then I began to see some progress.

So if you too find that there is some area in which you are not making progress despite taking the right steps, it could be a sign that you need healing at a deeper level, or that there is something buried within you or pushed down within you that needs to be brought to the surface. Seek to identify where a problem may have originated in your life, and to bring that for healing.

Footnote

You will not be able to take all twenty five steps at once. Identify the steps that are the most urgent for you to take, and then make a start in taking them. Pick out about three steps and start seeking to implement those. Work through the other steps later. **If you desire healing, then start co-operating with God.**

— —

Jesus asked him, "Do you really want to be healed?" John 5:6

I Want To Go To Heaven The Moment I Die

Don Piper went straight to the gates of Heaven without any need for a life-review. So too did Linnie Smith. Both had not merely a living relationship with Jesus, but were living the transformed life. This is God's plan for each of us also.

There are five possibilities when we die depending on how we have lived:-
1. Eternal damnation for those who reject God and are truly wicked.
2. The depths of Purgatory for those who barely escape hell; the middle levels of Purgatory for others who have serious matter to deal with.
3. The upper levels of Purgatory for those who love God but still have some matters to deal with or purification to undergo.
4. Heaven for those who are truly walking with Jesus.
5. Those who are living in deep union with Him, will not merely go straight to Heaven, but will continue to bring blessing on earth after their deaths.

To be able to go straight to Heaven the moment we die should be our minimum aim. Anything less is a failure. Going to Purgatory, even the upper levels, is a bit like failing an exam, but being allowed to do the repeats.

Not merely should our aim be to go straight to Heaven the moment we die, but our aim should be to live in such union with Jesus here on earth, that we will be so totally open to Him, that when we go to Heaven, we will be able to bring blessing here on earth. This should be our aim. Jesus has put it into our reach. It is God's plan for us. We have only to cooperate with God, to accept Jesus as our Saviour and to allow ourselves to be transformed by Him in order to go straight up. Learn to walk in deep union with Jesus, and not merely will you be able to go straight to Heaven, but from Heaven you will be able to bring powerful blessings on earth.

There is also the consolation of knowing that, if we aim for Heaven but fall a little bit short, our Purgatory experience will be mild, even beautiful. Continue to aim to so walk with Jesus that you will be able to go to Heaven the moment you die, and you can look forward with joy to the next life - even if you pass through Purgatory.

Jesus wants to take all fear of death, all fear of judgement, and all fear of God from those who are walking in union with Him. If you are walking with Him, He wants you to be able to look forward to eternal life with joy, even with excitement.

"I will spend my time in Heaven doing good upon earth."
St Therese of Lisieux

We Catholics are very slow to speak in terms of "being saved" and sometimes we find the manner in which other Christians use this phrase very off-putting - often with good reason because of the incorrect way in which some Christians use the phrase. They think that everybody who goes up to the altar and recites a prayer is guaranteed to go straight to Heaven.

If you desire to go to Heaven, without the risk of going through a painful process, then learn to walk with Jesus. But Jesus wants those who are sincerely walking with Him to know that they are going to Heaven. Paul said, "Believe in the Lord Jesus and you will be saved, you and your household." Acts 16:31. He did not say that you 'might be' saved. He said you **will be** saved. However he is using the word 'saved' here in the broader sense to include those who go to Purgatory. They too are 'saved'.

In 1 John we read, "I write this to you who believe in the name of the Son of God, that **you may know** that you have eternal life." 1 John 5:13. God wants you **to know** that you have eternal life. But it is clear from earlier in 1 John, that there are important conditions. For example, he says, "If any one says, 'I love God,' and hates his brother, he is a liar; for he who does not love his brother whom he has seen, cannot love God whom he has not seen." 1 John 4:19-20 RSV.

If you are full of hatred and bitterness, don't fool yourself. You will not enter Heaven until these have been dealt with. If you don't deal with them in this life, then you will have to deal with them in the next life. Worse still, you may find yourself in a place where they will deal with you.

The Bible is very clear on this:- if you are truly walking with Jesus, then God wants you to have total assurance that you are saved, but if you are compromising, then there will be eternal consequences. St. James said, "Accept and submit to the word which has been planted in you and can save souls. But you must do what the word tells you, and not just listen to it and deceive yourselves." 1 James 1:21b-22. But if you are truly walking with Jesus and living a love empowered life, then Jesus wants you to know that you have eternal life. **Some deeply spiritual people live in fear of judgement. This is not God's plan for them.**

In 1 John we read,, "Whoever confesses that Jesus is the Son of God, God abides in him, and he in God. So we know and believe the love God has for us." 1 John 4:15 -16a So if you are seeking to walk with Jesus, you can have total trust that Jesus is within you and that God loves you. But if you desire to grow in your union with Jesus, then renounce hatred and selfishness, and seek to grow in love, for "God is love, and he who abides in love abides in God, and God abides in him." I John 4:16b. So the first step is to accept Jesus into our hearts, the second step is to grow in love.

The next step is to have all fear of damnation taken away. St. John continues,

"Blessed and holy is he who shares in the first resurrection! Over such the second death has no power, but they shall be priests of God and of Christ, and they shall reign with him a thousand years." Rev 20:6 RSV

"In this is love perfected with us, that we may have confidence for the day of judgement. .... There is no fear in love, but perfect love casts out fear. For fear has to do with punishment, and he who fears is not perfected in love. We love, because he first loved us." 1 John 4:17-19 RSV

God desires to embrace you in His love, to pour His love into your heart, and to give you total assurance of Heaven. Why fear Him who desires to embrace you in love? He just wants to go on loving you, to permeate you with His love, to transform you by His love. If you truly walk with Him, then you can be totally assured of your eternal salvation. St. Paul is quite clear about this. He declared, "There is laid up for me the crown of righteousness, which the Lord, the righteous judge, will award to me on that day, and not only to me but also to all who have longed for his appearing." 2 Tim 4:8

It is a beautiful thing to have this assurance - that is so long as the assurance is well founded. You too can look forward to the "crown of righteousness" if you walk with Jesus. It is a beautiful thing to know that one is going to Heaven. But what, you may ask, if one seeks to walk with Jesus, but falls a little bit short? If you are genuinely seeking to walk with Jesus and not compromising, then the very worst is a brief visit to the upper realms of Purgatory. The visionary Anne tells us that she would be totally happy to spend time in the upper realms of Purgatory. It is a place of light and love, where one's eternal spirit is transformed - what could be described as God's beauty parlour for blemished spirits. Indeed some people who had near-death experiences, and who I believe were in the upper realms of Purgatory, actually think that they were in Heaven.

So, let those who walk with Jesus rejoice for, "When Christ who is our life appears, then you also will appear with Him in glory" Colossians 3:4. So rejoice! Renounce your fear of God. Start thinking of Heaven as the most wonderful place that one could go; a place of total unbelievable happiness. Let the thoughts of it lift your spirit.

Not merely will walking with Jesus bring us happiness in the next life, but it will also bring us happiness on earth. We have an eternal spirit that cries out for a living relationship with Jesus. Without a living relationship with Jesus, a key part of our inner being is dead. He and He alone is the Bread of Life, the one who can take away our inner emptiness. That is what Jesus meant when He said, "He or she who drinks of the water that I shall give will never thirst again" Jn 4:14. He said that to a deeply needy woman, a woman who in order to fill the inner emptiness in her life had turned to sex and relationships. **She had had five husbands and was now living with yet another man.** But it hadn't brought her happiness. She arrived at the well all alone under the heat of the midday sun. The

---

"There is laid up for me the crown of righteousness, which the Lord, the righteous judge, will award to me on that day, and not only to me but also to all who have longed for his appearing." 2 Tim 4:8 RSV

134

other ladies had gone to it in the cool of the morning. Perhaps her sadness had left her unable to get up early, but most likely, she was too ashamed of her lifestyle to join the other ladies. She was an outcast, a woman of ill-repute, a person that respectable women avoided. So she went to the well when nobody else would be there - but Jesus was waiting for her. He told her her life story. **While still in her mortal body she had her 'life-review''.** "Come, see a man who told me everything I ever did," she later told her neighbours, (John 4:29).

Barbara Harris Whitfield had the experience of being totally loved by God while experiencing her life-review during a near-death experience. But the woman at the well, a woman who had had five husbands, and so presumedly five divorces, and who was now living with another man, had this experience while still in her mortal body. She felt totally loved by Jesus even as she was shown the full truth about her sad life.

Jesus effectively told her, **"I am the one who can take away your terrible inner emptiness. I am the one who can take away the shame and give you new life."** Following her meeting with Jesus, the change in her was quickly obvious. The woman who had been too ashamed to join the other women in drawing water, went straight back and started witnessing to the whole town. That is the sort of change that happens when one truly encounters Jesus.

I too am a witness to the power of Jesus to take away inner emptiness. In my book, **"Answering God's Call"**, I have told my own story:- the struggle with inner emptiness, the struggle with suicidal desires, and then the night back in 1972 when God's love was poured into my heart, followed by coming to a deep sense of the indwelling Jesus. From my own personal experience of meeting Jesus and gradually learning what it is to walk with Him, I know that everything I write in this book about God's transforming love is true.

That does not mean that I was ready for Heaven in 1972? Far from it!! I still had many problems to deal with, much personal transformation to undergo. Likewise the woman at the well had encountered Jesus, but there was still work for her to do. She was no longer in danger of eternal damnation, and, if she continued her faith journey in any realistic way, no longer in danger of ending in the lower depths of Purgatory, but she still had quite an ongoing transformation to undergo before being ready for Heaven. She still had to reach out to those she had hurt, and she still had to do what was in her power to break the cycle of hurting in her family. There was work still to be done - either in this life or in the next life.

Yet to be ready to go to Heaven the very moment we die is within our grasp. Indeed to be able to so live that not merely will we go to Heaven the moment we

— —

"Whoever drinks of the water that I shall give will never thirst; the water that I shall give him will become in him a spring of water welling up to eternal life." John 4:14 RSV

die, but that we will be so open to God, that we will be able to spend our time in Heaven bringing blessing on earth is within our grasp. It is totally possible for us. If we decide that that is what we want, and then take the necessary steps to cooperate with the work of Jesus in our lives, then it will happen. The good news is that we don't even have to do the work ourselves, we just have to allow Jesus to do it for us and within us. But allowing Jesus to do it for us and within us, does involve practical steps on our part. **It is also most important that we not fool ourselves.**

Jesus said, "You shall love the Lord your God with all your mind, with all your heart, with all your soul and with all your strength" Luke 10:27 Jesus said that this was the first and most important commandment. He didn't say that was just for holy people. **He said that this was the very first COMMANDMENT.**

If you truly love someone, it will be felt deeply in your heart.
If you truly love someone, it will be expressed in the way you live.
If you truly love someone, spending time with them will be a joy.
If you truly love someone, you will often be thinking of them.
If you truly love someone, you will desire to please them.
If you truly love someone, you will seek to live by their standards,
even if their standards are high.
If you truly love someone, you will have their picture in a prominent place.
If you truly love someone, you will read what they have to say.
If you truly love someone, you will look forward to going to places
where you know that you will meet them.
If you truly love someone, you will not be ashamed to stand for them
or to speak on their behalf.

How can I claim to love God if I have time to read newspapers
or to watch TV soaps, but haven't time to pray? It is a nonsense!
How can I claim to love God, if I don't desire to grow in my
relationship with Him? Again it is a nonsense!
How can I claim to love God, if I rarely think about Him?
Again it is a nonsense!
How can I claim to love God, yet elevate following MY 'conscience' over
keeping HIS commandments? Again it is a nonsense!
How can I claim to love God, if I do not experience a desire to love and to
nourish all of His children? Again it is a nonsense!
How can I claim to love God, if I do not desire to introduce my family
and friends to Him. Again it is a nonsense!
How can I claim to love God, if I am living in a way that clearly contradicts
His teaching? Again it is a nonsense!

— —

"Believe in Me and out of your heart will flow rivers of living water."
John 7:38

136

How can I claim to love God, if I do not go where He has promised to be. Again it is a nonsense! How can I claim to love God, if I am not prepared to open to His light the full truth about my life, including the hurt I have caused to others.

There are, of course, degrees of love. It is possible to love God in one's heart while still compromising, or still confused in one's thinking, or still not measuring up to the true objective standard of love. But if one truly loves God, these imperfect responses will be gradually dealt with - though it may take years.

Many people believe in God, but they do not love Him. Before my experience of coming to a living relationship with Jesus in 1972, and of Him coming alive in my heart, I believed in God, I prayed regularly, I tried to keep the commandments, but I neither loved Him, nor had His love been poured into my heart.

Either you are in love with someone or you are not. If you are in love with God, then you will know it in your heart. The title of one of my little booklets is, **"The World's Most Amazing Experience - To have Jesus come alive within you."** Having Jesus come alive within you truly is the world's most amazing experience. It is the beginning of Heaven on earth. There is nothing else that this world has to offer that can compare with it. Only then do you understand what Jesus meant when He said, "I am the bread of life" and again what He meant when He said, "He or she who drinks of the water that I shall give will never thirst again." Our eternal spirit needs Jesus and was made for eternal union with Him.

Our mortal body has a hunger for a relationship with an earthly mate or spouse. But that hunger in our mortal body for an earthly companion is nothing to the hunger that is in our eternal spirit for Jesus. Having an earthly companion may lessen the intensity with which our eternal spirit experiences the craving for Jesus, but it does not take it away. But having a living relationship with Jesus is such that, if it truly blossoms in our spirit and then bubbles up into our heart and mind, it can take away our need for an earthly companion. We will then have a new capacity to love, and be able to bring this love to others, but we will no longer need the love of others in the same way. For us, Jesus suffices! Jesus becomes our everything! Our life centres around Him!

Then life itself takes on a new perspective. One experiences in a practical way what it is to truly be in love with Jesus; to truly love God with all one's mind, all one's heart, all one's soul and all one's strength. One experiences a whole new set of priorities. As Jesus becomes bigger and bigger in one's heart, other things grow smaller and smaller. One still sees the important things. Indeed one has more time for the important things, because the unimportant lose their meaning.

"He who loves father or mother more than me is not worthy of me; and he who loves son or daughter more than me is not worthy of me."
Mt 10:37 RSV

137

For example, I was once an avid newspaper reader, and that did have its place in my emotional and mental development. It is not good for a young person to be too quickly separated from the cut and thrust of debate. But as my relationship with Jesus developed and so too did my prayer time, my time for reading newspapers got less and less. When people became aware that I had stopped reading 'the papers', some felt a need to warn me that I would end up out of touch. Out of touch with what? It is now many years since I last bought a secular newspaper and I never felt more in touch with all that is important.

The one thing a person needs to be in touch with is one's eternal spirit. If one is not in touch with one's eternal spirit, then one is not in touch. **There is no person so out of touch as the person who is out of touch with their own eternal spirit.** And if one's eternal spirit is not in touch with God, then it is not in touch. But if one is in touch with one's eternal spirit, and if one's eternal spirit is in touch with God, preferably through a living relationship with Jesus, then one is in touch with what gives life meaning and direction. Then, too, one receives the strength to be in touch with everything that is important in life.

One does not, however, cut oneself off from reality. For example, I time my morning shave for when the radio news is on, and my supper for the shorter TV news in the evening, but that is it. Sometimes when I am giving Parish Missions, my host will present me with the daily newspaper - at least on the first morning! Sometimes I may glance through it for ten or fifteen minutes, but I will always come away with a sense of time and energy lost. It has reached the stage where my spirit will experience heaviness almost as soon as I pick the paper up. My spirit knows the truth. My spirit knows where the true source of life is - and it is not in the secular newspapers! Once recently when I picked up a Sunday newspaper, I suddenly got this tremendous realisation that there is more print in that particular paper, (and in many Sunday newspapers), than in the entire New Testament. Yet many have time to read a number of Sunday newspapers, but few have time to read even one chapter of the New Testament. Who then is out of touch with the source of life? Who truly loves God?

Those who do not experience this intimacy with God often have to find endless ways to fill their time. In Ireland we have a phrase for this:- "a good way to kill an hour". This phrase sums up exactly what is involved - killing time. For those who truly love God, there is no need to 'kill' time unless they are in extreme isolation. Time on one's own becomes instead a deeply valued opportunity to enter into communion with God.

——— —— —— —— —— —— —— —— —— —— —— —— —— —— —— —— —— —— —— ——

"I call heaven and earth to witness against you this day, that I have set before you life and death, blessing and curse; therefore choose life, that you and your descendants may live, loving the Lord your God, obeying his voice and cleaving to him, for that means life to you." Deut 30:19-20 RSV

God's Masterplan For Us

God's masterplan for us can be summed up as follows:-

Step 1. Jesus comes to live in our hearts.

Step 2. We learn to cooperate with Jesus in growing in our relationship with Him, and in becoming open to inner transformation.

Step 3. We become the hands of Jesus, the feet of Jesus, the eyes of Jesus, the ears of Jesus and the voice of Jesus in today's world.

Step 4. We continue to grow in our relationship with Jesus, and to become open to the transformation of our inner selves until such time as we are living in deep union with Jesus.

Step 5. We further continue this process until we more and more become the living presence of Jesus. Jesus speaks of this as "living in Me".

Using simple language that would have been understood by the people of His time, Jesus set out this masterplan using the image of the vine and the branches.

"I am the true vine, and my Father is the vinedresser. Every branch of mine that bears no fruit, he takes away, and every branch that does bear fruit he prunes that it may bear more fruit. You are already made clean by the word which I have spoken to you. Abide in me, and I in you. As the branch cannot bear fruit by itself, unless it abides in the vine, neither can you, unless you abide in me. I am the vine, you are the branches. He who abides in me, and I in him, he it is that bears much fruit, for apart from me you can do nothing. If a man does not abide in me, he is cast forth as a branch and withers; and the branches are gathered, thrown into the fire and burned. If you abide in me, and my words abide in you, ask whatever you will, and it shall be done for you. By this my Father is glorified, that you bear much fruit, and so prove to be my disciples." John 15:1-9 RSV

Things To Note From This Reading

1. The unity between the branch and the vine tree is to be our unity with Jesus. Either we are in union with Jesus or we are worthless.

2. It is the branches that bear the fruit, not the trunk. If there is to be fruit, it has to come through us. Remember that the next time you hear someone say, "I don't know why God doesn't step in and ...." We are the one's who are called to 'step in' and to implement God's will in today's world.

"He who conquers, I will grant him to sit with me on my throne, as I myself conquered and sat down with my Father on his throne." Rev 3:21 RSV

3. Jesus speaks of us "abiding in Me" or "living in Me". It is not just Jesus living in our hearts, but us learning what it is to live in Jesus. For this to happen, we need to be "born again of water and the Holy Spirit"; that is we need a complete inner transformation. We do not abide in Jesus as long as sin (contrariness, judgementalism, pride, bitterness, selfishness, lust, etc. etc.) are given permission to abide in us.

4. It is when we learn to "abide in Jesus" or "live in Jesus' that we will begin to bear fruit. "He who abides in me, and I in him, he it is that bears much fruit, for apart from me you can do nothing" John 15:5

5. It is when we learn to "abide in Jesus" or "live in Jesus' that we see our prayers answered again and again. "If you abide in me, and my words abide in you, ask whatever you will, and it shall be done for you" John 15:7.

6. Our union with Jesus is a bit like the blood flowing from our heart into our body. At this moment one's body gets the blood it needs for this moment. It does not get tomorrow's blood now. It continues to get the blood only so long as it remains in union with the heart. So too living in union with Jesus is something that has to be lived continuously, one moment at a time. It always involves looking towards Jesus, not self; glorifying Jesus, not self.

God is love. One cannot live in union with Him without committing oneself to a totally love centred life; without seeking to embrace love, to be transformed by love, to live in union with Love, and to be the living presence of Love in the world. God's commandments spring from love, and are designed to lead us into love. So having outlined His masterplan for us living in Him, Jesus then immediately links this teaching to living a life of love and to keeping the commandments. Living in union with Him, demands both embracing a love centre life and keeping the commandments.

"As the Father has loved me, so have I loved you; abide in my love. If you keep my commandments, you will abide in my love, just as I have kept my Father's commandments and abide in his love. These things I have spoken to you, that my joy may be in you, and that your joy may be full. This is my commandment, that you love one another as I have loved you. Greater love has no man than this, that a man lay down his life for his friends. You are my friends if you do what I command you. ..... You did not choose me, but I chose you and appointed you that you should go and bear fruit and that your fruit should abide; so that whatever you ask the Father in my name, he may give it to you. This I command you, to love one another." John 15:9 -14, 16-17, RSV.

Here we have the fullness of God's masterplan set out for us. It is beautiful. It is very challenging, and indeed gets more challenging as we study the implications.

- -

"Bless those who persecute you; bless and do not curse them"
Romans 12:10 RSV.

But it is also truly awesome. **You are called to become the living presence of Jesus in the world.** This, in a secondary sense, is the new incarnation. Jesus desires to be born again in us and through us. Human flesh and blood that we are, with bodies that once craved to sin, and that may still be that way inclined, Jesus is offering us the opportunity of total and immense transformation - and assuring us that we will come into it, if we are prepared to take the necessary steps to become open to His transforming power.

The visionary Anne speaks of God's rescue mission for the present era and how Jesus is coming back today. She says, "Jesus is returning as King. In this initial phase of the process, He returns through each one of us."

We have traditionally looked upon the return of Jesus as some big descent coming down from Heaven. Anne tells us that the way He is currently coming back is in the hearts and lives of those who are prepared to become His living presence in the world; those who are prepared to embrace what Jesus Himself called 'living in Him'. "Abide in Me and I will abide in you" John 15:4.

Anne says, "It is in this way that Jesus is restoring light to a world that has grown dark." She adds, "He is coming back in 'rescued people', one person at a time." In fact what Anne presents as God's Rescue Mission is the keystone of God's original masterplan or rescue mission - the only problem being that this keystone of God's masterplan, which we find especially in John's Gospel, and which St. Paul calls "the predetermined plan", has rarely been understood.

Through His death and resurrection, Jesus won for us, not just forgiveness for our sins, but the right to inner healing and transformation. See Romans 6. But the masterplan (or rescue mission) was even bigger than this. Jesus only came on earth once. **His masterplan however was that each of his followers become his living presence in the world.** This is what Jesus meant when He spoke of His followers doing even greater works once He went to the Father. While Jesus walked the earth, He could only live in one human body. Now He can live in every person who becomes truly open to Him.

There are different stages to this. First we invite Jesus to live within us, then we seek to become His living presence in the world. We set ourselves to become His hands and His feet. Jesus lived for thirty years as an ordinary person. He worked as a carpenter, tidied up after Himself, did all the usual household chores. So too we can be His hands and His feet in all the simple practical things of daily life. Even while we are still in need of much healing in our minds and hearts, we can still be His hands and feet in very practical ways.

The next step is to seek to become His eyes and ears. To become His eyes, we need to begin to see people as He sees them - with eyes of love. We cannot

— — — — — — — — — — — — .— — — — — — — — — — — — —

"For his sake, I have suffered the loss of all things, and count them as refuse, in order that I may gain Christ and be found in him" Philippians 3:8b RSV

become His eyes until all bitterness, judgementalism and prejudices have been dealt with. Having His eyes also involves having an eye for beauty and order, and also having a love for reading spiritual things. It also requires that we only read and watch what we are happy to have Jesus read and watch with us.

Becoming His ears, involves a growing capacity to listen to people. It also requires that we only listen to what we are happy to have Jesus listen to with us.

The next step is to seek to become His voice. What a see-change in speech that involves for many, even for many committed Christians. We can only truly become the voice of Jesus when there is a growing intimacy with Him in our hearts and minds and when we are being empowered by His love. God is love, but we find a thousand perfectly good reasons for replacing love with harshness in our daily transactions.

Only when the love of God has truly been poured into our hearts, and then we begin to act out of that love, and then on top of that, we begin to see the people around us as eternal spirits to be encouraged and helped on life's journey, will our voice even begin to be the voice of Jesus. The human heart and mind are very sensitive entities. There is a limit to what they can suffer before going into crisis mode. The person serving us in the shop or the person that we are serving, may have had a very bad day or a very tough life, or may just be very tired. A little thing may be enough to push him or her beyond their limits. Our calling is to approach every person with a desire to bring them blessing; to be bearers of love, not of pain and hurt.

One cannot truly become the voice of Jesus without also more and more becoming His heart and His mind. Many people have a devotion to the Two Hearts - the Immaculate Heart of Mary and the Sacred Heart of Jesus. But the union of the Immaculate Heart of Mary to the Sacred Heart of Jesus is a symbol of how our hearts are to be united with the Heart of Jesus. That requires a real inner transformation, identifying everything base or selfish in our hearts, and opening it to the light through Confession, then seeking to have our hearts cleansed and immersed in God's love.

Jesus called the Pharisees hypocrites, and even whitewashed sepulchres, because while they were good on the outside, their hearts had not been transformed. **If you desire to go to Heaven the moment you die, then seek the transformation of your heart.** Get in touch with what is happening in your heart. Get honest with yourself about selfishness, anger, greed, covetousness, lust, pride, laziness, indeed all the deadly sins. They are deadly because they poison the heart, and because if they control one's heart, then one's heart cannot be united with the

---

"A new heart I will give you, and a new spirit I will put within you; and I will take out of your flesh the heart of stone and give you a heart of flesh"
Ezekial 36:26 RSV

Heart of Jesus or become a temple of the Holy Spirit. The same applies to self-pity, meanness, self-seeking, selfish ambition, and cynicism.

God is love. God absolutely and utterly is love. He desires to pour His love into our hearts, but for that process to be completed, it is our task to recognise anything in our hearts that conflicts with love, and to bring it to the light so that we may be delivered from it. Yet even if there is much in your heart that needs to be brought to the light, do not allow satan to tempt you to despair. If you identify where you need conversion of heart, and then keep opening this to the light of Christ in Confession and again to His healing power in daily prayer, then have total trust in Jesus, for He can then work in you and through you even as you still struggle.

As well as having one's heart transformed, there is what St. Paul called 'having the mind of Christ' 1 Cor 2:16. That requires a complete make-over of our minds. "Be transformed by the renewal of your mind" Romans 12:2. The mind is super-active, always on the go, always coming up with fresh thoughts. Having it transformed is no easy task, yet once again the process is the same as with the transformation of our hearts:- learning to reflect on what is happening within our minds, to spot thoughts that are unworthy of a child of God and to bring them to the light. Renounce fearful or bitter thoughts, worrying, despair, judgementalism, acting on impulse, and sexual fantasising.

The second great movement that is required for one's mind to become the mind of Christ, is to move from thinking about self to seeing the bigger picture. Many deeply religious people remain very caught up in their own world. They may care for others, they may set out to do good, but in any given situation their minds are so caught up in their own concerns that they fail to see what is good and helpful for the people around them. It is like two people taking photographs. One is able to help the people being photographed to relax and smile. The other is totally caught up in his own task of taking the photo. Or like two people who at 10.30 pm think of making a phone call. One says to himself, "Perhaps someone is asleep" and leaves the phonecall until the next day. The other makes the phone call regardless - even if there is a young baby in the house. Or like two people driving down the street, when another person is seeking to enter the street from the side. On person rushes so that the person from the side street cannot get out ahead of him, the other stops and lets the person out. One could give example after example. To have "the mind of Jesus", we need to move from thinking of ourselves to be able to care for others in the practical situations of daily life.

Taking on the mind of Christ is truly a lifelong task. It requires such a miracle that it can only be lived one moment at a time, in deep union with Jesus Himself. That also means that every time we succeed in doing so, we are a living miracle.

"If anyone is in Christ, he is a new creation; the old has passed away, behold the new has come" 2 Cor 5:17 RSV

The Saints Knew This

I am not writing anything in this book that we do not find in the saints - when we start looking for it. The following quotations are just a tiny sample of the many quotations that I could have used. Some require meditation to grasp their meaning. Others are so simple that they just jump off the page. But they all confirm the five steps as set out in the previous chapter

Step 1. Jesus comes to live in our hearts.

Step 2. We learn to cooperate with Jesus in growing in our relationship with Him, and in becoming open to inner transformation.

Step 3. We become the hands of Jesus, the feet of Jesus, the eyes of Jesus, the ears of Jesus and the voice of Jesus in today's world.

Step 4. We continue to grow in our relationship with Jesus, and to become open to the transformation of our inner selves until such time as we are living in deep union with Jesus.

Step 5. We further continue this process until we more and more become the living presence of Jesus. Jesus speaks of this as "living in Me".

In St. Paul and St. John

"If any one is in Christ, he is a new creation; the old has passed away, behold, the new has come." 2 Cor 5:17 RSV

"It is no longer I who live, but Christ who lives in me" Galatians 2:20b RSV

"God is love and whoever abides in love abides in God, and God abides in him." 1 John 4:16 RSV

What The Early Christians in Jerusalem Were Told

"Now that you have been baptised into Christ and have put on Christ, you have been turned into the image of the Son of God. For God destined us to be his sons, so he has made us like to the glorious body of Christ. Hence, since you share in Christ, it is right to call you 'Christs' or anointed ones." Myst 3:1

What St. Hilary of Jerusalem said

"When Jesus was born as a man He took on human nature in such a way that it became inseparable from Himself, and He joined His human nature to his Divine nature in the sacrament of his flesh which He allows us to share. Therefore we are all one, because the Father is in Christ and Christ is in us. He is in us through the

"God in me! I in Him! Oh, this is my life!" St Elizabeth of the Trinity

flesh, and we are in Him; and, being united with Him, what we are is in God. He himself testified to us being in him through the sacrament by which we share in his flesh and blood when He said: '.... For I am in my Father, and you in me, and I in you.' ....

"We abide in Him and He abides in the Father, and while abiding in the Father He abides in us. In this way we are united with the Father. For while Christ is in the Father naturally ..., we too are in Christ naturally, since He abides in us naturally. How natural this union with Him is can be seen from his own words: 'He who eats my flesh and drinks my blood abides in me, and I in him'."

From his treatise on the Trinity, Bk 8:13-16

What St Elizabeth of the Trinity said,

"I think that in Heaven my mission will be to draw souls, by helping them go out of themselves to cling to God by a wholly simple and loving movement, and to keep them in this great silence within, that will allow God to communicate Himself to them **and transform them into Himself.**"

Again she said, "A soul united to Jesus is a living smile which radiates Him and which gives Him."

What St. Teresa of Avila said,

"Christ has no body on earth but yours,
No hands but yours,
No feet but yours,
Yours are the eyes through which Jesus wishes to look with compassion on the world.
Yours are the feet with which he desires to go about doing good.
Yours are the hands with which He desires to bless us now."

What Other Saints Said

"The Word of God, Jesus Christ, on account of His great love for mankind, became what we are in order to make us what He is Himself." **St. Iranaeus.**

"The Word of God became man that you may learn from a man how a man becomes a God." **St Clement of Alexandria**

"If a man no longer lives according to the flesh, but is led by the Spirit of God and is called son of God and is conformed to the image of God, he is described as a spiritual man. As the power of seeing is to be found in the healthy eye, so the working of the Spirit is to be found in the purified soul" **St Basil the Great**

"If we put aside the natural way of life, and surrender once and for all to the laws of the Spirit, it is incontrovertible that, by denying, in a sense, our own life and

— —

"He was made man that we might be made God." St. Athanasius

145

assuming the heavenly form of the Holy Spirit so that he becomes woven into our being, we are transformed, so to speak, into another nature. We are no longer just men but sons of God; we receive the name of heavenly men because we are made partakers of the divine nature." **St Cyril of Alexandria**

What Pope John Paul 11 said,

"The body, and it alone, is capable of making visible what is invisible, the spiritual and divine. It was created to transfer into the visible reality of the world, the invisible mystery hidden in God from time immemorial, and thus to be a sign of it." Pope John Paul 11, Feb. 20, 1980

St. Faustina's Prayer

Most Holy Trinity! As many times as I breathe, as many times as my heart beats, as many times as my blood pulsates through my body, so many thousand times do I want to glorify Your Mercy.

I want to be completely transformed into Your Mercy and to be Your living reflection, O Lord. May the greatest of all divine attributes, that of Your unfathomable Mercy, pass through my heart and soul to my neighbour.

Help me, O Lord, that my eyes may be merciful, so that I may never suspect or judge from appearances, but look for what is beautiful in my neighbours' souls and come to their rescue.

Help me, that my ears may be merciful, so that I may give heed to my neighbour's needs and not be indifferent to their pains and moanings.

Help me, O Lord, that my tongue may be merciful, so that I should never speak negatively of my neighbour, but have a word of comfort and forgiveness for all.

Help me, O Lord, that my hands may be merciful and be filled with good deeds, so that I may do only good to my neighbour and take upon myself the more difficult and toilsome tasks.

Help me, that my feet may be merciful, so that I may hurry to assist my neighbour, overcoming my own fatigue and weariness. My true rest is in the service of my neighbour.

Help me, O Lord, that my heart be merciful so that I myself may feel all the suffering of my neighbour. I will refuse my heart to no one. I will be sincere

— —

"It is not to remain in a golden ciborium that Jesus comes to us each day from heaven; it's to find another heaven, infinitely more dear to him than the first, the heaven of our soul, made to His image, the living temple of the adorable Trinity!" St Therese of Lisieux

even with those who, I know, will abuse my kindness. And I will lock myself up in the most merciful heart of Jesus, I will bear my own suffering in silence. May Your mercy, O Lord, rest upon me.
O my Jesus, transform me into yourself for you can do all things."
Diary 163

The bottom line and our mission impossible

Everything that I am writing in these chapters concerning the fivefold plan of Jesus is to be found in both the Sacred Scriptures and in the writings of the saints right down through the ages.

Our calling is nothing less than to become Jesus. Our personal identity still, of course remains, but just as Jesus was so united with the Father that He could say, "I and the Father are one" John 10:30, "the Father is in Me and I am in the Father" John 10:38 and 14:10, and "he who has seen Me has seen the Father" John 14:9; so too we are called to be so deeply united with Jesus, while yet maintaining our individual though transformed nature, that we can say, "Jesus and I are one," "Jesus is in me and I am in the Jesus", and "he who has seen me has seen Jesus".

That is our calling. There are no words to describe how awesome it is. Just look at your hands, and say to yourself, "these hands are meant to be the hands of Jesus". Then think of your voice, and say to yourself, with awe and trembling knowing how far short you have fallen, "this voice is meant to be the voice of Jesus."

This brings us face to face with our dilemma and our 'mission impossible':- before our voice can truly be the voice of Jesus, a mighty transformation needs to take place. We need to be utterly permeated by Love; to become so permeated by Love that we become love. This transformation is such that in human terms it is utterly impossible. We can only cry out with St. Faustina, **"O my Jesus, transform me into Yourself for You can do all things."** Diary 163

Yet we know that every moment we succeed in being united with Love and permeated by Love, we are being united with and permeated by the Power that created the universe. We also know that Love will always be stronger than evil, because God is love. Evil will have temporary victories. At the time, these victories may appear all powerful, but they are not. They are temporary. We must never give in to the temptation to fight evil with evil, for then evil is winning a victory in our own hearts. Instead, as we desire to become the living presence of Jesus, we seek to be totally permeated by Love, so that we become the living presence of Love in the world.

— —

"You are to become the body of Christ, his own flesh and blood."
(Pope Benedict speaking to the youth in Cologne.)

This Is Not Channelling

When we speak of Jesus living is us, and us becoming the living presence of Jesus, and becoming His hands and His voice, it is most important to realise that we are not talking about channelling.

Channelling is where people seek to open themselves to a spirit or an 'entity' as they tend to call them. In channelling, one seeks to act as a medium:- one seeks to allow an outside force to act through you. Sometimes this outside force is merely looked upon as an energy, and they may speak of "redirecting energy". No conversion is required for this process, no repentance for sin, no inner transformation. The true Jesus does not operate by channelling.

With Jesus it is totally different. We do NOT channel Jesus, though we are called to actually become a living channel; that is to actually become the living presence of Jesus. But we do not seek to act as a medium. What actually happens is much more profound. We seek to enter into a unity of love with Jesus. We seek to be penetrated right through by His love and His living presence; and then by the healing, cleansing and delivering power of the Holy Spirit. But that cannot happen without renouncing sin, and seeking to be delivered from it.

We speak of Jesus coming alive in our hearts. In reality what actually happens is more complex than that. Our heart is one of the key components of our spiritual soul through which our eternal spirit is conjoined to our mortal bodies. Our eternal spirit is spirit. It does not require our mortal body to exist, and will continue to exist when our mortal bodies die. **Our eternal spirit is capable of being utterly penetrated by the love of Jesus, leading to an intense union between our eternal spirit and Jesus.** When this happens, it will begin to impact on our spiritual soul - and the first place this is experienced is in our hearts. Thus we speak of Jesus living in our hearts - and indeed He does. When our eternal spirit is penetrated by God's love, our hearts become like a beautiful sittingroom with a warm fire - and the door open for Jesus to enter at any time.

Utterly unlike with channelling, the first step is repentance. The very first message preached by Jesus was, "Repent, for the kingdom of heaven is at hand" Mt 3:2 RSV. If there is big sin in your life, that is if, through your own fault, you have rejected God or brought serious hurt into the lives of others, it has to be repented of at a very early stage. Only then can your eternal spirit be penetrated by God's love. There is no other way. In the early stages, it does not have to be complete

---

"We were buried therefore with him by baptism into death, so that as Christ was raised from the dead by the glory of the Father, we too might walk in the newness of life." Romans 6:4 RSV

repentance. The complete recognition of all that is wrong in your life does not yet have to have taken place. But a certain basic degree of repentance is required. Where there is serious sin for which you are personally culpable, one cannot enter into this unity of love without at least a basic degree of repentance.

Where there isn't serious sin for which one is personally culpable, one may first be blessed with an experience of God's love, but to grow in this relationship, one needs ongoing inner conversion; gradually coming to recognise the full truth about one's life; gradually repenting of the totality of one's sinfulness; gradually coming into inner transformation. In this way one's mortal body is attuned to the relationship that now exists in one's eternal spirit with Jesus, and is attuned to God's will for one's life.

This is the total opposite to channelling, where there is often no recognition of sin, no call to repentance, and no inner conversion; often indeed the denial that there is such a thing as sin. For us, Jesus comes alive in our heart, but we do not channel Him. Instead we seek to be embraced and permeated by His love. What is involved is a unity of light and love.

Jesus came into the world through the incarnation. This could be referred to as primary incarnation:- Jesus, in the flesh, was truly man and truly God. We are called to live a life of deep union with Jesus, a union that is so deep, that Jesus Himself refers to it as "living in" Him or "abiding" in Him. This is possible by what could be termed "secondary incarnation". It is secondary incarnation in the sense that we do not become by our nature truly God; but it is incarnation in the sense that first our spirit and then our spiritual soul is penetrated and dyed through and through by God's love to such an extent that we become His living presence in the world.

Instead of operating as a medium, one is entering into deep union with Jesus, and He is transforming us, so that our very nature becomes more and more akin to His nature. In this unity of love and unity of spirit that grows and develops, we become His living presence in the world:- our heart becomes united with His heart, our mind becomes more and more His mind, and then our hands can be His hands, our feet His feet, our eyes His eyes, our ears His ears, our voice His voice. Is it any wonder that Jesus said that one needed to be born again to enter the kingdom of Heaven? In a very real sense the caterpillar has to turn into the butterfly, and a mighty metamorphosis is needed. Before we enter Heaven, our eternal spirit needs total transformation. If we walk with Jesus, this transformation will happen in this life - a transformation that begins with our inner spirit, or as we usually say, in our hearts, and then radiates to embrace our entire being.

— —

"The harder we strive in this world to give ourselves to the precepts of God, the more blessed shall we be in the life to come and the greater will be the glory which we attain in God's presence" St Ambrose.

149

Being Embraced By Love

"God is love" 1 John 4:16. That is the very essence of God. It is His very nature. At the heart of every genuine spiritual experience is a sense of being embraced by Love. At His Baptism in the Jordan, Jesus was embraced by the Father's love, "Thou art my beloved Son; with thee I am well pleased." John 1:11 RSV

Our eternal spirit was created for love. It has the capacity to be penetrated and permeated by love. In Heaven everybody is embraced by love and radiates love. Don Piper, in describing his experience of being ninety minutes at the gates of Heaven, says, "I felt loved - more loved than ever before in my life. ... When they gazed at me, I knew what the Bible means by perfect love. It emanated from every person who surrounded me. I stared at them, and as I did, I felt as if I absorbed their love for me."

In God's plan for us, that is His plan to redeem us, we can experience a very real foretaste of this tremendous love even while here on earth. In my own case, at the time of my spiritual experience in 1972, I was still full of anger and bitterness, and it took me many years to even desire to forgive those who had hurt me. By my slowness to forgive, I greatly slowed my own spiritual growth.

But it was Jesus who loved me first! The love of God was literally poured into my heart - even while I was still very much a sinner.
"We love, because He first loved us." 1 John 4:19 RSV
"God's love has been poured into our hearts through the Holy Spirit who has
      been given to us." Romans 5:5 RSV
"While we were yet sinners, Christ died for us" Romans 5:8b RSV

Jesus loves you. Jesus absolutely loves you. The heart of the Christian life is having one's inner being permeated and penetrated by Love, and then learning to be a bearer of this love. One of the three original secular meanings of the word, 'baptism', is to be flooded. In Baptism in the Spirit, our heart is meant to be flooded with the love of God and the living presence of Jesus.

It is only possible to truly love after one has been loved. This is true of ordinary human love in the first place. In the natural order of things, a child is meant to have a profound experience of being loved by its parents. If it receives this love, then it will be enabled to love others. If this love is missing, then it will be very hard for the child to love; though where a child isn't loved, all is not lost, because God can still step in with His love - and will do so if given the opportunity.

--- --- --- --- --- --- --- --- --- --- --- --- --- --- --- --- --- ---

"Beloved, let us love one another; for love is of God, and he who loves is born of God and knows God. He who does not love does not know God; for God is love." 1 John 4:7 RSV

Divine love is greater than human. It enables us to live at a new level, one that is heroic. Divine love, unlike human love, can be poured right into a person's heart. More correctly we could speak of it being poured into our eternal spirit, and of it then bubbling up or effusing up into one's heart. But how can we have it poured into our hearts? This is something which we cannot do for ourselves - or for anyone else. It is totally a gift from God; the work of Jesus and of the Holy Spirit. There are however things that we can do to become open to the gift.

1. Thirst

Right now the great Eternal Love is right there with you. Pause, allow your mind and heart to have a sense of being before the great Eternal Love, the almighty Love that created the universe. Desire to be embraced by this Infinite Love, to be penetrated and permeated by this Infinite Love, which is God.

"My soul thirsts for God, to experience the living God" Psalm 42:2

"O God, you are my God, I long for You,
My inner being thirsts for You,
My body cries out for You,
Just like the desert lands thirst for water. Psalm 63:1

When a person's spirit thirsts in this way, of course Jesus will respond. Jesus gave a personal promise on this himself. "If any one thirsts, let him come to me and drink. As the Scriptures promise, the one who believes in Me, 'rivers of living water shall flow from his heart'." John 7:37-38

So, if there is emptiness in your inner self, focus it totally on Jesus and on the eternal Love which is the Holy Spirit. If you feel inner loneliness, focus it totally on Jesus and on the eternal Love. Instead of feeling sorry for yourself, instead of saying "Nobody ever visits me" or "Nobody cares", start crying out, **"Jesus come to me. Flood me with your love".**

I say that as one who once felt such inner emptiness that it was like as if there was a bottomless hole deep within me. If you feel empty, it is Jesus coming alive within you that you need. It is the pouring of God's love into your heart that you need. Start inviting Jesus to come alive in your heart. You can use simple words like, **"Lord Jesus, I invite you to come alive in my heart. Make your home within me. I am sorry for all my sins. Heal and cleanse my heart, Lord Jesus, so that it will be a fitting home for You to live in."**

2. Seek Jesus Where He Is To Be Found

Jesus is indeed to be found in many places, especially in Mass and in Eucharistic Adoration, but some people, before they are able to commune with Him in these

---

"When you seek me with all your heart, you will find me, says the Lord"
Jer 29:13b-14a RSV.

places, need an actual experience of His love first. This may happen at a Prayer Meeting where people have expectant faith, or during Life in the Spirit Seminars where these are being run with expectant faith, or at Healing Services where these are being led with expectant faith, or at an event like a Marriage Encounter Weekend, or at places of pilgrimage where there is expectant faith - places like Medjugorje. These events act very much like the ignition on a gas cooker. All the parts are in place on the gas cooker, but even after the gas starts to flow, a spark is still needed to ignite the gas into a flame. So too your inner spirit, in some mysterious way, needs to have the presence of Jesus and the outpouring of the Holy Spirit ignited in a moment of special grace that most often occurs in an atmosphere of expectant faith.

3. Trust Jesus

If you have invited Jesus into your heart, then He has come!! Start trusting that that is so. Perhaps you will later experience an explosion of His love. It is beautiful when that happens, but remember Jesus is pure spirit. The explosion of His love, the sense of heat, while they certainly have a profound impact and bring very real healing, are not strictly necessary for Jesus to come alive in your heart. And while yes, I did have such an experience in 1972, that is now way back in the last millennium, and Jesus still lives in my heart today without any further experiences of heat.

Start trusting that Jesus has answered your prayer, that your eternal spirit has now been embraced by His love, and that you will grow in your relationship with Him over time, and that, if you continue in this path, Jesus will bless you in the ways most appropriate to your needs when the time is right.

4. Keep Embracing Love

"God is love" 1 John 4:16. We cannot be attuned to God without ourselves growing more and more in our capacity to love. "He who does not love does not know God; for God is love" 1 John 4:7 RSV. We cannot become the living presence of Jesus in the world without becoming the living embodiment of love in the world, for God is love. We are called to love as Jesus loved; to be a person of love in every situation. That is why it is so important to renounce bitterness, judgementalism, and prejudice. When hurt, learn to feel the pain, but do not let bitterness poison your spirit.

There are different kinds of love. There is how the ordinary person loves. That too comes from God, but it can be very limited. It is usually linked to the other person's worthiness of being loved, and can sometimes be quite selfish. It can love one person at the expense of another; it can be jealous, controlling, possessive,

---

"Believe that He loves you. He wants to help you Himself in the struggles which you must undergo." St. Elizabeth of the Trinity

insensitive, and can become quite bitter if unrequited. Those who operate out of God's love, on the other hand, desire the best for all people, even their enemies. Divine love is not dependent on the other person being nice or good. It does not seek for itself, and is not jealous or possessive or controlling, nor is it dependent on being requited.

To begin to take on the nature of God, (and to be ready to go to Heaven the very moment we die), we need to learn to love the Divine Way, yet this kind of loving is beyond our capacity. It is only possible when we are empowered by Love; when God's love has been poured into our hearts; when our eternal spirit is being baptised in love and permeated by love. This is the perfection to which we are called, not a perfection of outward performance, but one of being transformed by love. Coming into this union of love with Jesus requires a lengthy process of growth and of inner transformation. Whereas you may be tempted to beat yourself up over the times you fall short, Jesus will rejoice over every step you take. He will rejoice over every time that you succeed in moving to another level of loving, and over every act of love and kindness rendered along the way.

You will later discover that your every act of love and your every loving word, has an eternal significance. Some people, during their near death experiences have been shown how simple acts of love can start a process of love that just spreads out and out. Likewise, when we hurt people, that can cause a wave of satanic hurt to start spreading out to many people and a cycle of satanic hurt to start spreading down to future generations. But when we act in a loving way, that can start a wave of Godly love to spread out to others and a cycle of Godly love to spread down through the generations.

There will inevitably be people who will hurt us and people, perhaps even Christian leaders, whose actions we find incomprehensible. Our human nature will instinctively react negatively to them. When that happens, become aware of God's love for them, even mentally picture His love embracing them, and then seek to be united with His love. In uniting with God who is love, and in drawing your capacity to love from Him, another mighty victory for His kingdom will be taking place in your eternal spirit, and both your inner spirit and your spiritual soul will be being transformed by Love.

So seek to become love, for God is love.

— —

"If you love those who love you what reward have you? Do not even the tax collectors do the same? And if you salute only your brethren, what more are you doing than others? Do not even the Gentiles do the same? You, therefore, must be perfect, as your Heavenly Father is perfect."
Mt 5:46-48 RSV

What is Baptism in the Spirit?

Nicodemus was a deeply religious man, a man of prayer, a man who sought to live by God's teaching. Yet Jesus told him that he needed to make a complete fresh start; to be born again of water and the Holy Spirit. He needed to be transformed from the heart, to be embraced and permeated by love, and to learn to live a love centred life. We can best understand what Jesus meant by 'Baptism in the Spirit' and being 'born again of water and the Holy Spirit' if we understand how the word 'baptism' was then understood. Before the word Baptism came to be used in the religious sense, it was a secular word with three different meanings. The three original secular meanings of the word 'baptism' were,

1. To be immersed (or dipped into),
2. To be flooded,
3. In the textile industry for a garment to be dyed right through.

To Be Immersed

In Baptism, one's spirit dipped into the death and resurrection of Jesus. This has immense significance. St. Paul asks, "Do you not realise that when you were united with Jesus in Baptism, you were immersed into His death? Being immersed into His death, you can be transformed by the power of His resurrection, and so be enabled to live the new life. Jesus took with Him to the cross all your sinfulness, so that you might be set free from the power of sin." Romans 6:3-6

Jesus by His death has won for us the right to be set free of our compulsive and sinful tendencies. The victory is already there for us in Christ Jesus. But we need to take the steps to become open to it. An important element of Baptism in the Spirit is learning to take the steps to become open to this transforming power of Jesus. Instead of striving for perfection by one's own power, one identifies one's weaknesses and learns to open them for healing to the transforming power of Jesus. See the steps for healing on page 119.

To Be Flooded

A second original meaning of the word 'baptism' was to be flooded. In Baptism in the Spirit, our inner spirit needs to be permeated (flooded) by God's love, and then by the indwelling Jesus. This is for everyone - including you. In the words of Jesus, it is for "**anyone** (who) thirsts" and for "**whoever** drinks".
"**Whoever** drinks of the water that I shall give will never thirst again. The water

— —

"May Christ dwell in your hearts through faith, so that you, being rooted and grounded in love, .. may know the love of Christ which surpasses knowledge, and be filled with all the fulness of God." Eph 3:17-19

that I shall give him will become in him a spring of water welling up to eternal life" (John 4:14).

"**If anyone thirst**, let him come to Me and drink .... out of his heart shall flow streams of living water" (John 7:38).

Early saints, like St. **Hilary of Poitiers**, spoke of the streams of living water flowing from one's heart once one comes to a living relationship with Jesus. Around 365, he wrote, "When someone has drunk from the water of the Lord, then streams will flow from the heart of that person. So make sure that you drink the water of the Lord, so that the rivers will flow" (Tract on the Psalms).

To Be Dyed Right Through

The third original secular meaning of the word baptism was for a garment to be dyed right through. Just as the dye goes right through the garment, so too in our case, our entire being needs to be penetrated through and through by the healing, cleansing and delivering power of the Holy Spirit. I use the three words deliberately:- healing, cleansing, and delivering. In some parts of our inner selves, we require healing. We also need inner cleansing:- our memories, our conscience, and sometimes our hormones and emotions need cleansing. If we have compulsive tendencies, big or small, (and who doesn't have compulsive tendencies?) we need deliverance.

One may occasionally be touched by this healing, cleansing and delivering power by the direct gift of the Holy Spirit. When that happens, it is often like a current passing through one's body, and afterwards one knows that one has been healed, cleansed and delivered in, at least, a specific area. I experienced that in the area of my sexuality, which for years was a real struggle for me. While spending a couple of days in prayer by the seaside back around 1984, I happened to open a book. The words, "Celibacy is a gift" really lit up. At the same moment, it was as if a current passed right through my body cleansing me and setting me free from sexual compulsions.

In every other area of my life I had to learn how to become open to the healing, cleansing and delivering power of the Holy Spirit, identifying the areas in which I most needed it, and then learning how to become open to His power to set me free. The image the early Church Fathers used for this process was of putting a piece of iron into a fire, something they were very familiar with. As the heat penetrated the iron to its core, it became bright all through. This is the way the Holy Spirit works in the inner person.

Footnote
For a fuller treatment of Baptism in the Spirit and how to become open to it, see my booklet, "The World's Most Amazing Experience - to have Jesus come alive within you."

— —

"As the Father has loved me, so have I loved you; abide in my love."
John 15:9 RSV

Learning To Live As God's Child

In her early days in Calcutta, a journalist visited Mother Theresa, and was shocked and even repulsed by the condition of the homeless dying people that Mother Theresa was helping. "I would not do that for a thousand dollars" the journalist exclaimed. "I wouldn't do it for a million dollars!" Mother Theresa replied, but holding up her crucifix, she continued, "However I am happy to do it for Him."

When we learn to live as a child of God, it has a profound impact on how we see reality. The New Testament teaches what it is be a child of God, but there are four reasons why we Catholics are poor when it comes to reading the Bible.

1. There is no tradition of reading the Bible in most of our families.

2. The New Testament only begins to make sense when we not merely come to a living relationship with Jesus, but also begin to learn what it is to live in Jesus and to have one's life transformed by Him. Many passages in the New Testament are about having this relationship with Jesus, about living in Him, about having one's life transformed, but, if we are not experiencing these realities, how can these passages light up for us? Instead they just pass over our heads and become boring religious jargon.

3. The Christian is called to a heroic lifestyle that is only possible if one is having one's life transformed by Jesus. The challenges of this heroic lifestyle are set out by Jesus in the New Testament, but unless one is being empowered by Jesus, the standards just appear like impossible ideals. The New Testament will inevitably be boring to the person who is not trying to live by its teachings.

4. There are a small number of words in the New Testament that can best be understood when we understand their background - like the word 'baptism' Understanding the full significance of this one word opens up whole areas of both the spiritual life and the New Testament to us.

The New Testament sets out the teaching for how the child of God is to live. If we begin to live by this teaching, then it most certainly will not be boring. Who could call seeking to live by the "turning the other cheek" principle boring? Who could call phrases like "Unless you forgive others their trespasses, neither will your Heavenly Father forgive you yours" boring? Who could call the instruction that

— —

"**A new commandment I give to you, that you love one another; even as I have loved you, that you also love one another**" John 13:34 RSV

if your right hand causes you to sin, you are to cut it off, boring? Who could call the instruction that if you look at a woman lustfully, you have already committed adultery with her in your heart, boring? Who could call the instruction to love your enemies, boring?

The only person who could call these and the many other instructions in the New Testament boring is the person who is not seeking to live by them. Walking as a child of God is challenging. It is the spiritual equivalent of setting out to climb the highest mountain in the world, and who could call that boring?

Then there is the instruction that if at the altar you remember that your brother has something against you, you are to go first and be reconciled with your brother, then come back and bring your offering. An ancient Church document called "The Teaching of the Twelve Apostles, states "If any person has a quarrel with a friend, let him not join your assembly until they are reconciled, that your sacrifice may not be defiled." Think of how challenging that is! Think too of the change it would make within our communities if we started to live it!

To be a child of God, we need to take seriously and to seek to implement every sentence of Jesus recorded in the New Testament. Some small sections of St. Paul, like the instruction for ladies not to speak in Church, are related to the culture of his time, but apart from that, to be a child of God and to be ready to go to Heaven the very moment we die, we need to take seriously and to seek to implement the full teaching of the New Testament.

Of course, this is not possible by our own power. Indeed by our own power it is utterly impossible. To ask people to live by the teaching of the New Testament out of their own power, would be to place an impossible burden on their shoulders - and sometimes that happens. But this heroic living is possible by the power of Him who lives within us and only by the power of Him who lives within us - and then only when we begin to allow Him to transform our lives. Of course, we will fail and fall short many times. But the only person who truly fails is the one who gives up trying.

Sometimes Jesus was very explicit about what makes a person a child of God. "Blessed are the peacemakers, for they shall be called sons of God" Matthew 5:9 RSV. **If you desire to be a child of God, then become a peacemaker.** This may involve allowing oneself to be wronged. It will often involve letting things 'go', and a conscious decision to not return fire with fire, or evil with evil, or harshness with harshness.

Again Jesus said, "Love your enemies and pray for those who persecute you, so that you may be sons of your Father who is in Heaven; for he makes his sun rise on the evil and on the good, and sends rain on the just and on the unjust." Matthew

---

"If I speak in the tongues of men and of angels, but have not love, I am a noisy gong or a clanging cymbal. 1 Cor 13:1 RSV

5:44-45 RSV   This contrasts radically with the imperfect understanding of God we find in many parts of the Old Testament, which states, "On the wicket he will rain coals of fire and brimstone" Psalm 11:6 RSV. Running through large parts of the Old Testament is this belief that God punishes the bad. It is so ingrained into us that this is God's nature that we fail to see what Jesus actually said; that the Father "makes his sun rise on the evil and on the good, and sends rain on the just and on the unjust" (Mt 5:44-45), and that to be children of the Father, we too need to love those who are evil and unjust.

Unfortunately the parts of the Old Testament that proclaim the imperfect understanding of a God who punishes the bad are large and colourful, and they are regularly read in our Churches without adequate comment - including on Holy Saturday night.   Only with Jesus was the true image of God revealed, but unfortunately his teaching is often 'missed', leaving people still believing in a God who deliberately steps in to punish the wicked.   This has very serious consequences. Those who believe in a God who zaps the bad, will have no difficulty in waging war or even in carrying out terrorist attacks in the name of that same God. Those who believe in a God who wants his enemies killed, will not take seriously a God who says "Love your enemies", nor will they see any contradiction between saying their prayers and being vicious to their neighbour.

Many people are so attuned to the imperfect understanding of God in the Old Testament with all its colourful stories, that they have never really heard the radical message of Jesus. **They neither know that God is love, nor do they begin to understand the type of love-powered life to which Jesus calls us.** They have yet to embrace the God who "makes his sun rise on the evil and on the good, and sends rain on the just and on the unjust" Mt 5:45.

Affirming that God causes His sun to rise on the evil as on the good, is not to deny that those who walk in union with Jesus will become open to special blessing, or to deny that they will see their prayers answered in special ways. God's desire is to bless all people, and those who walk with Him take steps that facilitate the outpouring of God's blessing, so they do see prayers being answered. But they will not be protected from the normal trials of life. **Life is almost like a challenge course.** I print the monthly magazine, The Curate's Diary on two old bangers of printing presses, and then put it into booklet form using two second-hand booklet makers. Every month there are new challenges with the machinery. It is almost as if it is being said to me, "Now that you have sorted that problem out, see if you can overcome this one." That is exactly like life. As soon as one succeeds in overcoming one challenge, one is faced with a new one. It is in overcoming these challenges that one's inner spirit matures and grows. So see life as a challenge.

"If I have prophetic powers, and understand all mysteries and all knowledge, and if I have all faith, so as to remove mountains, but have not love, I am nothing. I Cor 13:2 RSV

Let your spirit rejoice every time you overcome a difficulty. Look forward with confident expectation of being able to overcome the new ones. Along the way one will meet people who have ended up broken by life's challenges or by their own selfish choices. Jesus tells us not to judge. Suppose you knew a woman who had had five failed marriages and was now living with another man, would you judge her or speak ill of her? If so, the person you have judged is the woman with whom Jesus sat down at the well in Samaria. **This woman had her life-review, while still in the flesh, by the well in Samaria - and she too experienced God's unconditional love in Jesus.** After her life-review with Jesus, she rushed back to her village and told everyone, "Come meet the man who told me everything I ever did." She is the first mass evangelist in the New Testament. Her experience of the unconditional love of Jesus transformed her life.

God is love. To be bearers of God's love, we too need to love people unconditionally. Jesus said, "Judge not and you will not be judged" Mt 7:1. If you desire to be a true follower of Jesus, then renounce all judgementalism and start practising unconditional love. Unconditional love sounds like a lovely concept, but it means that you seek to love even those who are most unlovable - the outcast, the abusive person, the rude person, the impatient person, the vulgar person, the selfish person, the mean person, the murderer, the thief, the abuser. This is so challenging that your first instincts may be to say that it is impossible. **Yes, in human terms it is utterly impossible.** One cannot love like this out of human strength. But God is love. When we become truly united with Jesus who is love, then His love within us can enable us to love like this. "God is love and whoever abides in love abides in God, and God abides in him." 1 John 4:16 RSV

When we take this on board, it revolutionises both our understanding of God and of what it is to be a child of God. **It also goes so totally against human nature that inevitably we will fail a thousand times.** But every time we succeed, a mighty victory is being won for God's kingdom in our hearts, and our eternal spirit is more attuned to the nature of God, more ready for entry into Heaven, and indeed more ready for such union with God in Heaven that we will be able to continue to bring blessings upon earth.

This way of living involves a life of deep and ever growing union with Jesus. This in turn requires excellent channels of communication with Him:- that is regular quality prayer, regular reflection on His teaching especially those parts that we find most challenging, and regular opening of our inner selves to His power. It is not possible to live this life for one hour without this continuous interactive union with Jesus. But if we are living in union with Him, then we will begin to see ourselves bearing very real fruit, and we will begin to see our prayers being answered again and again.

— —

If I give away all I have, and if I deliver my body to be burned, but have not love, I gain nothing. I Cor 13:3 RSV

A Little Girl's Dreams

In 1980, Denise Curtis gave birth to their first son, Ian. Then thirteen months later David was born with a hare lip and a cleft gum. Denise says, "The deformity of his tiny face was overpoweringly brutal. At first glance it appeared that a part of the baby's face was missing." Later as she sat in the dim light by the incubator watching him, she says "with his disfigured mouth he reminded me of a tiny injured bird. I came face to face with life at its most precious and at its frailest and I felt my heart simply melting. I was irresistibly drawn by his utter helplessness."

The doctors told her that his face could be fixed when he reached ten pounds, but he was only five pounds, and feeding him was to prove an enormous problem because of his disfigured mouth. Then when at last he had the operation, it was discovered that he was semi paralysed down one side. Later it was discovered that there was a serious problem with his blood. A bone marrow test was necessary, and it had to be performed under local anaesthetic. What a horrific ordeal for a two year old!! It left him with a real fear of needles and of men in white clothes.

When the results came back, they were very bad. Instead of a platelet count of 300, his was just 21. Likewise he was not producing nearly enough red cells or white cells. He had what is called severe aplastic anaemia. He would need treatment all his short life. Five years later, a little sister Hannah was born. She too suffered from severe aplastic anaemia. Now parents, Bryan and Denise had two special needs children to rear, plus, of course, Ian, the older brother.

Bryan was then an agnostic, Denise a committed Catholic. A time came when Bryan, worn out by combining work with hospital visits, felt a need to get away for a couple of days rest. He opted for Yugoslavia. Medjugorje was in the news, and Denise put a rosary beads into his case in the hope that he might go there.

One evening, while he was away, Denise sat down with her three children for prayer at the hour of the claimed apparition in Medjugorje. She lit a candle, then started to lead the children in the sign of the cross. Suddenly David interrupted her, "Mummy, Mummy, look at the candle. It's just after flashing three lights!" Denise says, "We all looked at the candle and it was no different to any other evening it had been lit." When the others began to pray David, normally a fidget,

---

"She was more brilliant than the sun, and radiated a light more clear and intense than a crystal glass filled with sparkling water, when the rays of the burning sun shine through it. .... We were bathed in the light which surrounded her, or rather, which radiated from her."
Sr. Lucia describing the first apparition of Our Lady to the three children in Fatima

had his eyes gently closed and sat perfectly still without joining in.

"Mummy he's not praying with us," Ian retorted indignantly.

"Oh never mind just ignore him," Denise sighed.

When the others finished praying, David continued to sit quietly. An atmosphere of peace had descended on the room, and the others sat watching David. Eventually he opened his eyes and declared, "He's gone."

"Who is gone?" Denise asked.

"Jesus is gone!" David replied and proceeded to tell a remarkable story. "After the three flashes of light from the candle, I saw a mist. As the mist cleared, Jesus was standing beside the candle. He wore a white robe and He had wounds on His hands and His feet. He then spoke to me and said, 'You are to pray and say the Rosary. You are a son of Mary.'"

David added, "Jesus then showed me the world of Medjugorje, it was like a moving picture. I saw a church with two high steeples. I then saw Jesus standing beside my Daddy. Daddy was wearing a necklace around his neck with a cross on it. When he returns home he will be leading the rosary in our family."

Afterwards David, instead of being his usual hyper self, remained seated as Denise took Ian and Hannah to bed. He was still seated in profound silence when she came back. Denise gently and quietly took him by the hand, and in silence, brought him to bed, tucked him in and left him in silent contemplation.

Meanwhile Bryan was having a profound conversion experience in Medjugorje. He returned home wearing a rosary beads round his neck as a 'necklace', just as David had seen in his vision. One year later he was received into the Catholic Church, and yes, he now leads the family Rosary.

David packed a lot into his short life of ten years. At his funeral, Fr. Cannon said that David gave a new meaning to the word 'handicap'. A golfer is handicapped because he is better than everybody else; so too is a horse. That's the type of handicap David had, Fr. Cannon said.

His death, though expected, brought great grief to his family, including to his four year old sister Hannah. One day Denise walked into the lounge. Hannah was already in it, but didn't see her come in. Somehow Hannah was after climbing up and taking David's photo off the wall. Denise overheard her say, **"David it is time for you to come back home. Jesus has had you long enough. You have to ask him to send you back home again. Please go and tell Him now."**

Denise felt that Hannah needed time and space to grieve in her own way, so she slipped out of the lounge without being noticed. Early the following morning, Hannah came bounding into her bedroom, and climbing into bed beside her, proceeded to share a remarkable dream she was just after having. "I dreamt I was in heaven. **Mummy do you know that nobody speaks in heaven, but yet they**

"Whoever welcomes a little child like this in my name welcomes me"
Mt 18:5

all understand one another? I was playing with David. Then Mary called me to her by means of her finger and asked me whether I would like to play with the baby Jesus. I nodded. She didn't ask David only me. I held her hand and we went into the stable together. I knelt and played with the baby Jesus in the crib. When I came out I saw David standing there with a small crown on his head. Jesus stood on one side of him and Mary joined him on the other. Mummy, David had to stay with Jesus in heaven, but I knew that I had to come home again."

Remarkable Hannah's description of communication in Heaven matches perfectly that of those who have had profound near-death experiences:- "**Nobody speaks in heaven, but yet they all understand one another?**" And this from a four year old child after a dream. We are far closer to the other side, and the other side is far closer to us than we realise. The part in her dream about playing with baby Jesus in the crib, looks on the surface like an ordinary child's dream, yet it is highly theological. In Heaven the saints, amongst other things, contemplate on the life of Jesus - and this is exactly how a four year old girl might contemplate it.

Six weeks later Hannah had another dream. They had just come back from a holiday during which they stayed in a mobile home. Denise says, "I was putting Hannah to bed and I mentioned David to her. She became animated and said, 'Mummy, do you know where David lives?'
"Before I could reply 'Heaven', she continued, 'David lives in Jesus' Sacred Heart! When we were in the caravan I had a dream. I dreamt that I was standing on a hill. I watched while the soldiers were nailing Jesus to the Cross. I then began to cry'."
Hannah then interrupted her story to ask, "Mummy who is that man that stands beneath the Cross with Mary - is his name Peter?"
Denise explained that it was not Peter but John.
Hannah then continued, "Well when he saw me crying, he left Mary's side and walked up to me and held me in his arms whilst we both watched what the soldiers were doing to Jesus. Then when Jesus was dying and He couldn't hold up His arms any longer on the Cross, I saw David walk up to the Cross and he held and supported Jesus arms. When Jesus died, David disappeared into Jesus' Sacred Heart and they all went up to heaven."

She dreamt "David disappeared into Jesus' Sacred Heart." Barbara Harris Whitfield, during her near-death experience, was immersed into God's love and permeated by it. Those who die in openness to Jesus are immersed into Jesus, while yet retaining their own identity. The image of going into the Sacred Heart of Jesus is a perfect symbol of how they are embraced by His love. As to the bit about David going to hold up the arms of Jesus, at first one may say, "But His hands were nailed to the cross." That however is to miss the amazing symbolism:-

— —

"Since we are surrounded by this great cloud of witnesses, the saints, let us throw off everything that holds us back, especially sin, and putting our eyes on Jesus, let us run life's race with total commitment." Hebrews 12:1

that when our suffering is united to that of Jesus, we are indeed helping to hold up His arms; our suffering is an extension of the suffering of Jesus. **Again what an insight for a four year old. It shows how open four year olds are to God when given a chance.** It is just totally natural for them to know Jesus as their best Friend when given the chance to do so.

In 2007, I was speaking to a group of five year olds in Kinnegad, Ireland. When I was finished speaking, a little boy put up his hand and said, "God is omnipresent." What a big word for a five year old!! Thinking perhaps that he didn't know the meaning of the big word that he had used, I replied, "That means that God is everywhere", opening my arms wide to emphasise the point. "I know that!!" he replied, with almost a tone of disgust that I could have thought that he didn't.

Children, not merely have an amazing openness to God, but also an amazing openness to understanding spiritual things. Sadly, however, a great number of children are suffering spiritual neglect today. Many are not introduced to God at all. Others get a brief introduction but then are left to their own devices, without anyone to guide them. We have only to read the stories of Angie Fenimore and Barbara Harris Whitfield to see how sensitive a child's faith can be. Angie lost the ability to trust God when she didn't see her prayers for her parents answered. Barbara became an atheist when her prayers for her mother were not answered.

The title of the booklet which I hope to write by 2010 is **"What every child has a right to know"**. That includes that they have an eternal spirit; that God is love and that He really loves them; that Jesus is inviting them to a special relationship with Himself; and that He has a special plan for their lives. It also includes teaching them from their earliest years about the wonders of Heaven, about how part of their family is already in Heaven, and about how one can become a living saint.

If we ourselves are true children of God, then we will have an immense desire to help our young people come to know and love God, and for them to come to know how much He loves them. **If you do not have this desire, then you have either never really met Jesus or are only in the very early stages of walking with Him .** "Once I have Jesus, I have to bring Him to others" Mother Theresa.

Footnote

The full story of the life of David Curtis is told in Denise Curtis' beautiful book, "A Song For David". Published by and available from Lulu.com. The book also includes the account of successful search for a bone-marrow donor for Hannah, who is now a mature adult.

— — — — — — — — — — — — — — — — — — — —

"Jesus did many other signs in the presence of the disciples, which are not written in this book; but these are written that you may believe that Jesus is the Christ, the Son of God, and that believing you may have life in his name." John 20:31 RSV

The Living In Jesus Association

In 2006, I started a little association for those who would like to commit themselves to seeking to live a life of deep union with Jesus. It is called **"The Living in Jesus Association"**. The Living In Jesus Association has six different stages, giving people the opportunity to start with a relatively small commitment and to then move up through the stages by degrees. In this way the words of St. Paul are fulfilled, **"We are being transformed from one degree of likeness to Jesus to another."** 2 Cor 3:18.

Stage One

We begin to pray for the grace to live a life of deep union with Jesus; that our hearts will be united with His heart, that our thinking and our attitudes will be transformed by the power of the Holy Spirit, and that we will be His hands, His feet, His eyes, His ears and His voice in our daily lives. Recognising that this will not happen by chance, we make a commitment to at least **an average** of 15 minutes of prayer daily. Not all prayer leads to transformation. Nicodemus was a man of prayer, yet Jesus told him that he needed to be born again. Jesus called religious people whose hearts had not been transformed, whitewashed sepulchres and hypocrites. **The type of prayer that counts is prayer that leads to inner transformation.** It is not about saying extra prayers, but about having one's life transformed through prayer. Many find my booklets helpful. **"To Pray With The Voice Of Jesus"** is specifically written for those who are willing to embrace this way of life. However the booklet "**A Shower of Blessings**" has perhaps greater potential to lead people into transformation, while **"Dear Lord, I'm Desperate"** is simpler and suited to people in the early stages of this journey. Many also find **"The Miracle Rosary"** very helpful - especially the CD version which enables on to turn driving time into quality prayer time.

Confession is another of the special gifts given to us by God to lead us into inner transformation. Those on stage one should aim towards monthly Confession, and should seek to get into the practice of making a frank and real Confession.

In this stage, while praying for the grace to be the hands, feet, eyes, ears and voice of Jesus, one starts by reflecting on what it is to be the hands and feet of Jesus in one's daily life. Jesus spent 30 years as an ordinary person, so we too can be His hands and feet in all the ordinary things of daily life. One then moves on to reflecting on what it is to be the eyes and ears of Jesus.

Stage Two

On the one hand we are growing in our capacity to spend time with Jesus and to relax with Him. On the other hand, we are becoming aware of the level of inner

---

"It is no longer I who live, but Christ who lives in me. This union with Jesus I live by ongoing faith." Gal 2:20

164

transformation that is required if we are to live a life of deep union with Him.

Even being the eyes and ears of Jesus has many implications:- what we read, what we watch, what we listen to, having an eye for the needs of others, having a listening ear, developing a love for spiritual reading, learning to be guided by God in one's decisions, etc. One of the ways in which we need our eyes and ears opened is to the word of God. If you are into reading at all, get a New Testament and start regularly dipping into it. A chapter a day is recommended, but if that seems too much, start with a paragraph a day. We also seek to have our eyes opened to the real presence of Jesus in the Sacred Host. The two disciples who met the risen Jesus on the road to Emmaus only recognised Him when He "broke the bread". Then "their eyes were opened and they recognised Him." Luke 24:31.

Having our eyes opened to the needs of those around us is also vital - being able to see the people around us as real human beings with needs and feelings. This in turn challenges us to break free from self-absorption. Then there is learning to listen to the prompting of the Holy Spirit as regards one's decisions. That is quite a process:- a process which should be approached with great humility, knowing that we will sometimes get it wrong. So be willing to be guided.

Those on Stage Two are encouraged to spend 30 minutes a day in prayer. This may sound a lot, but as you develop a spirit of prayer, it comes very easily - part of your prayer time can be as you walk, drive, work, lie in bed etc. One is also asked to get into the habit of going face to face to the priest in Confession when possible, and to go approximately monthly, making a full and frank confession.

Stage Three

For many dedicated Christians seeking to become the voice of Jesus requires enormous change:- an end to vulgar, bitter, hurtful, judgemental, negative, long-winded or boring talk; an end to falsehoods and gossip; an end to self-preoccupation in one's talking. It also requires setting oneself the target of using one's speech for expressing love, and for encouraging others.

Being the voice of Jesus also involves evangelisation. For the housebound and for contemplatives, evangelisation consists of ongoing prayer for evangelisation and seeking to be the presence of Jesus to those around you. For **parents**, the primary place for evangelisation is in the home and seeking to promote the Gospel in the school and parish. For **a person with big work commitments**, being the hands and voice of Jesus in the workplace may well be their chief way of evangelising.

Those on Stage Three are asked to spend at least **an average** of 45 minutes a day praying, though again part of one's prayer time can be as one walks, drives, works, lies in bed etc. One's prayer time should normally include reading a chapter of the New Testament each day, though again if that seems too much, start

— —

"If your eye is sound, the one who looks through it is God. And God is Love." Chiara Lubich

with a paragraph a day. **From stage three on**, one should seek to have a regular confessor, go to Confession about once a month, and share frankly and honestly what needs to be brought into the open. One should also briefly bring to one's Confessor all major decisions, especially if in a dispute situation.

Stage Four

As we continue to seek to be the hands, feet, eyes, ears and voice of Jesus, one becomes more and more aware that for this to happen, one's heart needs to be deeply united with the heart of Jesus. We can only become the heart of Jesus when we truly fall in love with Jesus. The first step is coming to a living relationship with Jesus; then coming to love Him; then coming to have Him as one's best Friend; then surrendering one's life to Him and to His will; then seeking the entire transformation of one's heart.

The Bible warns, "The heart is more devious than any other thing, perverse too" Jeremiah 17:9. Jesus further warned that it is from the heart that all sorts of evil desires come, and that to even look lustfully at a woman is to commit adultery with her in one's heart.   **At some stage in life, most people will be faced with a choice:-** am I going to renounce the desires of my heart and be guided by Jesus, or am I going to be guided by the desires of my heart and adapt the teaching of Jesus to fit my lifestyle.

God is love. To have the heart of Jesus, one's heart needs to be permeated by Love. This transformation of one's heart requires embracing a positive life of self-giving love; seeking to get rid of all bitterness, all selfishness, all inner anger, all judgementalism, all meanness, all envy, all jealousy; developing a thirst for spiritual things, and for leading others to Jesus. It requires also an end to self-seeking and to self-promotion, and a real surrender to God's plan for one's life. It requires seeking to break all links with what would be unworthy of Jesus.

If one's heart is united with the heart of Jesus, one will have a spirit of prayer, praise and thanksgiving, plus a love for Mass, the Scriptures and holy things. Those on Stage Four are asked to spend at least **an average** of an hour daily in prayer, though again this can include talking to Jesus as one walks, drives, works, lies in bed etc.

Stage Five

The closer we come to Jesus, the more aware we become of how much our thinking needs to change. Having "the mind of Jesus", 1 Cor 2:16, requires a "complete make-over of our minds," Romans 12:2. It requires for one's mind, one's attitudes and one's emotions to be penetrated by the healing, cleansing and delivering power of the Holy Spirit. It requires an end to worrying; an end to negative thinking; an end to bitter, vengeful and judgemental thoughts; an end to sexual fantasising; an

— —

"Run so that you may obtain the prize. Every athlete exercises great control in how they live, seeking to win a prize that will perish. We, however, do so in order to gain a prize that will never perish." I Cor 9:25

166

end to acting on every impulse; and an end to self-seeking.

It requires for one's mind to be permeated by God's love and surrendered to the guidance and inspiration of the Holy Spirit, so that one's thoughts will spring from the thoughts of Jesus, and one's prayers from the prayers of Jesus. It requires not just seeking to do the will of God in all things, but seeking to have the mind of Christ concerning all things. As one's mind is being transformed, one will begin to experience the prophecy of Jeremiah being fulfilled, "I will put my law within them and I will write it upon their hearts." Jer 31:33 RSV

Those on stage five are asked to seek the guidance of the Holy Spirit as to the length of time over and above stage four that they are to spend in prayer, taking into account their work and family commitments. Where family and work commitments make it possible, it is not unusual for people on stage five to spend an average of three hours in prayer daily. But where there are children to be cared for, or heavy work commitments, it may not even be God's will that one spend more than an hour in prayer.

Stage Six

One seeks to live a life of such total union with Jesus that one actually becomes Jesus. "You are called to become the body of Christ, His own flesh and blood," Pope Benedict told the youth (WYD 2005). St. Paul reached the stage of being able to say, "It is no longer I who live but Christ who lives in me" Gal 2:20.

One's top ambition becomes to live in total union with Jesus, to become His living presence in the world. For that to happen, one needs to be utterly transformed by love so that one becomes love incarnate.

While seeking to live this life of total union with Jesus, we realise that the 'fit' will never be total. In our case, the caterpillar never fully turns into the butterfly. St. Paul calls the bit that isn't fully transformed "the old self". This too keeps us humble; keeps us realising that this life can only be lived in total dependence on Jesus. **When we fall, regardless of which stage we are on, let us start again with total trust in God's love for us.**

Enrolment

By formally enrolling in the Living in Jesus Association, one is,
1. Making a definite commitment to this way of life.
2. Setting oneself definite targets.
3. Giving oneself the opportunity for real spiritual development.
4. Becoming united in spirit with the other members.
5. Responding to the desire of Jesus for the New Springtime.

"Not that I ..... am already perfect; but I press on to make it may own, because Christ Jesus has made me his own. .... Forgetting what lies behind and straining forward to what lies ahead, I press on toward the goal for the prize of the upward call of God in Christ Jesus." Phil 3:12-14 RSV

Start living the principles of "Living in Jesus", and you are part of the New Springtime!

One starts with a commitment for a year. After the year there will be the opportunity to take it on as a lifelong commitment. There is also the opportunity to progress up through the stages when one is ready.

Enrolment Prayer

Lord Jesus, I do desire a living relationship with You. I do desire to be part of the New Springtime. I now desire, with Your help, to start living in You. I will start at stage ..... and will then seek to grow.

I make this commitment for one year initially, and I pray for the grace that after the year I will be able to renew it for life.

Enrolment Form (Block Capitals Please)

(So as not to damage this page, please write these details on a sheet of ordinary paper.)

Name ....

Address ....

....

.... *Phone number*........................

Enrolling at Stage ....   *Age, if under 29,* ....

Send to Fr. Thady Doyle, Shillelagh, Arklow, Co Wicklow, Ireland.

A SMALL donation towards correspondence and the printing of literature for the Living in Jesus Association would be welcome with enrolment.

For further details on the Living in Jesus Association, see website, www. jesuspowerministries.org

Footnote

For a full list of books, booklets and CDs by Fr. Thaddeus Doyle, and for the current price list and how to order these by post, see the website, **www.jesuspowerministries. org.** This website also contains the list of his coming public retreats and engagements. If you can't remember name of website, go to Google and call up "Fr. Thady Doyle" or "Fr Thaddeus Doyle" or "The Curate's Diary".

— —

"There are many more things that I wish to say to you, but they would be too much for you just now. When you receive the Spirit of Truth, He will lead you on from here into the fulness of the truth."
John 16:12-13